Catholics and Radicals

The Association of Catholic Trade Unionists
and the American Labor Movement, from Depression
to Cold War

Douglas P. Seaton

Lewisburg
Bucknell University Press
London and Toronto: Associated University Presses

Associated University Presses, Inc.
4 Cornwall Drive
East Brunswick, New Jersey 08816

Associated University Presses
69 Fleet Street
London EC4Y 1EU, England

Associated University Presses
Toronto M5E 1A7, Canada

Library of Congress Cataloging in Publication Data

Seaton, Douglas P   1917-
    Catholics and radicals.

    A revision of the author's thesis, Rutgers University.
    Bibliography: p.
    Includes index.
    1. Association of Catholic Trade Unionists.
2. Trade-unions—United States. 3. Trade-unions and
communism—United States.   I. Title.
HD8055.A7S42   1980   331.88'0973   78-75204
ISBN 0-8387-2193-1

Printed in the United States of America

Contents

For my Mother and Father,
Shirely and Glenn Seaton

Abbreviations

ACA	American Communications Association
Actist	member of the ACTU
ACTU	Association of Catholic Trade Unionists
ADA	Americans for Democratic Action
AFL	American Federation of Labor
AFSCME	American Federation of State, County and Municipal Employees
AFT	American Federation of Teachers
CIO	Congress of Industrial Organizations
CLDL	Catholic Labor Defense League
CP	Communist party
CUU	Catholic Union of the Unemployed
District 50	United Mine Workers, nonmining employees
District 65	Distributive Workers' Union
FAECT	Federation of Architects, Engineers and Technicians
FLW	Fur and Leather Workers' Union
IBEW	International Brotherhood of Electrical Workers
IBT	International Brotherhood of Teamsters
ILA	International Longshoremen's Association
ILWU	International Longshoremen's and Warehousemen's Union
IUE	International Union of Electrical Workers
MDA	Members for Democratic Action
MMSW	Mine, Mill and Smelter Workers' Union
NMU	National Maritime Union

NRA	National Recovery Administration
PCA	Progressive Citizens of America
RU	Retail Workers' Union
SP	Socialist party
SWOC	Steel Workers' Organizing Committee
SWP	Socialist Workers' party
TWU	Transit Workers' Union
UAW	United Automobile Workers' Union
UE	United Electrical Workers' Union
UMW	United Mine Workers' Union
UOPWA	United Office and Professional Workers' Association
UPW	United Public Workers' Union
URW	United Rubber Workers' Union
USW	United Steel Workers' Union
UWU	Utility Workers' Union
WPA	Works Progess Administration

Preface

This book is the outgrowth of a long-standing interest in the American labor movement and in American radicalism. I have been especially curious about two related questions: Why is the labor movement in the United States uniquely conservative in comparison to its counterparts in Europe and Latin America, and why has radicalism failed to achieve strong organizational roots in the United States?

The standard explanations of this "American exceptionalism" have included the relative wealth of the United States, the impact of the frontier, of pluralism, or of political democracy, the possibilities for social mobility, and an American ideology of competitive individualism. As I investigated my questions, however, these explanations seemed increasingly inadequate. They were often presumptive or even tautological rather than persuasive, and in many cases were increasingly contradicted by the evidence (evidence suggesting, for example, that there was no more overall social mobility in the United States than there was in France in a comparable period). The assumption that American workers were somehow naturally conservative appeared inconsistent also with the genuine strength of radical movements at several stages in the history of the American labor movement. And it seemed, too, to sell short the energetic efforts of the conservatives to contain and defeat the radicals.

The "inevitable" conservativism of the American labor movement, like the inevitable shape of so many ideas and institutions in history, seems in fact to have been the outcome of serious ideological, organizational, and even physical conflict. I wanted to investigate this conflict and, since I was unsatisfied with the traditional

9

structural explanations of labor conservativism, to isolate some crucial actors and ideas on the conservative side. Who were the conservatives, I wondered? What relationship did they have to the radicals and to their defeats? What overall impact did the conservatives have on the labor movement?

As I studied these questions during the period of the organization and consolidation of the CIO industrial unions, the role of Catholics, especially Irish Catholics, came increasingly to my attention. The influence of the Church and of lay Catholic activists, some scholars have argued, was important in the conservative direction taken by the AFL unions in the late nineteenth and early twentieth centuries. I thought that this might be true for the CIO unions in the 1930s and 1940s also. The CIO had conducted massive organizing drives in 1937–38 and had consolidated these gains during World War II. The events of 1946–50 determined the political and ideological direction of this new labor organization for decades to come. The years 1937 to 1950 are thus crucial to any explanation of the conservative complexion of the American trade-union movement and I thought the role of Catholic activists during these critical years might have been a pivotal one. The study which follows is the result. In it I try to demonstrate that Catholic influence was indeed of crucial importance in the consolidation of conservative leadership, policies, and practices in the industrial unions which emerged from the upheavals of the 1930s.

This study is a revision of a dissertation prepared at Rutgers University under Daniel Walkowitz and Warren Susman. I owe both of them, as well as Norman Markowitz and Wells Keddie, a considerable debt for their suggestions and direction. I am especially grateful for the careful editorial criticism of Daniel Walkowitz and the encouragement which both he and Louis Galambos offered me. I would also like to acknowledge the assistance of George and John Donahue and other members of the ACTU, who interrupted their current activities to spend time with me in my study of their organization. I am grateful, too, for the assistance of my secretary, Dianne Ruppert, and researchers Charles Becker, Todd Johnson, and Robert Kaplan. Lastly, I want to thank my wife, Hilory Soltanoff, for a great many things in addition to her encouragement, ideas, and work on this book.

Catholics and Radicals

1 † The Eighth Crusade:
The Catholic Church and Socialism

The relationship of the Catholic Church and the American working-class movement is an important, but relatively neglected story. The history and doctrine of the Church itself have received attention from scholars, especially those who are Catholics.[1] The Church has also been investigated as an influence in family history, ethnic allegiance, education, politics, and in "social questions" like contraception and abortion. Yet, despite the fact that the Catholic population has been predominantly wage-earning, and union membership between one-third and one-half Catholic, there have been very few studies of the role of the Church in the development of the labor movement.[2] The work that has been done has stressed one or two significant incidents, such as the Henry George mayoral campaign in New York in 1886 or the dispute over secrecy and radicalism in the Knights of Labor, or the impact of an individual priest or layman.[3] There have been very few works, however, dealing with the general Catholic contribution to the labor movement, especially after 1900.[4]

A major reason for this inattention is that the role of the Church in the American labor movement has been much less visible than it has been in many European and Latin American countries. In Italy, France, Germany, and Spain, as in Chile, Argentina, and Mexico, the Church was propelled into an active role in the labor movement by the strength of socialists and other radicals in the unions. In these countries and others the unions were organized and led by socialists and the working class gave its allegiance to radical political parties. As industrialization and urbanization proceeded, the working class became an ever-more substantial proportion of the population. The Church, whose traditional adherents had been rural and agricultural, was thus faced with a crisis. Not only was it "losing" the working class (this loss was largely metaphorical, since most western European workers were never active Church members), but they were being lost to a movement and an ideology which Catholics regarded as antithetical to Christianity, morality, and civilization.

Despite the gravity of this crisis, the Church was slow to endorse trade unionism as a means of rebuilding support for the Church among industrial workers. The unions, in Europe, were too closely identified with socialism and the Church hierarchy shared in the general upper-class view that unions themselves were conspiracies interfering with "harmonious employer-worker relations." The encyclical *Rerum Novarum* of 1891 finally endorsed workers' organization, but Leo XIII still preferred guilds which would unite employers and employees within the same organization. The only unions which might receive qualified Church approval were "unmixed" unions, those whose membership did not include socialists, the irreligious, or those of other faiths.[5]

This policy of quarantining the socialists was coupled with an active campaign against their influence. The first labor encyclical, Pius IX's *Nostis et Nobiscum* of 1849, was largely a polemic against socialist doctrines. Both *Rerum Novarum* and the later social or labor encyclicals maintained this fire against the left wing.[6] Leo XIII's pastoral letter *Quod Apostilia Muneris* of 1878 stated the reasons for the belated papal endorsement of unions as follows:

> Because the socialist sectarians recruit particularly among men who work in diverse industries or who rent their labor . . . it seems to us opportune to encourage societies of workers and artisans which, instituted under the guidance of religion, would be able to make all of their members content with their lot and resigned to labor and also to help them lead a peaceful and tranquil life.[7]

The Church's foray into the labor movement was thus designed largely as a counter-force to the activity of the socialists, rather than as a drive for the amelioration of the workers' condition.

The primacy given to hostility to the socialists by the Catholic Church had several sources. Doctrinally, there were serious conflicts with the socialists over atheism, materialism, collectivism, authority, the state, and private property. Organizationally, the socialists were in competition with the Church for the individual allegiance of workers, intellectuals, and others. Politically, the socialists were revolutionary while the Church opposed social revolution and barely regarded itself even as evolutionary. Socially, the Church fathers drew their major support and most of their own members from the aristocracy, peasantry and bourgeoisie, while the main weight of the socialist movement was drawn from the working class. Whatever its proximate causes, the Church's hostility to socialism took on something of the character of a crusade. Many Catholics proudly viewed their Church as the "first and foremost" of the forces arrayed against the socialists and believed the struggle to be one of good versus evil, civilization versus anarchy, and even God versus Satan. [8]

This struggle was no less sharp in the United States than in Europe or Latin America, though there were different conditions which altered both the form of the Church's activity and the prospects for success. Most important were the multidenominational and multiethnic character of the American working class and the nonsocialist leadership of the labor movement. While the Church would have preferred Catholic unions, which were organized in Quebec, the minority status of Catholics in the United States made this strategy both difficult and dangerous. [9] Such formations could not really function as trade unions, would invite the hostility, not only of anti-Catholics, but of the trade-union leadership, whose direction paralleled that of the Church, and would divide conservative forces and thus increase the strength of the socialists. [10]

This dilemma was the underlying issue in the dispute over the Catholic position on the Knights of Labor in the 1880s. [11] Cardinal Taschereau of Quebec had condemned the Knights for their secrecy and membership oath, which conflicted with the sacrament of confession, and for their radicalism. Cardinal Gibbons of Baltimore, who shared the general Catholic position on socialism, nonetheless realized that for Catholics to abandon the Knights of Labor was to surrender the leading American labor organization to the radicals. Fearing a general papal pronouncement against the Knights, he interceded with the pope and with Terence Powderly, Grand Master of the Knights, to effect a compromise. As a result, the Knights disavowed their policy of secrecy and Catholics were permitted to join.[12]

The crucial consideration in granting this imprimatur to the Knights was the struggle against radicalism in the labor movement. The American hierarchy and the pope were apparently satisfied with Grand Master Powderly's announced intention to rid the labor movement of the "violent element, the element of radical men who want to found a society of atheistic anarchy."[13] The Churchmen believed that Catholics, if permitted to join the "mixed" Knights of Labor and AFL unions, would be an important ally of the conservative forces in the labor movement. If they were not permitted to join, and if the Church attempted to organize its own Catholic unions, the existing unions would be in grave danger of socialist domination. The exemption from the obligation to join only Catholic unions granted by the pope to American Catholics was intended largely to preclude just such a socialist victory.[14]

The threat of a socialist-led American labor movement was a real one from the 1880s up until 1917. The Socialist Labor party (SLP) and the anarchists were important influences within the Knights of Labor and support for political action, the "cooperative commonwealth," and industrial unionism was widespread among the Knights. The SLP declined because of sectarianism and a dual unionist approach, but the Socialist party (SP) became a more serious threat to conservative unionism within the AFL than the DeLeonites had ever been. Socialists were among the national leadership of many of the important AFL unions, including the Brewery Workers, the Western Federation of Miners, the ILGWU, the Amalgamated Clothing Workers, the International Typographical Union, the International Association of Machinists, the United Mine Workers, and even Gompers' own union, the Cigarmakers. Socialists led several of the important city and state AFL bodies and regularly won more than a third of the vote on policy questions and election of officers at AFL national conventions. On one occasion they were even able to deny the presidency to Gompers.[15]

Opposition to the socialists inspired the Church to condone Catholic membership in mixed unions in the United States, but the Church's role in the struggle against the left was an active one as well. The cardinals and bishops pronounced against socialism as a "rampant heresy" and the common enemy of all Catholics.[16] Cardinal Gibbons argued that Catholics must "throw the whole force of the Church against the further progress of the [socialist] movement."[17] It was particularly important, thought Gibbons, that the labor movement be convinced to reject the socialists, who sought to make the unions "subservient to their own selfish ends, or convert it into a political engine."[18] The statements and writings of the hierarchy were paralleled by the sermons and pastoral letters of the parish priests and the activities of a wide range of Catholic institutions and publications. As the Reverend William Kerby of Catholic University put it,

> The Church has entered the conflict as the avowed enemy of Socialism. Our colleges teach against it, we lecture and write, preach and publish against it. We have abundant official pronouncements against it, and an anxious capitalistic world looks to the Church for the anticipated set back that Catholicism is to give to Socialism.[19]

Opposition to socialism was a serious duty incumbent on all Catholics and, according to Catholic historian Vincent McQuade, "was acknowledged by devout Catholics to be the fundamental issue" within the unions.[20]

The Catholic labor tradition, of course, has not been a monolithic one. There were dissenters to the official Church policy of opposition to socialism. Several important socialist union officials, including J. Mahlon Barnes of Gompers' own Cigarmakers' Union and Frank J. Hayes, president of the UMW in 1907–1909, were Catholics and there were significant numbers of rank-and-file "Catholic socialists."[21] Priests, too, strayed from the hierarchy's position on socialism. Reverend McGlynn functioned as campaign manager in Henry George's socialist race for New York mayor in 1886, despite the position of Thomas S. Preston, vicar-general of the Church in the United States, that the Church "would deeply regret the election of Mr. George" because of his "unsound views." McGlynn was excommunicated for his unrepentant activity on behalf of George.[22] This was the fate also of Thomas Hagerty, the revolver-toting "wobbly priest," who was an important strategist of the Industrial Workers of the World (IWW). Reverend Thomas McGrady of

Kentucky lectured at the socialist Boston School of Political Economy.[23] The Church hierarchy and the preponderant majority of clergy, however, held to the official position that socialism was a "heresy" and the greatest enemy of Catholics.

Nor was opposition to socialism confined to clerics. Lay Catholic organizations, including the German Catholic Central Verein, the Knights of Columbus, the Militia of Christ for Social Service, and the American Federation of Catholic Social Services, were actively involved in the struggle against the SP. German-speaking socialists were numerous and the Central Verein, a German Catholic social and benevolent society, was energetic in opposing their influence within the German community. The Verein published against socialism, blacklisted left-wing unions, and opposed socialist candidates for political and union office, and its efforts were paralleled by those of Catholic organizations in other ethnic communities. The Knights of Columbus also published pamphlets against socialism and sponsored speaking tours by ex-socialist Catholic converts.[24]

The major and most active Catholic lay organization committed to a fight against socialism, however, was the Militia of Christ for Social Service. The Militia of Christ was organized in 1910 and focused almost entirely on the struggle against socialism within the AFL unions. The Reverend Peter Dietz, a Central Verein veteran, was its founder and peripatetic national organizer. Dietz had received his baptism of fire in the struggle with socialism at the 1909 Ohio AFL convention, where he led the Catholic and conservative forces against the socialists, led by Charles Ruthenberg. The socialists won the important convention votes and the disgruntled Dietz led the conservatives in a bolt from the convention. The Militia enlisted as members many important Catholic AFL leaders, including four AFL vice-presidents and six international union presidents, and the small staff was able to use its impressive list of letterhead members to great advantage in their lobbying against socialism with union officials and convention delegates. Dietz himself was a fraternal delegate to every AFL convention from 1909 to 1917. After the formation in 1917 of the American Federation of Catholic Societies he continued his anti-socialist activities under the aegis of the Federation's Social Services Committee.[25]

Dietz's purpose was to develop "a disciplined array of responsible Catholic trade unionists, prepared to act in concert at a moment's notice . . . to *take hold* of the labor movement."[26] Such a "coup," of course, never occurred. It was unnecessary, largely because the AFL leadership were perfectly willing to work with conservative Catholics. Most of them were conservative Catholics themselves and their policies dovetailed with those supported by the Church.[27] Church leaders did not wish this support to be taken for granted, however, and repeated warnings were addressed to AFL unionists which underlined the terms of such support. Bishop John Carroll of Helena, for example, told the AFL convention delegates in 1913 that Catholics would be obliged to withdraw from the federation if it were to adopt "any theory of economics . . . that must incur the enmity of the Church."[28] Such threats were not idle ones, even when the "theories" involved were merely "educational" rather than "economic." When in 1912 the AFL took the relatively mild step of condemning the Spanish government's execution of Francisco Ferrer, an educator and opponent of clerical control of the schools who was a socialist, a storm of protest arose from the clergy and one Catholic periodical even stated editorially that "our workmen who are Catholics should withdraw from the AFL."[29]

The extensive Catholic campaign against the socialists within the AFL unions and on behalf of the policies of the AFL leadership, including opposition to minimum wages, eight-hour legislation, industrial unionism, and independent political action by labor, was an important factor in the conservative direction of the AFL. David J. Saposs, writing in 1933, argued that the influence of the Church "explains, in part at least, why the labor movement in the United States differs from others, and why it has become so reactionary."[30] Marc Karson, who made an intensive study of the Church's role in the struggle with the socialists in the AFL, concluded that Catholicism "has been a vital force accounting for the moderate political position of American labor" in the period 1900 to 1918.[31] Repression during World War I, the division of the socialist movement, and the entrenchment of the AFL leadership, assisted by the Catholic forces, reduced the socialist threat during the 1920s. Though the Verein, the Knights of Columbus, the American Federation of Catholic Societies, and other Catholic organizations continued their polemics against socialism, the campaign did not have the urgency it had in the prewar decade. This urgency returned only with the onset of the depression, the gains of the organized left during the 1930s, and particularly the organization of the CIO.

World War I and the depression wrought some important changes in the Church's position on the labor movement and social and economic reform. The war had provided extensive experience with government intervention in social and economic policy and this had soothed the fears common to Catholics and others of such activity by the state. Such intervention, it was now apparent, need not be "socialist." Indeed, it might be quite necessary to forestall further advances by the radicals. The Russian Revolution, of course, contributed to the popularity of an ameliorationist perspective in some quarters, while the steel strike of 1919 and the Seattle general strike of the same year impressed a certain urgency on the discussion of reconstruction policy.

The Church, responding to these changes, felt compelled to depart from its earlier hostility to state intervention and legislative protection for workers. In 1919 the Conference of American Bishops published the "Bishops' Program for Reconstruction," which gently broke with previous Catholic opinion by endorsing public housing, minimum wages, social security, and a number of other measures of state intervention in social and economic life.[32] The depression reinforced this support for state activity in areas where the Church had traditionally resisted governmental action as socialist. The works of Monsignor John A. Ryan, who argued extensively in support of New Deal measures, were the foremost expression of this altered Catholic approach.[33]

The reforms which the Church espoused in the 1930s were never socialist, however, and the Catholic hierarchy remained an obdurate enemy of the socialists and especially of the burgeoning communist movement. The authors of the "Bishops' Program" denounced the socialists and communists and viewed their own program as an alternative to Leninist revolution or British Labour party—style socialism.[34] Ryan also dissociated his program from the socialists and criticized them extensively.[35] In 1937 Pius XI, worried over the rising strength of the communists in Spain, the Italian underground, and the French Popular Front, issued the encyclical *Divine Re-*

demptoris. The encyclical charged the communists with materialism, atheism, denial of natural law and rights, violence and demagoguery, and held that they represented the leading heretical force.[36]

Anti-socialism and particularly anti-communism remained the "fundamental issue" for Catholics in the unions in the 1930s then, just as they were in the early 1900s. But the organization of the CIO demanded a change in the strategy and tactics of the Catholic forces in the labor movement. The Church had stood solidly behind the conservative AFL leadership in its struggle against the socialists. A majority of the AFL officers were Catholics, as were a majority of the membership, and the craft unions were held to be the embodiment of Catholic views on the labor movement.[37] The highly skilled AFL unions, often including subcontractors, resembled the guild organizations which Catholic theoreticians continued to promote.[38] The AFL leaders were cautious of state intervention in the economy and opposed industrial unionism and political action by labor. They were conservative, loath to strike, respectable, and impervious to radicalism in any form.

These qualities, however, did not have much appeal among the industrial workers, who wondered "what use the AFL was if it couldn't help them get organized."[39] The AFL's opposition to militance and industrial organization, and its frequent sabotage of the organizing efforts of industrial workers in the early 1930s, instead alienated these workers by the hundreds of thousands.[40] By 1937, when this discontent became focused in the organization of the CIO, the Church could no longer afford this exclusive commitment to the AFL if it hoped to continue to have an important influence on the American labor movement.

Radicals of every stripe, and particularly the communists, played a significant role in the organization of the CIO.[41] The industrial workers had been spurned by the AFL, and in turn they spurned the craft unions. Under depression conditions, with faith in capitalism considerably undermined, there was a distinct possibility they would turn to radical leadership. While the CIO leadership was hardly radical, it was forced to accept the support of the socialists and communists as organizers and activists.[42] For the first time since before World War I, the left was building a genuine base within the unions, and there was no guarantee that the radicals might not manage to win leadership of the CIO.

For the Church this situation was distinctly ominous. In many respects it was analogous to the situation in the AFL before World War I when the socialists led several unions and won forty percent of convention votes, and in some ways was distinctly worse.[43] The industrial workers were less likely than the relatively privileged craft workers to adopt the tenets and style of business unionism. The depression conditions contributed to left-wing sentiment in a far more serious way than the relatively prosperous, if erratic, conditions from 1900 to 1914. Even the enormous faith in Franklin Roosevelt did not prevent the emergence of serious third-party sentiment and activity in California, New York, Wisconsin, and Minnesota.

Furthermore, the communists were a much more serious challenge than the socialists had ever been. William Z. Foster, a leader of the CP in this period, had led the 1919 steel strike and was widely thought to be one of the best union organizers the United States had ever seen. The communists were more disciplined than the Debsian socialists had been, too, and did not tolerate factionalism in their ranks. The popular-front strategy, comparatively well suited to conditions in the United States, had also replaced the more esoteric formulations of the CP of the 1920s. The party membership, which never exceeded 100,000, had nonetheless an enormous impact on the unions since the members were generally spirited, hardworking, and disciplined, as even their worst enemies were quick to admit. The prestige the communists derived from the example of the Soviet Union, unaffected as it was by the worldwide depression, was considerable as well.

The strength, position, and prospects of the CIO left, then, were quite impressive in 1937. A number of factors contributed to a potential radicalization among unskilled and semiskilled workers, not the least of which was the complete loss of faith in the AFL and, by implication, in business unionism itself. If the Catholic Church were to influence the direction of the new industrial unionism, it was imperative that it build a presence within the CIO independent of the old structure of influence in the AFL. This was the role played by the Association of Catholic Trade Unions (ACTU), founded "around a kitchen table" in New York City in the winter of 1937.[44]

The early Actists (as the ACTU members called themselves) had gathered first under the auspices of the *Catholic Worker* organization to study the popes' social encyclicals. Some of them were well acquainted with Catholic social doctrine, while one had merely found a discarded copy of the *Catholic Worker* in a subway and become interested. John Cort, a Harvard graduate, intellectual, and convert to Catholicism, had made an intensive study of Catholic social doctrine and was dedicated to the point of asceticism, while others had more practical motives. Martin Wersing and Edward Squitieri, for example, were extremely affected by the case of a Utility Workers Union (UWU) member who, fired for union activity, killed himself in despair of finding work. They were both UWU members and had determined that they would help to organize other workers so that such incidents could not recur. Some Actists worked in unorganized industries and intended to learn what they needed to organize them. Others were members of well-established craft unions, but wished to help industrial workers build their own organizations. One, George Donahue, had been victimized by the gangster methods of Joseph Ryan's International Longshoremen's Association (ILA) and was interested in cleaning up that union. Some, including the transit workers and social workers, were members of left-wing union locals and planned to arm themselves for a campaign against the communists.[45] Whatever their immediate motives, the Catholic unionists soon became "convinced that in the labor encyclicals of Leo XIII and Pius XI there was a program that would not only solve the problems of the American labor movement, but bring order out of chaos in American industry."[46]

The Actists moved very quickly from study to action. Their first year was devoted to an extensive campaign of strike and CIO organizing support work. They initiated several workers' schools in the New York metropolitan area, began publication of a newspaper, formed a speakers' bureau to propagate Catholic social doctrine, and won the support of much of the U.S. hierarchy. Before the close of 1938 the ACTU had established chapters, schools, and a union infrastructure in New York, Boston, Detroit, Pittsburgh, San Francisco, and New Jersey. During the thirteen years in which it was active the ACTU was to become a significant force in the U.S. labor movement, particularly the CIO. The Actists ultimately established twenty chapters, tutored tons of thousands of local union activists and officers, organized an extensive network of union conferences and caucuses, published several newspapers, conducted legal defense, union support and organizing work, and elected members and supporters to local and international union office. The Actists and their supporters were to play a crucial role in the political struggle in the CIO in the late 1940's and the impact of their theory, practice, and personnel continues to be felt in the labor movement and in industrial relations generally. The ACTU proved to be a worthy heir of the Militia of Christ for Social Service in its role as a Catholic vanguard in the conflict with the radicals and on behalf of conservative union policies.[47]

NOTES

1. See, for example, Aaron Abel, *American Catholicism and Social Action* (Garden City, N.Y.: Hanover, 1960), Aaron Abel, "The Reception of Leo XIII's Labor Encyclical in America, 1891–1919", *The Review of Politics* 7, no. 4, pp. 164–95; Robert Cross, *The Emergence of Liberal Catholicism in America* (Cambridge, Mass.; Harvard University Press, 1958); Charles Bruehl, *The Pope's Plan* (New York: Devin-Adair, 1939); Joseph N. Moody, *Church and Society: Catholic Social and Political Thought and Movements, 1789–1950* (New York: Arts, 1953); Daniel A. O'Connor, *Catholic Social Doctrine* (Westminster, Md.: Newman Press, 1956); Richard Camp, *The Papal Ideology of Social Reform* (Leiden, Holland: J. Brill, 1969). On Catholic anti-communism, see also Don Crosby, "Angry Catholics" (Ph.D. diss., Brandeis University, 1973), and Peter Irons, "America's Cold War Crusade" (Ph.D. diss., Boston University, 1972).

2. A study by the Survey Research Center of the University of Michigan in 1959 found that thirty per cent of union family heads were Catholics, compared to eighteen per cent of family heads generally. These results may be an underestimate since students of the American labor movement generally believe that one-half of the AFL and even more of the CIO membership were Catholics. Derek C. Bok and John T. Dunlap, *Labor and the American Community* (New York: Simon and Schuster, 1970), p. 46; Marc Karson, *American Labor Unions and Politics* (Carbondale, Ill.: Southern Illinois University, 1958), p. 221; Selig Perlman, *The Theory of the Labor Movement* (New York: Macmillan Co., 1928), p. 169; Norman Ware, *Labor in Modern Industrial Society* (New York: Heath, 1935), p. 35; Len DeCaux, *Labor Radical* (Boston: Beacon, 1970), p. 393; Philip Foner, *History of the Labor Movement* 3 vols. (New York: International, 1964), 3:112.

3. Henry Browne, *The Catholic Church and the Knights of Labor* (Washington, D.C.: Catholic University, 1949); Henry Browne, "Peter E. Dietz: Pioneer Planner of Catholic Social Action, *The Catholic Historical Review*, January 1948. pp. 448-56"; Mary Harrita Fox, *Peter E. Dietz, Labor Priest* (South Bend, Ind.: Notre Dame, 1953); Abel, "Ryan", *The Review of Politics* 8,

no. 1, pp. 128–34.; Francis Broderick, *Right Reverend New Dealer* (New York: Macmillan Co., 1963); Patrick W. Gearty, *The Economic Thought of Monsignor John A. Ryan* (Washington, D.C.: Catholic University, 1953); Allen Raymond, *Waterfront Priest* (New York: Holt, 1955).

4. Some attention has been given to the Church's impact on the ethnic communities, but most of it has ignored the effect on working-class attitudes and trade-union practice. See, for example, Oscar Handlin, *Boston's Immigrants* (Cambridge, Mass.: Belknap Press of Harvard University Press, 1959) and Victor Greene, *For God and Country* (Madison, Wisc.: State Historical Society of Wisconsin, 1975). Later work has often focused on the trade-union and working-class components of ethnic life, but has downplayed the role of the Church in shaping them. See Victor Greene, *The Slavic Community on Strike* (Notre Dame, Ind.: University of Notre Dame, 1968). Protestant Christianity, on the other hand, has always been understood as an influence in working-class economic and political action, both in this country and in Great Britain. See E. P. Thompson, *The Making of the English Working Class* (London: V. Gollàncz, 1963). The only studies dealing directly with the Catholic Church and the American labor movement in this century are a chapter in Marc Karson, *American Labor Unions and Politics* and an article by David Saposs, "The Catholic Church and the Labor Movement", *Modern Monthly*, May, June 1933, pp. 225–230; pp. 294–298.

5. Camp, *Papal Ideology*, pp. 113, 115.

6. See ibid., pp. 55–60, for a discussion of the vehemence and consistency of the Church's denunciation of the socialists. Catholic social doctrine is discussed at greater length in the following chapter.

7. Ibid., p. 112.

8. Ibid., p. 50.

9. The Catholic unions of Quebec enrolled 6,325 members in 1912, Fox, *Peter E. Dietz*, p. 77.

10. Cross, *Liberal Catholicism in America*, p. 117.

11. On the Knights of Labor and the Church, see Browne, *Catholic Church and the Knights of Labor*.

12. Saposs, "Catholic Church and the Labor Movement," p. 230; Cross, *Liberal Catholicism in America*; Fox, *Peter E. Dietz*, pp. 13–14; Browne, *Catholic Church and the Knights of Labor; Jubilee*, September 1954, pp. 5–6.

13. Saposs, "Catholic Church and the Labor Movement," p. 230.

14. Cross, *Liberal Catholicism*, p. 117, Karson, *American Labor Unions and Politics*, p. 269.

15. On the Socialist party and the AFL see James Weinstein, *The Decline of Socialism in America* (New York, Monthly Review Press, 1967); David Shannon, *The Socialist Party of America* (New York: Macmillan Co., 1995); Ira Kipnis, *The American Socialist Movement, 1897–1912* (New York: Columbia University Press, 1952); John Laslett, *Labor and the Left* (New York, Basic Books, 1970); William Dick, *Labor and Socialism in America* (New York: Kennikat Press, 1972).

16. Marc Karson, "Catholic Anti-Socialism" in John M. Laslett and Seymour M. Lipset, eds., *Failure of a Dream?* (Garden City, New York: Doubleday, 1974), p. 154.

17. Allen S. Wil, *Life of Cardinal Gibbons, Archbishop of Baltimore* (New York: E. P. Dutton, 1922), pp. 258–59.

18. Karson, "Catholic Anti-Socialism," p. 166.

19. William Kerby, "Aims in Socialism," *The Catholic World* 85, p. 511.

20. Vincent McQuade, "American Catholic Attitudes on Child Labor Since 1891" (Ph.D. diss., Catholic University, 1938), p. 50.

21. Foner, *History of the Labor Movement*, 3:116; Saposs, "Catholic Church and the Labor Movement," pp. 296–97.

22. Saposs, "Catholic Church and the Labor Movement," pp. 295–96; John Commons, *History of Labour in the United States* (New York: MacMillan Co., 1935), 2:453–56.

23. Fox, *Peter E. Dietz*, p. 27.

24. Karson, *American Labor Unions and Politics*, pp. 263–64. On the Verein see also Philip Gleason, *The Conservative Reformers: German American Catholics and the Social Order* (South Bend, Ind.: Notre Dame, 1968).

25. On Dietz and the Militia see Karson, "Catholic Anti-Socialism," pp. 169–74; Fox, *Peter E. Dietz*, Browne, "Peter E. Dietz: Pioneer Planner of Catholic Social Action."

26. Fox, *Peter E. Dietz*, p. 63.

27. Karson estimates that half of all the AFL vice-presidencies and sixty-two of the international union presidencies, including all but one of the five largest unions, were held by Catholics in the period from 1900 to 1918, Karson, *American Labor Unions and Politics*, pp. 221–24.

28. *Proceedings of the 1913 AFL Convention*, pp. 207–10.

29. Foner, *History of the Labor Movement*, 3:123–24.

30. Saposs, "Catholic Church and the Labor Movement," p. 225.

31. Karson, *American Labor Unions and Politics*, p. xi.

32. For the text of the "Bishops' Program" see John A. Ryan, *Social Reconstruction* (New York: Macmillan Co., 1920), pp. 217–38; see also my discussion in chapter 2.

33. The best-known of Ryan's works are *Social Reconstruction, A Better Economic Order* (New York: Harper's, 1935), and *A Living Wage* (New York: Macmillan Co., 1906). On Ryan see Patrick Gearty, *The Economic Thought of Monsignor John A. Ryan* (Washington, D.C.: Catholic University, 1953); Broderick, *Right Reverend New Dealer*; Abell, "Ryan."

34. Ryan, *Social Reconstruction*, pp. 220, 223, 235.

35. Ryan, *A Better Economic Order*, pp. 126–46.

36. Camp, *Papal Ideology*, p. 102.

37. On the proportion of Catholics among AFL members and officers see Karson, *American Labor Unions and Politics*, pp. 221–24; Perlman, *Theory of the Labor Movement*, p. 169; Norman Ware, *Labor in Modern Industrial Society*, p. 35; DeCaux, *Labor Radical*, p. 393; Foner, *History of the Labor Movement*, 3:112.

38. Ryan, *A Better Economic Order*, pp. 154–55, 177–83; Camp, *Papal Ideology*, pp. 112–13; *Labor Leader* 1, nos. 18, 21.

39. DeCaux, *Labor Radical*, p. 191.

40. Said AFL President Green, "We do not foment strikes. . . . We get what we can by going to the employer and asking for it." The AFL generally procrastinated in organizing industrial workers, refused to grant them industrial union charters, offered them second-class membership, and often simply ignored them. "AFL Executive Council Minutes," January 15–29, 1936, pp. 33, 36, 119; Irving Bernstein, *The Lean Years* (Boston: Houghton-Mifflin, 1960), pp. 83, 88, 89, and *The Turbulent Years* (Boston: Houghton-Mifflin, 1970), p. 355; DeCaux, *Labor Radical*, p. 191.

41. As noted previously, Communist party leadership became dominant in unions repre-

senting between fifteen and twenty per cent of the CIO membership between 1941 and 1946, Bernstein, *The Turbulent Years*, p. 783; Max Kampelman, *The Communist party vs. the CIO* (New York: Praeger, 1957), p. 45.

42. John L. Lewis, of course, was a Republican, and so was Philip Murray, a pious, conservative Catholic who supported the industrial-council plan of the popes.

43. On the Socialist party in the AFL see sources listed in note 15.

44. A number of terms used in this study require definition. "Conservative" is used to denote those who generally support the status quo with respect to private property, management prerogatives, and power arrangements in American society. "Conservatives" in the labor movement may favor wage increases, industrial cooperation, unionization, or regulatory legislation, but draw the line at independent political activity by labor, expropriation or nationalization of property, transfer of management or personnel decisions in industry to labor, class conflict and the general objectives of the "radicals." In political terms conservatives are unwilling to work with any component of the left wing, except insofar as may be necessary to defeat more significant left-wing forces. The primary aim of conservatives is the defeat of the "radicals." "Right wing" is synonymous with conservative for our purposes. "Radical," for the purposes of this study, means those who oppose the status quo in industry and politics and favor independent political action of labor, expropriation of productive property, a leading role for labor in production and supervision in economic life, class conflict between labor and capital, an increasing share of wealth for labor, and ultimately socialism as a political, social, and economic system. Radicals reject any alliance with conservatives. "Left wing" denotes those holding such views, including members of socialist organizations, including the Communist party (CP), Socialist party (SP), Left Socialist party, and Socialist Workers' party (SWP). "Progressive" is used to denote those who, while rejecting the ultimate goal of socialism, share more in common with the radicals than with the conservatives in immediate goals. Progressives accept intrusions on private property and management prerogatives and support independent political activity by labor. They accept class conflict as a political instrument and are willing to work politically with radicals against conservatives, and unwilling to work with conservatives against radicals. "Center left" is an equivalent term, while "center" refers to those who are undecided in position, serving some instrumental objective, or opposed equally to the objectives of the conservatives and the radicals. "Reactionary," as occasionally used in this study, denotes those who explicitly favor a return to some past form of social, economic, or political organization. "Communism" in this study refers to those associated with the Communist party. "Socialism" refers to the Socialist party while the uncapitalized form refers to the more general objectives of socialism. References to the "Church," "hierarchy," "diocese," "parish," and to ecclesiastical titles should be understood to refer to the Roman Catholic Church. "Actist," a self-descriptive acronyn, refers to a member of the ACTU.

45. John Cort, "Catholics in Trade Unions," *Commonweal*, May 5, 1939, p. 34; Cort, "Ten Years of ACTU," *Commonweal*, May 23, 1947, p. 143; Interview with George Donahue, July 22, 1974; *Labor Leader* 1, no. 1; 1, no. 38; 2, no. 1; *Michigan Labor Leader* 2, no. 14.

46. *Labor Leader* 1, no. 24.

47. The Association of Catholic Trade Unionists, dominated, like the Church itself, by Irish Catholics, was the officially sanctioned "voice of Catholic labor" in this period and was certainly the largest and most important of the several Catholic groups whose work had impact

on the labor movement. Accordingly, I have focused almost entirely on that organization, except for the discussions of historical background and Catholic social ideology generally. Though there were other important sources of Catholic influence on the labor movement (the parish priests, the schools, the hierarchy, Catholic periodicals, and a number of Catholic social service agencies) which paralleled and reinforced the work of the ACTU, the Actists focused the impact of these disparate authorities and gave them credibility and political shape within the labor movement.

2 † Catholic Social Doctrine: Harmony Between the Classes

The Catholic social doctrine which guided the ACTU in its organizing efforts had been developed largely since the promulgation of *Rerum Novarum* in 1891, though it had been grafted onto roots which went back to the founding of the Holy Roman Empire. *Rerum Novarum* itself had no more than sketched a response to the industrial conditions which occasioned it. The encyclical argued that the workers had been abandoned to the mercy of a laissez-faire state which ignored the teachings and organization of the Church. The remedy was not to be found in class conflict or socialism, since the "classes should dwell in harmony and agreement," but rather in a resuscitation of the role of the Church in social life. Reciprocal rights and duties of employers and workers would guarantee social peace and "social justice." Contracts would be respected, "just wages" paid, a day's work performed, violence and property damage avoided, and human dignity assured. Insofar as labor organization was concerned, guilds which united labor and management were the best solution. Unions of workers alone could only be tolerated if they were nonsocialist and Catholic, but in Great Britain and the United States Catholics would be permitted to join mixed unions. [1]

The popes who followed Leo XIII offered some embellishments to his encyclical, but the major task of developing a workable social program fell upon the national churches. The churches devised their programs according to the precepts of the Church, the stipulations of *Rerum Novarum* (1891), and later *Quadragesimo Anno* (1931), and their own local conditions.

In the United States this task commenced on a national scale with the publication of the Bishops' Statement on Reconstruction of 1919. This document was explicitly a response to the reconstruction programs of the British Labour party, the American Quakers, and the AFL and implicitly a response to the Russian Revolution and to unsettled labor conditions at home.[2] The bishops cautioned that they meant to suggest "no profound changes in the United States," rather a "practical and moderate program."[3] Among the measures endorsed were a national employment service, colonization of veterans on government land, the "smallest practical limits" on the number of women workers, continuation of the War Labor Board, a "living wage," municipal housing, restraint of monopoly, minimum wages, a social-security system, and "labor participation in industrial management." Such reforms were necessary, the bishops argued, to assure efficiency and justice and to establish "an industrial and social order that will be secure from the danger of revolution."[4]

None of the important recommendations of the Bishops' Statement on Reconstruction were implemented in the post–World War I period. Employers and the government elected a more militant rather than a "cooperative" approach to class relations in the 1920s and the slogans of "Open Shop," "The American Plan," "Bolshevism," and "Prosperity" buried that of "Social Justice." The labor upsurge of 1919 was buried also and even the heretofore secure AFL unions experienced a calamitous decline in membership. From 5,047,800 members in 1920 the AFL sank to 3,622,000 in 1923.[5]

A number of Catholic social theoreticians kept the torch burning during the 1920s, despite the inhospitable atmosphere. Foremost among these was Monsignor John A. Ryan, economist, teacher, social theoretician, and activist, who "was to lead United States Catholic social thinking until his death in 1945."[6] Ryan published a lengthy commentary on the Bishops' Statement on Reconstruction in 1920 entitled *Social Reconstruction*. Previous to that, in 1906, he had published *A Living Wage* and he followed with a work entitled *A Better Economic Order* in 1935. Ryan had worked closely with Reverend Peter E. Dietz of the Militia of Christ for Social Service and had headed the Social Services Department of the American Federation of Catholic Societies.[7] He was a faculty member of the first Catholic labor school, Xavier, which was founded in 1911, and he was to assist the ACTU closely in its own work. Ryan developed the most comprehensive American statement of Catholic social doctrine and was generally credited as "the father of the Church's labor program in the United States."[8] His ideas, which will be examined in some detail, demonstrate that, even at its most liberal, Catholic social doctrine was a consistent adaptation of the Church's fundamental conservatism in social and economic matters.

The Church's social doctrines were actually an amalgam of several different traditions and themes. Elements from classical economics and the traditional defense of private property were present, but so were sweeping pronouncements against monopoly, usury, and the greed and materialism of capitalist society. Concern for hierarchy, stability, and harmony often collided with commitment to charity, spiritual reform, and voluntary ethical action. Utopian medievalism and modern corporate state theory interpenetrated with ideas on the redistribution of property and the reform of economic dependency, material deprivation, and spiritual malaise. There were contradictions and ambiguity in the resulting combination and the component elements coexisted with a certain degree of mutual checkmate.

The Church broached some ideas which implied truly sweeping social changes. But the essential content and impact of Catholic social doctrine was conservative. The Church had basic social and ideological commitments to conservatism and, though the logic of many of its ideas was radical, it tended to retreat from the implications of those ideas. Dependence on voluntarism for the implementation of the more radical measures, too, while the state was to see to order, property, and stability, weakened the more radical components of the Church's eclectic social doctrine, as did the uncompromising hostility to socialism itself. Since the implications of certain ideas were socialist, these ideas simply remained undeveloped. The Church did not wish to offend the powerful, either, and it shrank from recommendations which would arouse their opposition. The potentially critical aspects of Catholic social ideology tended therefore to be submerged by the conservative.

The Church's position on the institution of private property in the means of production was one of unqualified support. Both *Rerum Novarum* (1891) and *Quadragesimo Anno* (1931) were plain in their arguments on behalf of individual ownership of productive property.[9] The encyclicals held that the major error of the socialists was their denial of the "natural right" to private property.[10] Catholics had a duty to expose this error and to defend the institution of private property. "Do not abolish private property" was the command of Pius XII in one Papal letter addressed to workmen, and American Catholics affirmed this right in their own commentaries on the social doctrines of the encyclicals.[11] The authors of the Bishops' Program of 1919 were careful to explain that the reforms they contemplated would not mean the "abolition of private ownership." They argued against the demand for heavy taxes on excess profits and wealth and similar taxes on fallow land which were contained in the AFL reconstruction program of the period on the grounds that this implied "confiscation" of private property.[12] Similarly, Monsignor John A. Ryan, the most authoritative Catholic social and economic theorist, argued in his writings that "private property is morally right."[13]

Catholic doctrine held that private property was the just reward of labor and was necessary to human welfare and the development of human potential.[14] Since there was a prior "imperishable right to a livelihood from the common bounty of nature," however, it might seem that the Church offered hope to the proponents of collective enterprise.[15] Not so, argued Ryan. Since men were "unequal in their individual powers and needs," common ownership would deny the more productive the fruits of their labor.[16] Therefore, between socialism and private ownership, "every Catholic must be for private ownership no matter how much we may criticize its present distribution."[17]

Property rights and the right to a livelihood were to be reconciled through Aristotle's dictum that "it is best to make property private, but to have the use of it common."[18] This might seem to guarantee no more than the right of the propertyless to labor for the propertied, a right already secured by necessity. Ryan, however, argued that since the right to a livelihood was "superior to and limits the right to private ownership," the former was the source and the moral authority for three crucial checks on the rights of property: the right to "just wages," the limitation of profits to no more than a "fair return" on capital, and the doctrine of "fair prices."[19]

While the moral standing of the claim to just wages had its source in the right to a livelihood, its specific origin was as a corollary to the whether relative affluence implied higher than "just" wages, and if so, what this higher rate was, and whether it was a right or a privilege, were continually to plague Catholic social theorists.

The Bishops' Program further complicated the wage question by introducing the notion of a "family wage," to be paid to all adult males, which would permit an adequate livelihood for an average family. Female workers, on the other hand, were to be paid a wage sufficient only for individual support.[27] The bishops' belief that the family was the basis of moral life and that therefore "the proportion of women in industry ought to be kept within the smallest practical limits" led to this endorsement of unequal pay as an inducement to traditional family life.[28] The "family wage" concept was not, however, designed entirely to wed women to the home. It was tacked onto the doctrine of a "livelihood" wage because the theoretical basis of the latter was the support of the worker alone. His work guaranteed him an enforceable moral claim to an income sufficient for maintenance. His family, however, did not enter into this ethical formula.

Ryan inherited these deficiencies in the "livelihood" doctrine. He argued, in 1920, that the "proportion of women in industry should be kept as low as possible," since their proper place was in the home and industrial work was harmful to "their health and morals."[29] But his understanding of the injustice, divisiveness, and downward wage pressure inherent in differential rates of pay led him to support the concept of equal pay for equal work.[30] Instead of embracing the concept of a "family wage," he modified the doctrine of a "just" or livelihood wage to include the support of a family. His reasoning was that both the personal dignity of the worker and the right to life presupposed a moral life. Since the maintenance of a family was an "essential condition of moral life," a living or just wage had to provide for a family. Ryan, however, continued to assume that the head of such a family was invariably male and that women workers were a temporary aberration.[31]

Ryan further modified the concept of a living wage, which had been traditionally interpreted as a subsistence wage, by tying it to the trend of economic development and civilization generally. Different periods brought different wants and needs and therefore different qualitative standards of justice. In twentieth-century older doctrine of "just prices." Under the conditions of artisanal production the "just price" had been the pri guaranteed the cost of production, including labor. The "common estimation" was usually held to be the "just p Since there was relatively little inflation, slight economic gro a traditional labor-intensive productive process regulated guilds through much of the medieval period, this analogy serve enough. The "just price" prevailed except in periods of fami war. When scarcity threatened a rise in prices, the secula religious authorities, or the people themselves, as in the traditi bread riot, acted to bring them down again to the level of comn estimation. [21] The only pressure was upward and the cost of labor w always met.

With inflation, however, the common estimate lost its utility as price-regulating mechanism. In addition, Ryan continued, the wage system undercut the simple relationship between the price of a commodity and the cost of labor. In applying the old procedure under the new economic conditions, "prices" for labor which were below subsistence could be justified as meeting the criterion of common estimation. [22] This led nineteenth-century Church authorities, including von Ketteler, Pascal, and Manning, to tie the idea of just wages instead to the right to a livelihood. [23] Since labor, they argued, is necessary to life and since life is a moral duty, then it follows that the worker has a right to a livelihood from his labor. This was the line of argument used by Pope Leo XIII in the encyclical *Rerum Novarum* in 1891. Here it was held that the just wage was one that "is enough to support the wage earner in reasonable and frugal comfort." [24] If the worker was not receiving such a wage, even if under the terms of a purportedly voluntary wage contract, he was the "victim of fraud and injustice." [25] Just wages, therefore, were not necessarily the prevailing wages.

While this was theoretically a more flexible approach to the question of just wages, the practical difficulties of determining what they were to be were enormous. The Bishops' Program of 1919 offered support for state minimum-wage laws to meet the requirements of justice, but held that in the affluent United States "just wages" were only a minimum which could and often should be exceeded. [26] The problems of defining just wages, of determining

America, he reasoned, it would hardly be just to limit the worker to a bare subsistence income. Increasing levels of production and consumption made the idea of a "subsistence" income an inherently unjust one. Workers who aspired to the "middle class" would hardly be content with an income that provided for no leisure activities, luxuries, or recreation.

Instead, the worker ought to have an income adequate to provide "that amount of goods which will enable a human being to live as a human being, rather than as an animal, even a well-fed animal."[32] This would include income "sufficient" to meet the needs of an average family for food, clothing, shelter, health care, recreation, social intercourse, religious obligations, education, organizational dues, taxes, insurance, utilities, culture, vacations, tobacco, alcohol, books and magazines, as well as savings for accidents, ill health, and old age.[33] The difficulty in ascertaining what would be "sufficient" income for these purposes was admitted by Ryan. While he offered an estimate of 600 dollars in a work of 1906, in his later writings he confessed, "I do not know how anyone would go about forming a set of standards or rules by which to determine with any degree of accuracy what would be a completely just wage in the case of any group of workers."[34]

A number of problems remained unresolved even after Ryan's modifications of the living wage doctrine. One problem was presented by the ambiguity in the terms themselves. The living or just wage was a descriptive rather than an analytical concept. Precision in calculating such wages was impossible. Attempts to do so mired hopelessly in a welter of detail: how many rooms constituted "adequate" shelter, what was a "decent neighborhood," how many bottles of beer were "adequate" or consistent with a "moral life," how much life insurance was "reasonable," how many suits were "sufficient," what was a "frugal" diet, etc.? Variable family size continued to suggest differential wage rates, despite the endorsement of equal pay for equal work, and the picture was further complicated by a recurrent notion that a livelihood wage varied according to "one's station in life."[35] With such a plethora of factors to consider, the practical application of the livelihood or just-wage doctrine was elusive.

Another difficulty with the just-wage concept was a lingering tendency to describe it in terms of subsistence. This had been the original definition and, despite modification, the flavor of austerity remained. While Ryan's budget included recreation, "holiday" clothes, and vacations, the recurrence of the phrases "reasonable and frugal," the "minimum sufficient," and "adequate" suggested that austerity and justice were nearly synonymous. This abstract and austere notion of justice conflicted with and often overwhelmed Ryan's idea that a livelihood wage varied with levels of civilization. Since nearly all American workers were at a subsistence level or better, the effect was to blunt the critical force of the just-wage concept and increase its utility as a doctrinal rationale for the prevailing wage rates.

Perhaps the greatest deficiency of the just-wage doctrine, however, was its lack of any connection to the productive process. The employer found an economic rationale for prevailing wages in the marketplace and in his competitive position. Labor, as a commodity, had its price, which varied according to market conditions, not abstract justice. The Marxist, too, had an economic rationale. Since workers were the source of production and capital merely the reflection of past production, the workers had a just claim to their entire product, as well as the ownership of capital.

Unlike the Marxist, however, the Catholic social theorist did not locate the just-wage concept in production, nor did he accept the labor theory of value.[36] Neither did he credit market explanations of labor's price. His justice was not analytical or quantifiable. Instead, it was an abstract notice of what was sufficient to a decent human life. If workers' productivity increased threefold, this had no necessary relationship to the determination of a just wage. Since workers under modern industrial conditions could produce the equivalent of a subsistence wage in a fraction of their working day, the actual struggle for justice was a struggle over the division of the remainder of their product. To the degree that the just wage doctrine defined a near-subsistence-level wage as the just wage, it militated against recognition of this struggle, much less its successful prosecution. Thus the just-wage doctrine tended to rationalize much lower wage rates than would be justified by the workers' productivity. Obviously such a doctrine was of limited utility to most industrial workers, though it suggested potentially important increases for the most poorly paid.

If justice was less than fully served in the question of wages, Catholic doctrine did attempt to address it from the opposite angle, that of profits. Laissez-faire in profits or in any other area of economic activity was a fallacious doctrine, according to the Church, which merely secured "the liberty of the strong to oppress the weak and to injure the common good under the cover of 'free' contracts."[37] According to Church doctrine, the capitalist had to learn that "wealth is a stewardship, that profit making is not the basic justification of business activity, and that there are such things as fair profits, fair interests and fair prices." From the point of view of Catholic social doctrine, economic activity was carried on to secure equal access to the fruits of production. Profits were not the motivating factor, and insofar as capitalism put these above the rightful claims of workers, it was in error.[38] Indeed, the employer "has no right to interest on his investment until his employees have obtained at least a living wage."[39]

As we have seen, however, a moderately efficient employer could receive substantial profits, and still claim to be meeting the rather vague requirements of the living-wage theory. Insofar as "fair profits" were defined as profits made after payment of a "living wage," this doctrine, too, would share in the imprecision and shortcomings of the "living-wage" concept. Ryan did strive for a more precise definition. In 1920 he estimated that five or six percent would constitute an adequate return on investment.[40] In 1935, under depression conditions, he suggested that one or two percent might be "most in harmony with the common good."[41] Coupled with Ryan's endorsement of heavy taxation of excess profits, this latter definition might have meant a substantial redistribution of income.[42]

This possibility was diminished, however, in a series of caveats that justified higher profits in nearly every case in which they might occur. The major exemption from the prohibition on excess profits was to be granted to efficient producers.[43] Ryan's argument paralleled those of classical economists David Ricardo and Adam Smith. Efficient producers had a "right" to any excess profits in recompense for their entrepreneurial skill. Their efficiency was assumed to benefit the consumer through lower prices and the worker through more jobs and higher pay. The capitalist who had "earned" a million dollars in this way, then, had a "right" to it.[44] This argument severely undercut the effect of the fair-profit doctrine. Since no particular measure of efficiency was contemplated other than profit itself, the way was paved for businessmen's claims that high profits per se demonstrated their efficiency and thus were justified.

A second serious problem with Ryan's exemption of the efficient producer from the "fair profit" doctrine was his ready acceptance of the capitalist commonplace that the sole cause of increased efficiency was entrepreneurial skill. Increased efficiency, from the vantage point of the industrial worker, usually meant "speed-up." Even in those rare cases in which improved machinery results in both increased production and a slackening of the pace of work, the worker could be said to be the ultimate source of the increased product, just as his labor is said to be the source of the capital for the machinery itself. Thus it would seem illogical and unjust to assign the proceeds from exceptional efficiency exclusively to the owners of the enterprise. Ryan noticed a similar problem in the case of idle or absentee owners ("dead capital") versus active managers. Where active managers were the stand-ins for entrepreneurs, he argued that they, rather than the owners, should receive the rewards of increased productivity.[45] The workers, however, apparently had no such claim. While charity and the theory of competition might "suggest" that the excess profits resulting from increased efficiency be shared with the workers and consumers, they had no enforceable "right" to any share at all.[46] Indeed, the modifications in the Catholic theory of "fair prices" by the authors of the Bishops' Program of 1919 and by Ryan himself tended to reinforce the position of monopoly enterprise vis-à-vis the consumer and the worker.

Where production methods were static the identification of fair prices with the price of common estimate was a reasonable mechanism for limiting the unjustifiable upward advance of prices in time of scarcity or speculative hoarding. Under industrial conditions, however, increased production could make even the prevailing prices a source of excess profits. Even cutting prices less than would be warranted by increased efficiency could be seen as unjust. In this situation the price of common estimate was no guide to fairness or justice.

Rather than attempt to modernize a theory of price regulation, however, the Church tended to drop it altogether, except as a sort of general reproof against "extortionate profit." Ryan, heavily influenced by the National Recovery Administration (NRA), argued against any stronger form of price regulation. Since, Ryan thought, the inefficient producer had to be protected in order to preserve jobs, the only permissible form of price regulation was the setting of maximum prices that would guarantee the most inefficient a fair rate of return.[47] Since such prices would secure the high profit rates of the efficient or the monopolistic, they hardly constituted price regulation at all. They were rather a "fair trade" mechanism which prevented the lowering of prices. Thus the fair-price doctrine was diluted until its effect was quite the reverse of the original purpose: legislative authority for the highest possible prices. The fair-price doctrine, rather than offering an alternative to a problematic theory of fair profits, instead reinforced its worst effects. Excess profits could not be touched because they were the rightful reward for efficient enterprise and because to do so through price regulation would mean the elimination of inefficient producers.

Church doctrine, then, defended the institution of private property as a natural right and as necessary to human welfare, but since there was a prior right of all persons to a livelihood from nature, property had a social obligation to charge "fair prices," pay a "living wage" and secure no more than a "fair return" to capital. By means of these three checks the institution of private property was to be reconciled with the common good. As the foregoing analysis suggests, however, these rights offered very little in the way of resistance to the power of property.

The fair-price doctrine had become so diluted that it was no more than a justification for monopoly profits. The living wage doctrine, while retaining more critical potential, was vitiated by its lack of connection to increased productivity, its near-subsistence definition and the near impossibility of its practical application. The concept of fair return to capital was undercut by the exemption of the most efficient producers and the difficulty of distinguishing these from monopoly profit-takers. Despite the intention to construct a case based on Catholic ethics for industrial social justice, very little of such a case was made.

If indeed each of these conceptions could be used without much difficulty by those who might seek to justify prevailing wage rates, high prices, and high profits, with what was the Catholic social activist to arm himself in the fight for social justice? One answer might have been an identification of the workers' interests with justice and the acceptance of class conflict as the means to secure it. Every tenet of the Church, however, stood in the way of such a theory. Class conflict, according to Leo XIII, could not be a remedy for inequities since the classes "should dwell in harmony and agreement."[48] "Society," he had written, "can be cured in no other way than by a return to Christian life and Christian institutions."[49] The Bishops' Program of 1919 reaffirmed this ethical and voluntary approach to social injustice in its concluding call for "a reform in the spirit of both labor and capital."[50] A Christian social order would embody this spiritual reform and replace class conflict and social injustice with harmony, understanding, and reciprocal action.

The prospect of a peaceful ushering in of the millenium was no doubt an attractive one. How it was to be accomplished without mandatory curbs on the practitioners of social injustice, short of a miracle, was another matter. The Church's answer to this problem was reciprocal, voluntary action. *Rerum Novarum* had contained a sketch of the reciprocal rights and duties of capital and labor that served as the basis for later programs centering on cooperative industry, profit sharing, co-management, or a full-blown occupational or corporative organization of society. But the step from theory to practice was a large one and along the way these programs tended to be despairingly discarded as unworkable or transmuted from voluntary programs into authoritarian ones.[51]

Ryan's discussion of the various reciprocal schemes commenced from the proposition that wage earners "should be given the effective opportunity of achieving the status of ownership."[52] Since property was a natural right and a necessity for human welfare and development, the propertyless class was without the full means of human development. This was at once a misfortune for these proletarians and a social peril since the propertyless were bound to develop resentment and even class consciousness.[53] The solution was a wider spread of ownership.

The medieval orientation of Catholic social thought encouraged notions of the resuscitation of the family farm and artisinal production as a means to this increase in property owners. The Bishops' Program of 1919, for example, had unsuccessfully sought to promote homesteading by returning veterans, claiming that this would be "one of the most beneficial reform measures that has ever been attempted."[54] The depression brought a renewed interest in such homesteading and handicraft schemes, and these were promoted by the *Catholic Worker* organization and the Catholic Union of the Unemployed, among others.[55] They were largely a form of stopgap relief, rather than a long-lasting property reform measure, however. Ryan, too, believed the "family farm" to be the "most desirable socially," but he did not consider homesteading or handicraft production to be much of a solution to the restricted ownership of property.[56]

He favored, instead, cooperative industry as the "most desirable and democratic arrangement."[57] Cooperative production would combine the functions of worker and capitalist and thus end the dependency inherent in a propertyless condition. Cooperative firms would provide workers with a basis to express their "desire to exercise some controlling influence on their environment."[58] They would encourage "a sense of responsibility for the welfare of the employing concern," and thus make workers feel "more like a partner and less like an antagonist" to the firm.[59] It was important, too, that cooperative enterprise would encourage workers to "turn out a larger daily product."[60].

While cooperative enterprise as a means of speed-up might have received a lukewarm reception from workers, there was a radical thrust in Ryan's discussion of cooperative ownership. Though Ryan might echo the promise of the Bishops' Program of 1919 that "no profound changes in the U. S." were contemplated by Catholic social theory, his criticism of the wage system and endorsement of its abolition through total cooperative enterprise did seem to imply profound changes.[61]

Ryan, however, was unwilling to follow through on the radical implications of his support for cooperatives, just as he was in the case of the doctrine of fair profits. He eschewed expropriation, even with compensation, as a vehicle for cooperatization since all private property was sacrosanct. Workers, even if willing, would not have the capital to organize cooperatives. This, certainly, was the lesson of previous attempts to organize cooperatives in the United States. Since capitalists were unlikely to undergo cooperatization willingly,

Ryan considered the cause lost. Cooperative enterprise on any scale, he wrote, "cannot be hoped for in the near future."[62]

Several other, more limited solutions had better prospects in Ryan's opinion. Profit sharing was already practiced by a number of corporations and might be extended without great difficulty. According to Ryan, the best form of profit sharing was the division of all surplus profits, after the payment of "fair wages" and salaries and a reasonable rate of interest, among workers and managers. "Idle capital" would not share in the proceeds, beyond its "reasonable rate of interest."[63]

When combined with some form of labor co-management, Ryan felt that such a profit sharing scheme could be nearly as effective as cooperative industry in ameliorating the dependent condition of the laborers. The Bishops' Program had indicated the areas in which it would be reasonable to expect labor to share in decision making with management. These included "the control of processes and machinery; nature of the product; employment and dismissal of employees; hours of work; rates of pay, bonuses, etc.; welfare work; shop discipline; relations with trade unions."[64] If divisions of surplus profits were to be combined with this degree of control it is apparent that a radical change would be wrought in economic life.

Once again, however, no sooner was the conclusion reached that radical change would be necessary than the retreat was sounded. Co-management and profit sharing, too, foundered on the shoals of property rights. Workers had no "right" to this profit-sharing arrangement, nor, in the Church's view, did they have a right to co-management.[65] Both co-management and profit sharing, then, depended on the voluntary surrender by the capitalists of a portion of their power and profits. Despite his belief in the possibility of spiritual reform, Ryan did not seem to think this eventuality any too likely. He therefore concluded that "labor sharing in management is unlikely to be widely adopted by business corporations."[66]

With cooperation, profit sharing, and co-management reduced to the practical status of dead letters, very little was left of the Church's program of reciprocal action and spiritual reform as a means of social justice. Ryan thus retreated to advocating an extension of the profit-sharing and workers' representation plans initiated by employers. Among the exemplary programs he cited were those of

Standard Oil of New Jersey and Hart, Schaffner and Marx.[67] Profit sharing under such company plans involved encouragement of optional stock purchases by employees, sometimes at a small discount. In some plans the stock purchases were mandatory and deductible from the pay envelope. Obviously, the number of shares involved did not constitute a controlling interest. The effect of such plans was to cultivate employee loyalty on the cheap and to secure a little extra capital in the bargain.

The Standard Oil plan was an even unlikelier candidate for exemplary social justice. Instituted in the aftermath of the Ludlow Massacre of 1914, it was partly a public-relations gambit and partly insurance against unionization.[68] Its main component was a legislature elected by the employees. Though it was highly touted as embodying the best principles of democracy and rational economics, the Standard Oil plan was at best no more than an elaborate employee-consultation system. No decisions binding on the corporation could be made by the legislature, whose members were in large measure supervisory workers. The major impact of the Standard Oil plan was as a prototype of the company unions of the 1920s.[69] Ryan may have believed that cooperation on the employer's terms was better than none at all, but his endorsement of a company union as the epitome of fruitful capital-labor cooperation certainly gave a rather conservative cast to the doctrine of reciprocity.

The Church's program for the reorganization of society along corporative or industrial-council lines carried this conservative direction even further. Leo XIII's encyclical *Rerum Novarum* had endorsed guilds as a solution to industrial conflict in 1891, but the most extensive Catholic discussion of corporative doctrine was Pius XI's encyclical of 1931, *Quadragesimo Anno*. According to Pius XI, "Sound prosperity is to be restored according to the true principles of a sane corporative system which respects the proper hierarchic structure of society." The occupational groups would unite employers and workers, who would be "fused into a harmonious unity inspired by the principle of the common good." This plan involved placing the organizing, planning, and day-to-day administration of the economy in the hands of the "occupational groups" in each industry, with a minimum of state interference.[70]

The doctrine had originally been developed by conservative Catholic social activists in Italy and Austria in the late nineteenth century as a reaction both to socialism and the liberal state, and was literally reactionary in the sense that its purpose was the restoration of feudal forms of social organization. The model for this corporative restoration was the guild. Whereas, according to the corporatists, unions, and employer associations divided the classes and promoted class conflict and special interest, a new guild organization of economic life would combine all occupational groups and institutionalize reciprocal action. While the state was an inorganic and artificial organization attempting to regulate economic life from without, the guilds would be voluntary and organic, and would constitute rational self-regulation of the economy.[71]

Such an arrangement of social life would preserve private property and entrepreneurial initiative and at the same time promote a responsible role for workers in the running of the economy.[72] Reciprocal action through the guilds would guarantee fair wages, prices and profits and would avoid the evils of monopoly, maldistribution of property, concentrated power, and an unchecked bureaucratic state. Alienation and powerlessness would be ended through a "gradual hierarchial order" of subsidiary organizations between the individual and the state.[73] All of this would be accomplished under the guidance of the Church, which would assure the restoration of moral life.

The guild or corporative program did address itself to the alienation, powerlessness, dependency, and lack of purpose in capitalist society, in addition to material deprivation. In this sense it might be seen as critical social theory. Certainly many of the changes envisioned were sweeping ones which would threaten established interests, especially in the political system. At the same time, the solutions proposed were thoroughly conservative. The practical problems, too, were enormous. The corporative program suffered from all of the difficulties which beset the doctrines of "fair" prices, profits, and wages and, in addition, presented entirely new problems to the Catholic social activist which made the former seem minor in comparison. Modifying a doctrine such as the just wage, whose roots were in the thirteenth century, for twentieth century application was difficult enough, but reviving an extinct form of social organization was near impossible.

Two severe problems with the guild plan were its stress on hierarchy and its failure to assign any role to the unions.[74] Hierarchy was a positive good in the corporative program and was seen as an antidote to the instability and uncertainty of modern life. The contentment with one's lot in life that established hierarchy was to produce, however, was not likely to be attractive to workers with expectations of mobility, democracy, and equality. These ideas had no place in the guild organization of society. Nor did the unions. While Catholic doctrine in the late nineteenth century had grudgingly accepted a role for "unmixed" unions, unions, that is, consisting only of workers, the Church's preference had always been for guilds, which mixed employers and employees.[75] Despite the endorsement of unions, the preference for guilds came to the fore again in the corporative program. Since class harmony was to be restored, no class organization would be necessary. Hence the unions were to have either no role at all in the corporative order or a distinctly minor one. To a worker who felt that his union was his sole source of protection this was certainly a suspicious feature of the Christian social order.

There was a close connection, too, between the Church's corporative program and the syndicate structure of Italian Fascism. Mussolini claimed to be following the guidelines of the Church in his corporate state. Indeed, Pope Pius XI was sympathetic to the "special syndical and corporative organization" of Italian Fascism.[76] Franco, too, had the support of the Church in his armed rebellion and corporative program.[77] The doctrine had obvious utility to the Fascist regimes since it minimized political and social conflict and stressed a somewhat mystical unity and harmony. Since corporativism combined economic representation with hierarchy, discipline, and undisturbed property relationships, it was an ideal alternative to the potentially volatile and revolutionary system of political representation.

While American Catholic social theorists were naturally cautious about citing the Fascist regimes as examples of the Christian social order to come, they often betrayed a certain sympathy for them, especially when compared with socialism or communism. Ryan, for example, concluded that "the fascist system has some good features," among them the rejection of individualism and liberalism, the stress on unity, and the corporate features of the regime, including joint employer-worker associations and the "substitution of occupational for geographic representation in the Chamber of Deputies."[78] In contrast, Ryan found no good features in socialism or communism. "As a method of economic reconstruction," he argued "socialism would involve society in far greater evils than those from which it now suffers."[79]

The problems with socialism were many in Ryan's opinion. Class conflict and materialism were the fundamental and irredeemable errors. Flowing from these were the problems of lack of "adequate incentives," inefficiency, despotism, "concentration of power," and "a very great lessening of contractual liberty" and the "liberty to own," as well as other civil liberties.[80] Ryan took up the capitalist case against socialism, despite his own critique of individualism and excess profits, in arguing that competition and profits were the best organizer of economic life.[81] In a further striking reversal of his brief on behalf of cooperative enterprise, he indicated that "the average man will work hard at them [industrial tasks] only when compelled by sheer necessity, such as the fear of losing his job."[82]

Ryan was backed into this conservative position by the absolute anathema on socialism. There were obvious parallels between the Church's most sweeping policy suggestions and those of socialism. To admit that there might be areas of agreement, however, would open the door to serious discussion of the socialist alternative, and thus undercut that most "fundamental issue" of the Church, opposition to socialism.[83] Ryan's solution was to admit to no similarities and to reject the socialist alternative out of hand.[84] Since any other approach to socialism would tend to praise it with faint criticism, he retreated to the stock commonplaces of the capitalist polemic against socialism: tyranny, the sanctity of contracts, laziness, and inefficiency.

Once again, fear of radicalization or, in this case, of radical company tended to exacerbate the conservative direction in Catholic social doctrine. Thus, while socialism was "out of bounds" in any consideration of the elements of a Christian social order, Fascism was not. And since Fascism included such commendable features as respect for private property, hostility to the left, national unity and purpose, and a corporative organization of society, it was even worthy, to that degree, of emulation.

The corporative or "occupational groups" program for social reorganization never became much of an issue in the United States, either in the political arena or in the unions. The conservative nature of the program, embodied in its stress on hierarchy, authority, contentment with one's social position, guarantees for private property, class harmony, and the abolition of politics, coupled with the sectarian limitations of a Church-superintended society and the Fascist connections of corporationism, made corporatism singularly unattractive to most liberal, labor, and radical opinion. At the same time, conservatives and property owners found corporativism too sweeping for their own purposes. It was at once too radical and too conservative for business endorsement. The Fascists had their own secular ideology and organizations. In the absence of popular support for the guild program, its supporters were reduced to pointing out parallels between the "occupational groups" plan and the NRA or the AFL-sponsored partnership programs of the 1920s in the garment industry.[85] Since labor was unrepresented on 530 of the 559 NRA boards and had pressed partnership in the garment industry largely as a stopgap to union-busting and runaway shops, these parallels did little to increase support for the guild program among unionists.[86]

This lack of popular support for a voluntary corporative order led to a more favorable view of the state as a catalyst for the process than the guild program had originally provided. Corporativism was supposed to limit severely the arena of activity of the state and presumably remove it from the economic field altogether.[87] Without the requisite voluntary action, however, this goal remained distant at best. In fact, despite the Church's suspicion of the liberal state, American Catholic social theorists had assigned it an extensive role in social policy since World War I. The Bishops' Program of 1919 had indicated support for child labor laws, minimum wages, a national unemployment service, continuation of the War Labor Board in some form, municipal housing and power, price regulation and social insurance, despite the belief that a voluntary "reform in the spirit of both labor and capital" was the essential item in any program for social justice.[88]

Ryan, too, believed that "self-help" was the "more desirable method of social betterment."[89] But he was also a fervent supporter of the New Deal and a vigorous proponent of state intervention.[90] While the state might be "inorganic" and its role in the economy an artificial and stopgap one, it was better than nothing. Thus, many of the functions assigned in corporative theory to voluntary guild organizations were, in practice, given over to the state. Not all, however, for neither Ryan nor any other Catholic social theoretician was willing to grant the state the power to direct economic activity.[91] The proper sphere of the state, in Ryan's opinion, was to set boundaries and provide against the exigencies of unemployment, accident, and old age. To the degree that the state had a more positive role to perform, its limits had been reached with the NRA, the Wagner Act, and a more progressive taxation policy. The corporative program, therefore, tended to be dissolved into a general endorsement of the New Deal program. As a result, corporative theory lost much of its already limited value as a guide to further action.

Despite the failure of the corporative program to become a live issue in public life, it remained the maximum program of Catholic social activists. It continued to be the fullest expression of Catholic social theory and tended to shape the reaction of Catholic social activists to other issues.[92] Its unique contribution was the guild model for economic life. This model was based upon and reinforced the ideas of class harmony and of cross-class cooperation, and thus promoted mediation, hostility to the strike, and the cross-class anti-communist front. The corporative program exacerbated the tendency among Catholic social activists to look backward rather than forward for solutions to industrial problems, a tendency which most often led them either to practical impasse or conservative policies. The tendency to voluntarism was also buttressed by the guild program, which made social justice the prisoner of spiritual reform and voluntary action by the practitioners of social injustice themselves. The "occupational groups" program thus shared with Catholic social theory generally the lack of an agency of social change, while it shrouded this problem with appeals to charity and the common good.

Corporativism, to a greater degree than other components of Catholic social doctrine, stressed the values of hierarchy, authority, and contentment with social station and thus undervalued equality, democracy, and mobility.[93] The guild program incorporated and extended the general anathema against class conflict and socialism, whose effect was uniform Catholic hostility to workers' militance in their fight for social justice, and the isolation of Catholic proponents of such militance.[94] The ideological resuscitation of guilds also tended to undermine the function of the unions and the independent role of workers generally, while it provided justification for company unions and a partial endorsement of Fascism. The themes of "harmony" and "unity" and the opposition to conflict resulted also in the dilution of those measures which, while consistent with justice and the common good, were unlikely to be voluntarily adopted by American business. Private property was inviolate in the corporative plan, as it was in other elements of Catholic social doctrine.

In summary, then, Catholic social doctrine had severe limitations as a guide to "social justice." Fundamental problems in capitalist society, including material deprivation, concentration of power and property, excess profits, alienation and powerlessness, fair prices and wages, lack of purpose, and spiritual malaise were analyzed and addressed. But the Church's fundamentally conservative commitments to private property, entrepreneurial autonomy, harmony, cross-class cooperation and voluntarism, and its unwavering hostility to socialism tended to undercut both the analysis and the more sweeping prescriptions proposed. Catholic social doctrine, therefore, in the context of the 1930s and 1940s, was a conservative ideological influence on the labor movement.

NOTES

1. Camp, *Papal Ideology*, pp. 83–90.
2. Ryan believed that, had the measures suggested in the Bishops' Statement been adopted, "the unprecedented unrest of 1919" which fed "revolutionary agitation and bolshevism" could have been avoided. Ryan, *Social Reconstrcution*, pp. 39, 217–22.
3. "Bishops' Statement on Reconstruction," in Ryan, *Social Reconstruction*, p. 223.
4. Ibid., p. 235.
5. Bernstein, *The Lean Years*, p. 84.
6. *Jubilee*, September 1954. Other important Catholic commentators on social doctrine

included Bruehl, *The Pope's Plan*, John F. Cronin, *Catholic Social Action* (Milwaukee: Bruce, 1948); Joseph Hussline, *The World Problem: Capital, Labor and the Church* (New York: Kenedy, 1918); John Paul, *Production for Use and Not for Profit* (Washington, D.C.: Catholic University, 1931). Ryan, however, by virtue of his extensive theoretical contributions, his influence on his students and peers, and his leading role as director of the Social Welfare Department of the American Federation of Catholic Societies, was generally acknowledged to be the most authoritative spokesman for the Church on social issues. For this reason he was selected to give the keynote speech at the ACTU's first national convention in September 1940, and to assist the organization in its activities. See *Labor Leader* 3, no. 17.

7. Fox, *Peter E. Dietz*, p. 49; *Michigan Labor Leader* 7, no 17.

8. Jules Weinberg, "Priests, Workers and Communists," *Harper's Magazine*, November 1948, p. 53. For further reading on Ryan see Broderick, *Right Reverend New Dealer*, Gearty, *Economic Thought of Monsignor John A. Ryan*, Abell, "Ryan." On Ryan and the ACTU see *Michigan Labor Leader* 2, no. 9, 7, no. 17; *Labor Leader* 1, nos. 4, 5, 19, and 24, 3, nos. 4 and 12; *Cleveland Free Press*, August 30, 1940, p. 1.

9. See Camp, *Papal Ideology*, pp. 80–96.

10. See the debate between Max Schactman and Reverend Charles Owen Rice, "Marxism vs. Catholicism," *New International*, January 1949, p. 5; and Ryan, *Social Reconstruction*, p. 236.

11. Camp, *Papal Ideology*, p. 106.

12. Ryan, *Social Reconstruction*, p. 220.

13. Ryan, *A Better Economic Order*, p. 150.

14. Ibid.

15. Ryan, *A Living Wage*, pp. 26–7.

16. Ibid., p. 75.

17. Ryan, *Social Reconstruction*, p. 211.

18. Ryan, *A Living Wage*, p. 70.

19. Ibid., p. 67.

20. Ibid., p. 30.

21. For an account of the traditional "bread riot," see George Rude, *The Crowd in History*, (New York: Wiley, 1964), pp. 19–33.

22. Ryan, *A Living Wage*, p. 31.

23. Ibid., p. 34.

24. Ibid., pp. 32–33.

25. Ibid., p. 33.

26. Ryan, *Social Reconstruction*, pp. 226–28.

27. This policy, of course, assumed that male wage earners either were the heads of families or would soon be and that women were neither the heads of families nor earning wages necessary to the support of others. See Ryan, *Social Reconstruction*, p. 230.

28. Ibid., pp. 225–26.

29. Ibid., p. 41.

30. Ibid., p. 42.

31. Ryan, *A Living Wage*, p. 118.

32. Ryan, *Social Reconstruction*, p. 65.

33. Ryan, *A Living Wage*, pp. 132–36, *Social Reconstruction*, pp. 65–66.

34. Ryan, *A Living Wage*, p. 150; *Social Reconstruction*, pp. 51–52.

35. This concept skewed the "livelihood wage" upward for professionals and businessmen and downward for laborers. See *Labor Leader* 3, no. 4.

36. Schactman, "Marxism vs. Catholicism," p. 4.

37. Ryan, *A Better Economic Order*, p. 111.

38. *Labor Leader* 2, no. 16.

39. This, however, was an unenforceable right as far as the worker was concerned. See Ryan, *Social Reconstruction*, p. 257.

40. Ibid., p. 196.

41. Ryan, *A Better Economic Order*, p. 159.

42. Ibid., p. 107.

43. Ryan, *Social Reconstruction*, p. 194; quotation from the "Bishops' Program for Reconstruction," quoted in *Social Reconstruction*, p. 236.

44. Ryan, *Social Reconstruction*, p. 198.

45. Ibid., p. 196.

46. The rights of property, in contrast, were always enforceable, either directly or through the agency of the state. See Ryan, *Social Reconstruction*, p. 194.

47. Ibid., pp. 56–58.

48. Camp, *Papal Ideology*, pp. 80–90.

49. Ryan, *Social Reconstruction*, p. 237.

50. Ibid., p. 237.

51. Falangist Spain, Fascist Italy, and Vichy France adopted portions of the Church's "guild" or "corporate" program and the Church regarded the Italian corporate state, at least in its first years, as worthy of emulation in certain respects. Camp, *Papal Ideology*, pp. 80–90; Ryan, *A Better Economic Order*, pp. 121–25.

52. Ryan, *A Better Economic Order*, p. 161.

53. Ibid., pp. 164–65.

54. Ryan, *Social Reconstruction*, p. 225.

55. See, for example, statements by members of the ACTU's Catholic Union of the Unemployed, *Labor Leader* 1, nos. 6, 7, and 13.

56. Ryan, *A Better Economic Order*, p. 154.

57. Ibid., p. 162.

58. Ibid., p. 163.

59. Ibid., p. 162.

60. Ibid.

61. Ryan, *Social Reconstruction*, p. 223.

62. Ryan, *A Better Economic Order*, p. 162.

63. Ibid., p. 165.

64. Ryan, *Social Reconstruction*, p. 232.

65. *Labor Leader* 3, no. 3; Ryan, *Social Reconstruction*, p. 157.

66. Ryan assumes here that any such arrangement would be a voluntary one. There is no question of state intervention to promote co-management. See Ryan, *A Better Economic Order*, p. 174.

67. Ryan, *Social Reconstruction*, p. 150.

68. For a firsthand account of the Ludlow strike and the inauguration of the Standard Oil plan, see Barron Beshoar, *Out of the Depths* (Denver, Colorado: The Colorado Labor Historical Committee and the Denver Trades and Labor Assembly, 1942).

69. The growth of the company unions, inspired by Standard Oil's example, encouraged by the postwar open-shop drive, and fed by the wreckage of disaffiliating AFL locals, was extremely rapid in the 1920s, especially when compared to the declining AFL membership. See Bernstein, *The Lean Years*, pp. 84–85.

70. Camp, *Papal Ideology*, p. 39.

71. The most important of these groups were the Italian Opera dei Congressi and the German Volksverein, which were active in organizational and educational work until the early 1900s. Camp, *Papal Ideology*, pp. 110–36.

72. Ryan, *A Better Economic Order*, p. 179.

73. Ibid., p. 178.

74. Ibid., pp. 124–25, 179.

75. See Camp's discussion of *Rerum Novarum*'s stress on guild organization, *Papal Ideology*, p. 113.

76. Ryan, *A Better Economic Order*, pp. 124–25.

77. Hugh Thomas, *The Spanish Civil War* (New York: Harper's, 1961), p. 182.

78. Ryan, *A Better Economic Order*, pp. 124–25.

79. Ibid., p. 126.

80. Ibid., pp. 126-30.

81. Ibid., pp. 126, 128.

82. Ibid., p. 128.

83. Opposition to socialism was so characterized by Catholic historian Vincent McQuade in his "American Catholic Attitudes on Child Labor Since 1891," p. 50.

84. Ryan, *A Better Economic Order*, pp. 126–46.

85. Ibid., pp. 183–86; *Labor Leader* 1, no. 40.

86. *Labor Leader* 1, no. 13.

87. Ryan, *A Better Economic Order*, p. 178.

88. Ryan, *Social Reconstruction*, pp. 222, 225, 226, 228, 229, 231, 233, 237.

89. Ibid., p. 202.

90. Ibid., pp. 62–114.

91. This tradition of hostility to the state derived from the Church's experience with European anticlerical liberalism, especially in Italy.

92. The ACTU viewed the issues of price controls, profit sharing, wages, monopolies, union-management relations, violence, class conflict, the NLRB, and the NRA all through the prism of the corporativist program. See, for example, *Labor Leader* 1, nos. 40 and 45; 3, no. 7; 2, no. 11; 1, nos. 6, 10, 21, and 27; 3, nos. 7, 12, and 4; 7, nos. 4, and 11; 8, no. 4; 7, no. 8.

93. See Ryan's discussion of the corporative state, *A Better Economic Order*, pp. 121–83.

94. Indeed, the guild program's institutionalization of class cooperation and class hierarchy was an explicit repudiation of class conflict and socialist theory.

3 † "Tear Down the Barricades of Class War": The ACTU's Catholic Apostolate to Labor

The ACTU's formation in February 1937 paralleled a number of important developments which were to shape the young Catholic action organization is its "apostolate" among American workers. The Reverend John P. Monaghan, Irish-born pastor of Saint Mary's parish in Staten Island and the first ACTU chaplain, recalls the flavor of the period:

> It was February 1937. A new and vigorous trade union movement was rising out of the terrible discouragement of vast unemployment and low wages with a great assist from a new national legislative policy (The Wagner Act) favoring collective bargaining.
>
> The ink was literally drying on the first great industrial union contract in America's short industrial history—(after a new and revolutionary type of strike called a "sit-down strike") between General Motors and the United Auto Workers, CIO. Socialists were an unmoored force in the American labor movement—the Socialist Party having split asunder the previous year (1936) over Marxist Socialism versus the peaceful social advances of the New Deal—with the trade union wing leaving the party behind in the belief that Socialism had no real meaning or practicality for American wage earners.
>
> Meanwhile, two other significant forces were on the move—the bootleggers (the new aristocracy of the Prohibition era) and the Communist Party. The first group, powerful then in political life and in certain business circles, found itself without any real function as Prohibition ended and the beer and liquor traffic became legal. Its manpower, police and political connections were obvious assets to be exploited in some new fields.
>
> Meanwhile, the Communist Party was undergoing some changes in

tactics. Dismayed by the growth of non-red unions throughout the world and the acceptance of peaceful social reforms by workingmen here, in France, Brazil, and elsewhere, the Communists decided at the Seventh World Comintern Meeting (1935) to abolish their own revolutionary unions and move in to control the new, growing unions in the democratic countries.

The former Prohibition beer barons, observing the sprawling, ofttimes directionless new growth of the labor movement and the efforts of the Communists to infiltrate and control, decided to move in themselves to dominate unions where they could and, at the same time, exploit employers' resistance to unions and their fear of Communism.

It was in this economic, social, and political climate that eleven young Catholics gravitated to the *Catholic Worker* and there formed the Association of Catholic Trade Unionists, the ACTU.[1]

This then was a period of great opportunity for organization among Catholic workers and the first members of the ACTU represented that opportunity in the diversity of their trades, backgrounds, education, and union affiliation. They included brushmakers, dock workers, carpenters, journalists, social workers, seamen, teamsters, government workers, utility workers, transit drivers, and milkmen. Their education ranged from grade school through Harvard and law school. Most of them were Irish, a few Italian or German, and all of them were male. They ranged from early twenties to early fifties in age. Most were American-born, though several were Irish- and one English-born. All but one were raised in the Church and nearly all had attended Catholic schools.[2] They were members of several AFL and CIO unions and one independent union.[3]

Whatever their particular background, all of the early ACTU members had been affected by the great organizing drives of the CIO and believed that the Church had a major role to play in the American labor movement. "At that time," recalled John Cort, "the Catholic Church, for all its tremendous numbers and wonderful organization, touched the union movement hardly at all. Then as now it was obvious to many that trade unionism, in America as in Europe, might well hold the answer to the future. Something was surely wrong if the Church were to have nothing to say about that answer." This lack of Catholic presence was hardly the case with respect to the AFL unions, of course, but Cort had in mind the new CIO unions, centered in the crucial mass-production industries and destined to become as important as the craft unions. These industrial unions had not been greatly influenced by the Church and the fledgling ACTU hoped to provide that influence.[4]

The *Catholic Worker* organization offered the Actists initial instruction in the social encyclicals, some union contacts, and a living example of Catholic dedication to the workers. Their headquarters on Mott Street in Manhattan served as a meeting place for the ACTU and as a school for weekly classes in the labor encyclicals which the Actists began immediately to conduct for other Catholic workers. Cort and Patrick Whelan lived in the communal *Catholic Worker* household for several years. After a few months, however, the ACTU moved to its own quarters. The new organization needed more space and it soon developed differences with the *Catholic Worker* organization over direction and strategy.[5]

The Actists respected the dedication of the *Catholic Worker* partisans, but disagreed with their stress on rural cooperatives and handicraft industry as a solution to social and industrial problems. The *Catholic Worker*, they thought, was "unrealistic" and "escapist." It offered no strategy or program for work within the unions and concentrated instead on creating cooperative alternatives in isolation from the industrial system and from the vast majority of Catholic workers. The Actists, citing the social encyclicals' defense of private property, also opposed the *Catholic Worker*'s position in favor of workers' ownership of the means of production. As Dorothy Day of the *Catholic Worker* recalls it, the ACTU also "disagreed with our indiscriminate assistance in strikes where there was a strong Communist influence, and our loss of the opportunity to get our own men into positions of advantage in order to influence others" in the unions. The parting was amicable, however, The Actists continued to utilize copies of the *Catholic Worker* in their educational efforts and Dorothy Day continued to address their meetings.[6]

The newly independent ACTU then set about constructing its own organization and developing strategy for its work in the labor movement. Of one thing they were certain: "We were not going to start a dual labor movement by setting up Catholic unions." The ACTU, in fact, altered its original name, the Catholic Trade Union Association, in order to avoid even the impression of "dual unionism". The ACTU would be an organization of Catholics who were members of bona fide CIO, AFL, or genuinely independent trade unions. The organization would be based on the ideals of the social encyclicals *Rerum Novarum* (1891) and *Quadragesimo Anno* (1931), and "other recognized Catholic authorities." Its purpose would be

> to foster and spread in the American labor movement sound trade unionism based on Christian principles, first by bringing to Catholic workers in particular, and all workers in general, a knowledge of these principles, and, second by training leaders and supplying an organization to put these principles into practice.

Since Pius XI, in *Quadragesimo Anno*, had stated that "side by side with these nonsectarian trade unions there must always be associations which aim at giving their members a thorough moral and religious training," the ACTU believed it was under "direct mandate from the highest authority of the Church—the Vicar of Christ on earth" to engage in these activities.[7]

The ACTU's classes on the encyclicals and its early strike-support work, coupled with the approval and encouragement of the Church hierarchy in the New York area, brought it many new members. The organization expanded to Boston, Pittsburgh, and Detroit in 1938, followed by Rochester and Corning (New York), San Pedro (California), Toledo, Cleveland, San Francisco, Glassport (Pennsylvania), Newark, Oklahoma City and Ponca City (Oklahoma) in 1939 and South Bend, Chicago, Milwaukee, Saginaw and Bay City (Michigan) in 1940–1941. The total number of chapters ultimately reached twenty-four and the membership 10,000. The addition of "associate members" (non-Catholics), clerics, professionals and other nonunionized sympathizers, supporters and members of ACTU conferences in particular industries and unions, students and graduates of the ACTU's extensive network of labor schools, and readers of the national *Labor Leader*, the *Michigan Labor Leader*, and the periodicals of other chapters and ACTU-supported union caucuses brought the number of ACTU supporters nearer to 100,000.[8]

This group of ACTU members and supporters was not merely an extension of the tiny group of original Actists. Expansion and activity brought changes in the background, union affiliation, ethnicity, education, sex, and political sophistication of the ACTU support base. In general, the ACTU membership became more industrial and more diverse in occupations and union membership. Their educational level decreased and their ethnic background became more varied, though the Irish remained dominant. The new members also included more women. The general trend was for the membership to become more conservative and more anti-communist, though it is impossible to determine which, if any, of these factors was involved in this trend. It seems most likely that this tendency was determined by the internal life of the organization and by external events in the unions and the country at large, rather than by any factor peculiar to the newer members. As the ACTU increasingly focused on the struggle against the communists and as anti-communism became more prevalent and more obligatory in the unions, the organization tended to recruit more anti-communist conservatives. When pressure on the left wing became extremely intense in the 1945 to 1950 period, the ACTU also began to gain a harvest of repentent, or at least intimidated, former Catholic leftists. Many of these, following the pattern of former-radicals generally, became extremely, if perhaps defensively, anti-communist.

The original group of Actists was overwhelmingly, about ninety percent, Irish. As the organization expanded, so too did the ethnic backgrounds represented. Catholics of French descent joined or worked with the ACTU in Boston, New Orleans, Saginaw, and Detroit. Italians, Poles, and Ukrainians furnished recruits in Pittsburgh, Glassport, Cleveland, Chicago, New York, Toledo, Akron, and San Francisco. Catholics of Scottish or English descent became members in New York, Boston, and Maryland. German Catholics furnished members and supporters in Milwaukee, New York, Chicago, Newark, Camden, Philadelphia, and Detroit. A few blacks became members in New York, Chicago, and Detroit. The Irish, however, remained by far the dominant group. A survey of names of ACTU members and officers, convention delegates, conference members, and participants in ACTU activities, representing most of the chapters, suggests that Irish Catholics consistently made up at least seventy-five percent of the membership. All of the members in Seattle were Irish and the seventy-five percent figure was exceeded in Boston and New York, where ninety percent of the membership was Irish. The officers of ACTU chapters were even more preponderantly Irish than the members generally, though the Cleveland, Detroit, and Milwaukee chapters were headed by German Catholics and the Glassport ACTU by a Polish Catholic.[9]

Whatever their ethnicity, ACTU members were quite observant in their Catholic faith. The ACTU had its own prayer ("Jesus the Worker"), patron saint (Saint Joseph), and catechism. Each chapter had a chaplain, an important officer in the ACTU, who reported regularly to the bishop. Members of the ACTU were constitutionally required to be devout, to pray, and to hold to the teaching of their Church and the observances of their faith. Each new member's faith and morals were inspected by the chaplain, who also secured a report from the parish priest. Retreats, nocturnal adoration meetings, communion breakfasts, and special masses were regular chapter functions and, indeed, often drew more participants than the chapters' secular activities.[10]

The unions which the ACTU actively supported varied considerably in their ethnic composition. In general the ACTU tended to support unions, locals, or groups within locals which were Catholic, though usually far fewer in proportion than in the ACTU itself. Seamen and longshoremen in Seattle, San Francisco, Boston, New Orleans, and New York and the transit workers, domestic workers, and municipal workers in both Boston and New York were largely Irish Catholic and the ACTU was heavily involved in their struggles for union recognition and improvements. In other trades and localities the proportion of Catholics, and especially of Irish Catholics, dropped considerably. When the ACTU supported electrical workers, newspaper workers, steel workers, telephone workers, professional workers, mine workers, or auto workers, as they often did, they worked with unions whose membership was Catholic in about the proportion that Catholics represented in the unions and the working class generally. In such cases ACTU conferences enrolled up to fifteen percent "associate," non-Catholic members who shared ACTU views, especially their anti-communism. The union caucuses in which the ACTU participated contained even more non-Catholic workers, in several cases a majority. On a number of occasions the ACTU worked closely with the largely Jewish workers of the hat, fur, and garment trades and with the majority Protestants of the printing and newspaper trades. The

ACTU on several occasions supported Protestant and Jewish candidates for union office against Catholics who were regarded as either communists or grafters.[11]

A much higher proportion of these new Actists and ACTU supporters were industrial workers than was true of the first members of the ACTU. The Detroit membership consisted of auto workers by a large majority, while the Cleveland, Pittsburgh, and Toledo Actists were heavily steel workers. Electrical workers joined the ACTU in New York, Schenectady, South Bend, and Pittsburgh. Rubber workers were dominant in Akron and glassworkers in Corning. The original ACTU members, though they were oriented to the CIO, were AFL union members by a factor of two to one. The new members were CIO industrial-union members by about the same proportion. Even the chapter in New York, a city dependent on trade, commerce, and publishing whose major industry, garment making, was largely Jewish, reached a ratio of 50:50 AFL to CIO members.[12]

It is more difficult to establish the educational background of ACTU members and supporters. The original membership was relatively highly educated. There were several college and law-school graduates among the first members and a high proportion of white collar, newspaper, and social workers. Though there were accretions of college-educated workers among the new ACTU members, especially in the Newspaper Guild, UOPWA, and FAECT, the vast majority of the new recruits did not have a college background. A probable majority were not high-school graduates. Consequently, the newer members were less theoretically inclined than the original students of the social encyclicals who founded the organization, and less politically sophisticated. Since the original members retained their leadership role within the New York ACTU and their control of the *Labor Leader*, friction could and did result.[13]

Perhaps the most striking change in the membership composition of the ACTU was not ethnic, occupational, or educational, but sexual. The original group of Actists was entirely male. As the organization branched into the retail, insurance, office, government, and domestic sectors, it began to recruit women workers. Indeed, it found many more than it expected in industrial work also. Women workers ultimately made up approximately fifteen percent of the ACTU membership and there were many more relegated to traditional "auxiliary" duties. Women performed the basic office duties of the organization and organized the social functions of the chapters. The ACTU chapter secretary was invariably a woman. This pattern was not always consistent, however. The Detroit and Boston chapters were both led by women for a time and women wrote columns for both the *Labor Leader* and the *Michigan Labor Leader* (later the *Wage Earner*). Women were also active in organizing efforts among retail workers and domestics.[14]

The increased ACTU membership included a great many local, county, regional, state, and international CIO union officers, whereas the original group of Actists had all been rank-and-file unionists. Several of the first members themselves became union officials. George Donahue was to serve successively as local business agent, international organizer and international vice-president of the RU. Martin Wersing became president of local 1212 of the UWU. ACTU members actively sought union office. Their schools were especially designed to prepare supporters for union leadership and, indeed, a large proportion of the labor-school graduates either were or became union officers. In addition, the ACTU conferences and caucuses focused on union elections and were often able to elevate their members to office.[15]

At the base of this ACTU network were hundreds of Actists serving as members of grievance committees, and as stewards and picket-line captains. At the local union level the ACTU was represented by officers in every major and most minor CIO and AFL unions. They were especially strong in the TMU, the UWU, the USW, the UE, the UAW, the RA, the NMU, the RU, and the Newspaper Guild. Some of these positions were powerful ones. ACTU members were the presidents of the UE's largest local, number 601 of Pittsburgh, and the largest UAW local, number 600 of Detroit, which was the largest local union in the world. Its 60,000 members outnumbered most of the international unions of both the CIO and the AFL. The important Detroit and Chicago units of the Newspaper Guild were also ACTU-led.[16]

ACTU members were also delegates to the representative union bodies at the city, county, state, and regional levels and to union and CIO conventions, and were international officers of several unions. Ralph Novak was president and Robert Stern secretary-treasurer of the Newspaper Guild. Actist Joe McCusker was a UAW regional director, and Joe Fischer was president of the UWU. Donahue and Martin Kyne were RU vice-presidents. Dick Horigan and Dave Keefe were international organizers for the Telephone Workers and the Stock Exchange Workers, respectively. Paul Jennings, the president of the International Union of Electrical Workers (IUE), Joseph Beirne, the president of the ACA, and John Cuddan, head of the TWU Joint Board, were ACTU supporters.[17]

One other category of ACTU supporter, a very important one, was the clerical member. The original ACTU secured a very able chaplain, the Reverend John Monaghan, who was the first of a large number of ACTU members and supporters who were members of the clergy. In a sense, the ACTU's clerical supporters included the entire body of ordained Church personnel. The Church as a whole supported their mission. The bishops of the dioceses formally approved the chapters and supervised their work and parish priests were often important supporters and publicists (though some conservative priests actively opposed the work of the ACTU). More narrowly construed, the ACTU's clerical supporters included those who served as chaplains, subscribed to an ACTU periodical, taught or lectured before ACTU meetings or classes, joined in organizing and union support work, or acted as mediators during an industrial dispute at the request of the organization. These numbered about 350. Adding those clerics who indicated support for the ACTU in an organizational publication, pastoral letter, or Church periodical would multiply this number several-fold. Several supporters were Protestant ministers.

These clerics represented many orders, though Jesuits were especially prominent and performed many duties for the ACTU. The chaplains were particularly important since they made up half of the ACTU's National Council, ministered to the membership, and determined the good faith and genuine Catholicism of new members. In some cases, including Pittsburgh, New Orleans, and Baltimore, they were the most prominent chapter leaders. The clerical supporters of the ACTU, of course, were both male and college-educated. If the ACTU membership as a whole was largely Irish Catholic, the clerical supporters were even more so. Ninety percent of the clerics who worked with the ACTU, and whose names are recorded in ACTU periodicals, reports, or literature, were Irish Catholics, many more of them Irish-born than among the lay members. The remainder were almost all Germans with a sprinkling of French or French-Canadians.[18]

There were Catholics, of course, and those of Catholic upbringing, who did not support the ACTU or the Church's conservative social doctrines. From the time of the first mass Irish immigration in the 1840s there had been radical Catholics who favored socialism, or what the Church regarded as socialism, and who resisted the Church's influence in the labor movement and in politics. The Fenians and the Molly McGuires had been Irish Catholics. There were Irish, Polish, German, Italian, Ukrainian, and Lithuanian Catholics, even clerics, among the members of the Single Tax movement, the Socialist and Socialist Labor parties, the Populist party, and the Industrial Workers of the World. Several prominent socialist leaders in the AFL, including a vice-president, Max S. Hayes, were Catholics and the most important socialist-led unions, the Brewery Workers and the Machinists, had substantial numbers of Catholics among their membership. Many of the martyrs of the American left-wing labor movement, including Tom Mooney, Sacco and Vanzetti, and some of its most colorful figures, such as Elizabeth Gurley Flynn, Kate O'Hare, and Reverend Hagerty, were of Catholic heritage.[19]

This minority tradition of Catholic radicalism continued in the 1930s and 1940s. The largest left-wing CIO union, and the fourth largest in the CIO, was the UE. Half of the UE's membership as well as its left-wing president, Albert Fitzgerald, were Catholic. Approximately eighty percent of the membership of the TWU was Catholic, as were its left-wing leaders Mike Quill, union president, and Austin Hogan, president of the largest local. A large proportion of the members of both the ILWU and the NMU were Catholic and so were their left-wing presidents, Harry Bridges and Joseph Curran. Indeed, Catholics were prominent in all of the left-wing CIO unions except the Fur and Leather Workers (FLW) Union, which was almost entirely Jewish. Ben Gold, the FLW president, was the only important left-wing union leader who was not Catholic in background.[20]

Many of the Catholic members of these unions, of course, were indifferent or hostile to their left-wing leadership and would support the ACTU's activities against them. Many others, however, supported their leadership, either from radical convictions or because they were good union leaders. The Actists reserved their strongest criticism and their most dire threats of excommunication for these "renegade" Catholics, since in the ACTU's view it was a "mythical stupidity" that "a true Catholic can at the same time be a Communist." The Church, of course, supported the ACTU on this count. The ACTU's clerical supporters argued that Catholic workers were forbidden to join left-wing organizations or "freely" to support leftist union leaders. On the contrary, Catholics had a duty to "join the ACTU" and oppose radical union leaders. Since the penalty for consistent support of the left was "automatic excommunication," the result of these arguments was to cow many faithful Catholics who were, at the same time, left-wing in sentiment. During the late 1940s, many of the more prominent Catholic leftists in exposed positions were under extreme pressure to recant and many, Mike Quill and Joseph Curran among them, did so. Several of them ostentatiously rejoined the Church, if they had left it, and a number joined or worked with the ACTU.[21]

The organizational structure of the ACTU developed eclectically until 1940, when the first full-scale ACTU national convention, representing ten chapters, adopted "Articles of Federation." The Articles of Federation largely confirmed the purpose, practice, and structure of the ACTU as it had evolved since 1937. The commitment to the social encyclicals was reaffirmed as was the determination to remove communist influence from the unions. Chapters were to be "autonomous" and coextensive with the diocese. The role of the bishop and the chaplain in approving formation of a chapter, screening members, and supervising activities, first set out in the New York ACTU constitution, was extended to the national organization.[22]

The National Council was to be the supreme authority within the organization between conventions. Its members were to include all ACTU chaplains and between one and three elected representatives, depending on chapter membership, from each chapter. The position of national director was created and Victor Lopinto, a member of the FAECT, was elected to the post. The requirement that members, except nonvoting "associates," be Catholics was confirmed and the chapters, the National Council, and the national director were each given the right to discipline and expel members. The national director also had the authority to suspend chapter accreditation. The convention passed resolutions endorsing national defense preparedness, organizing the unorganized, and labor unity, and directed ACTU members to "expose those who espouse all forms of Communism, Fascism and Nazism." The New York ACTU office was to double as national ACTU headquarters and the *Labor Leader* became the official national organ of the ACTU, though several other chapter periodicals continued to appear.[23]

This structure was to serve the ACTU essentially unchanged for the life of the organization. Chapter organization was left to the local units. Most of them emulated the New York ACTU in providing for a president, vice-president(s), secretary(s), treasurer, an educational or publicity director, and an executive board to include these officers plus a number of elected representatives. Membership meetings decided policy and these typically met weekly or biweekly. The larger chapters also provided for a number of committees. The Detroit ACTU, for example, had committees charged with arrangements, membership, education, publicity, and correspondence as well as a sergeants' committee. Special committees would also be organized for large rallies or for particular strikes and organizing drives. ACTU members in individual unions also met as ACTU conferences to plan strategy and tactics to further the ACTU's work in those industries. These conferences would become extremely important ACTU bodies. The Detroit ACTU regarded them as "the fundamental unit of the ACTU" and they tended generally to supplant the chapter structure during intense activity in a particular union.[24]

Though the 1940 convention was, on the surface, a relatively harmonious affair, there were disagreements and frictions among the chapters. A significant division involved resentment in Chicago and Detroit over the leading role of the New York ACTU. Resistance to what Thomas Doherty, Detroit ACTU secretary, referred to as New York's "drive toward centralization" was the reason for the adoption of a federal structure and chapter autonomy at the convention, and centrifugal pressure continued to affect the organization. The Detroit and Chicago chapters tended to develop "satellites" among the smaller Midwestern chapters, and the national organization was plagued by financial difficulties, lack of personnel and information, isolation from the Western and Midwestern chapters, and lack of authority. The Chicago and Boston groups finally split from the ACTU to form separate local organizations, though they remained "fraternal" in their relations with the ACTU. The Newark group, however, was denied chapter status at the 1940 convention because "there were some among the petitioners who do not subscribe to the philosophy of the ACTU." Part of the explanation for interchapter tension was personal, but political disagreement was involved also. Some of the chapters were less willing, or not yet ready, to concentrate as heavily on anti-communism as did the New York organization. The "New York boys" saw "a red behind every telegraph pole," complained Harry Read, president of both the Chicago ACTU and the Newspaper Guild in that city. This particular disagreement evaporated within a year, however, as the Chicago and Detroit chapters completed their organizing period and shifted priority to the struggle against the CP.[25]

This same rhythm, in fact, characterized the development of the ACTU in New York. The initial priorities involved in building an organization and assisting the union-recognition drives of the new CIO and newly expanding AFL unions left little room for ideological anti-communism. The tendency of union-organizing work was to unite everyone, rather than divide them along political lines, and to oppose the employers and their allies, rather than other workers. To join a union-organizing drive was to join a "united front" of all political viewpoints and to attack others within that united front was very bad form indeed. The ACTU in New York, though it remained anti-communist in theory and belief, tended to adjust to this reality during its first year of work. The urgencies of the organizing drives tended to draw out the latent "progressive" sentiments of some ACTU members, or at least a calculated toleration for leftists. Hard work by radicals on behalf of the unions tended to mute criticism of the left also, while the resistance of employers to employee organization made it difficult to retain a cheerful belief in employer-employee cooperation. Some individual Actists during this early period began to sound like socialists, and the ACTU as a whole rejected red-baiting and issued hearty condemnations of "savage industrialists."[26]

For a time, though only for a time, it seemed as though the ACTU were being transformed into a radical, even a socialist organization. In January 1938, for example, Michael Gunn, an AFL brushmaker who was one of thirteen members of the first ACTU executive board, wrote a letter to the Catholic *Brooklyn Tablet* in which he endorsed the labor theory of value. Gunn wrote:

> Money never produced anything at any time. In boring rock the workman swallows rock dust; in welding he risks his eyesight; in mining and building he risks his life; the investor risks nothing but money, and even the money he risks is only the representation of wealth created by former laborers.

In the same month, in a discussion of the workers' right to job security, the ACTU *Labor Leader* stated that:

> workers must gain seats on the Boards of Directors, shares in ownership, in the profits, in the management, not because it is necessarily the only way, but because it will probably be the only way they can insure for themselves job security or social justice that is something more than an abstraction.

While profit sharing was consistent with the pope's plan, the ACTU often went considerably further than this, including demands for workers' "control of the tools of production." In another instance, the second meeting of the ACTU-organized Catholic Union of the Unemployed indicated its opposition to "private ownership, when such ownership is excessive and harmful to the common good."[27]

The point was made in verse in another January issue of the *Labor Leader*. Mary Harrison offered a poem entitled "Job Security and Jam," in which she castigated those workers who accepted

> job security and jam, to go with the crumbs,
> that fall from their masters' tables
> (they tend to accept the capitalist evaluation of their
>   function, a factor, with others, in production for profit.)
> They should rather re-evaluate their own function and decide
>   whether they want to be,
> well oiled cogs in a machine (that is, well paid wage slaves)

or completely human, having something to say about the tools
they will use,
about the kind, as well as the amount, of work they will
do, and what purpose it will serve.
They should secure a share in management (for which the
closed shop is needed),
and a share in the profits, which could not be made without
them.[28]

This virtually socialist position seemed at time to be the official
one of the ACTU, as when a delegation of four ACTU officers—Cort,
Donahue, Michael Gunn, and Patrick Whelan—attended the 1938
Catholic Conference on Industrial Problems. They first heard
Monsignor John A. Ryan and others speak on employer-employee
cooperation and union recognition, the conference themes. But at
the plenary session the ACTU officers urged the conference to issue
a Catholic condemnation of capitalism, "for its exploitation of
producers without regard to human rights." The conference, though
it indicated opposition to racism, "war mongering," imperialism,
and "economic dictatorship" (by which they meant unregulated
economic laissez-faire), would not go so far as to endorse this
socialist demand.[29]

Many of the activities of the ACTU in these early months had the
effect of encouraging this "progressive" trend among the member-
ship. The first year saw ACTU members actively engaged on the
picket line in several strikes, a number of them very hard-fought.
The ACTU aided strikers at Woolworth stores in Manhattan, the
Todd Shipyards in Brooklyn, the Krug Bakery chain, and the
Schraeger Cigar Stores. A long and bitter strike of the Newspaper
Guild at the *Brooklyn Daily Eagle* involved John Cort, Bill Callahan,
Mike Gunn, and other ACTU members in picket-line duty, strike-
support meetings, parades, and mediation efforts for several months
before it was settled on December 23, 1938. ACTU assistance was
also given to striking UE members at the Metropolitan Engineering
Company, to the organizing efforts of the Household Employees'
Association and to another Newspaper Guild unit at the *Long Island
Daily Press*.[30]

Actists helped win severance pay for cafeteria workers at
Teachers College of Columbia University and picketed with striking

checkers at the Weisbecker Grocery chain during 1938. A strike of the United Retail Employees local 1199 against the Whelan Drug chain received substantial ACTU aid as well. These efforts had the effect of establishing the union credentials of the ACTU and providing ACTU members with a baptism of fire, and they resulted in some important recruits. Martin Kyne, the president of the United Retail Employees at Weisbeckers, for example, joined the ACTU and later became a member of the executive board. The head of the Newspaper Guild at the *Brooklyn Daily Eagle*, Barry Mullady, became a "friend of the ACTU." This union-support activity found the Actists in bitter conflict with intransigent employers and thus provided little sustenance for the idea of employer-employee cooperation. Employers' use of red-baiting and patriotic or conservative appeals also tended to promote skepticism about these ideas among partisans of the unions and to solidify unity among the workers involved, irrespective of ideology. A particularly bitter conflict in Jersey City intensified these trends within the ACTU.[31]

In January 1938 Mayor Frank Hague was leading a systematic campaign to keep the CIO out of Jersey City. His mainstays in this battle were appeals to God and country and the specter of communism. But his actual motives were somewhat different, according to the editor of the ACTU newspaper, the *Labor Leader:*

> Long a haven for sweatshop employers fleeing from union organization in other states, New Jersey, and especially Jersey City (to Hague's great profit) has become the home of industrialists determined to put up a savage battle before they see their last happy hunting ground invaded by these terrible Communists.

This situation in itself was hardly unusual. After a year's experience in union-support work the Actists, despite their ideological commitment to employer-employee cooperation, had grown used to employer hostility and they were not unacquainted with political and police favoritism either.[32]

What made the ACTU's position, in this case, an agonizing one was the uniform support for Hague's anti-union efforts among the Catholic clergy and their parishioners, including the Catholic leadership of the AFL. The Reverend Dennis Comey, president of Saint Peter's College and one of Jersey City's most prominent

Catholics, supported Hague as did every Catholic cleric in the city, with one exception. Robert Lynch, the Irish Catholic president of the Jersey City Central Labor Union (AFL), called the CIO a "red army" and the largely Catholic local AFL was in the forefront of opposition to CIO organizing efforts in the city. The Catholic War Veterans mobilized as vigilantes against the CIO. Indeed, it might have seemed that the only pro-CIO forces in town were the ACTU and the Communist party.[33]

This unlikely alliance, even though indirect, was hardly comfortable for the ACTU, and it made them a target of red-baiting themselves. But the Catholic activists were unshaken in their position. They castigated "the willingness of Catholics to join a fight against Communism" and the resulting clerical support for Hague's anti-CIO campaign. "What Hague is really fighting," argued the *Labor Leader*, "is the dirty-red, un-American attempt of the CIO to gain a living wage and a little sorely needed economic security for the workers of Jersey City and New Jersey." The *Labor Leader* quoted Cardinal Mundelein's criticism of those "selfish employers of labor" who "cry out against Communism while themselves practicing social injustice." Such politically motivated anti-communism, they felt, was designed to frighten workers away from the CIO and impugn the legitimacy of those who supported unionization. The proper response of unionists, thought the Actists, would be to avoid and ignore such comments as divisive and diversionary.[34]

Before the CIO finally succeeded in establishing a beachhead in the "employer's paradise" of Jersey City, Actist John Cort was assaulted, pro-CIO Congressman John O'Connel narrowly escaped a beating, and Sam Macri, an assistant regional director of the CIO, suffered a broken jaw and a concussion to the accompaniment of suggestions that he "go back to Russia." Several other members of the ACTU, including George Donahue, a longshoreman, Dan Laughlin, a teamster, and Victor Lopinto, a union engineer, were red-baited and harrassed by the police or "unidentified persons" who confiscated their leaflets and told them to get out of town.[35]

The experience in Jersey City, combined with a year of ACTU union-support activity, had the effect of calling into question some crucial components of Catholic labor doctrine and tradition among a portion of the membership and encouraging some virtually heretical alternatives. Though the Actists' opposition to communism and the Communist party was unshaken, the practical dynamics of the struggle to organize in the face of red-baiting and employer opposition tended to undercut any public stress on anti-communism. Many Actists were simply unwilling to deflect their fire from employers to the communists, whatever their disagreements with the latter, and they defended, as well, the radicals' constitutional right to advocate their position.[36] The *Labor Leader's* comment that "if something is right it deserves support even if the *Daily Worker* and J. Pierpont Morgan also support it" even hinted of parallel if not "united front" activity with the communists, though such common action continued, in fact, to be rejected.[37] The ACTU's position on Communism, in any case, might seem ambiguous, at least to the more uncompromising anti-communists. Beyond encouraging fraternizing with the enemy, the events in Jersey City had also promoted alienation among allies. The Church and the AFL were the mainstay of any moderate approach to the labor movement, yet in Jersey City both had opposed CIO organization.

The Actists early on attacked many of the corrupt and inactive locals of the AFL in New York City and had usually supported CIO unions in representation contests with the AFL. But despite their orientation toward industrial workers, the ACTU did not favor the permanent organization of a separate CIO. Indeed, they were clearly sympathetic to those elements of AFL ideology which converged with their own notions of "social peace" and capital-labor partnership. The influence of the Church had been great in the AFL and the organization conformed to the conservative demands of Catholic labor doctrine. In the Actists' schema the CIO would complement the inertia and conservatism of the AFL, while the AFL balanced the volatility and radicalism of the CIO. Yet, despite the lack of any real jurisdictional dispute and the presumptive sympathy of the Catholic AFL officialdom for the Church's stand on organizing industrial workers, the AFL stood shoulder to shoulder with the employers to resist the CIO "invasion" of Jersey City. As the centrist position became increasingly untenable in the course of the Jersey City campaign, so too did a sympathetic view of the AFL.[38]

The conservative role of the Church hierarchy during the Jersey City campaign was even more unexpected for the ACTU. The ACTU was dedicated to Catholicism and had the support of many important clerics. Their ideology, as they saw it, came directly from the social encyclicals. A considerable body of Catholic commentary and voluntary activity had established that it was the "duty" of good Catholics, especially the clergy, to support union organization. Therefore, the monolithic nature of the opposition to the CIO by the Jersey City Catholic establishment was especially appalling to the ACTU. Not a single priest could be found who would publicly support even the right of the CIO to organize in Jersey City, much less offer support for the organizing itself. The local Catholics red-baited the CIO and accused John Brophy, CIO director, of membership in the Communist party, even though he was a practicing Catholic whose son was enrolled in a seminary. Clerics refused to talk with *Labor Leader* reporters and joined in the general imputation that they too were communists.

Apart from the emotional shock of this split among the faithful was the practical fact that the conservative clergy were a crucial source of "ignorance and misinformation" about the CIO among the Catholic two-thirds of the Jersey City population. Opposition from employers, the press, and the political machine was to be expected, but for the Church itself to provide the margin of victory for an "American form of Hitler's fascism" was disturbing indeed. Since the ACTU counted on the Church to act as the consolidating force in its pro-union, pro–social justice, centrist position, the defection of most of the Church in Jersey City clearly jeopardized this position.[39]

The Jersey City campaign thus threw the ACTU's commitment to a "straight down the middle" position into question among a portion of the membership and provided an unprecedented challenge to several fundamental principles of Catholic social doctrine. Despite its moderate commitment, the ACTU found its support for unionization, social justice, and the CIO propelling it into active opposition to employers, clerical conservatives, and the AFL, and something akin to critical tolerance of the left wing in the unions. It remained to be seen whether this direction enjoyed the support of the membership as a whole and whether the group was willing to entertain the consequences of the position they had developed. What was certain was that the "straight down the middle" position had led to an impasse. The ACTU could move rightward, it could move leftward.

But "equal opposition" to the left and the right had proved impossible. Whatever the ACTU ideology of the middle way might demand now or in the future, the actual movement of events left no such course open for the ACTU or for Catholic workers generally. The Gerson affair of January–March 1938 was to provide the decision.[40]

NOTES

1. John Monaghan, "ACTU," ACTU files, pp. 1–2. On the significance of this year see Walter Galenson, *1937: The Turning Point for American Labor*, reprint No. 120 (Institute of Industrial Relations, University of California, Berkeley, Calif.: 1959).

2. Cort, "Catholics in Trade Unions," p. 34; Interview with George Donahue, July 22, 1974; *Michigan Labor Leader* 2, no. 14; *Labor Leader* 1, nos. 1 and 38, 2, no. 1.

3. *Michigan Labor Leader*, 2, no. 14; interview with George Donahue, July 22, 1974; *Labor Leader* 1, no. 24.

4. Cort, "Ten Years of the ACTU," p. 143.

5. Monaghan, "ACTU," ACTU files, p. 1; *Michigan Labor Leader* 2, no. 14.

6. Interview with George Donahue, July 22, 1974; Dorothy Day, *The Long Loneliness* (New York: Harper's, 1952), pp. 220–221.

7. "Constitution of the ACTU," ACTU files, p. 1; Monaghan, "ACTU," ACTU files, p. 3; *The ACTU: A Catholic Apostolate for Labor*, (New York: ACTU, 1940) p. 4–5; Cort, "Catholics in Trade Unions," pp. 34–35; Camp, *Papal Ideology*, p. 126.

8. "Report of the National Director," May 30–June 2, 1941, ACTU files, pp. 3–5; *Michigan Labor Leader* 2, no. 14; *Labor Leader* 2, nos. 13 and 17, 3, no. 3; Reverend John M. Hayes to Paul Weber, April 4, 1939, Detroit ACTU Collection; *The Gist Mill* 1, no. 1.

9. *Michigan Labor Leader* 1, no. 2, 3, no. 22, 4, no. 19; *Labor Leader* 1, nos. 1, 15, 18, 19, and 22, 3, no. 9; interview with George Donahue, July 22, 1974.

10. "Articles of Federation," ACTU files, pp. 1–3; *Labor Leader* 3, no. 5, 5, no. 5, 6, no. 2, 10, no. 6.

11. Weinberg, "Priests, Workers and Communists," pp. 49–56; list of members of ACTU Transit Conference, ACTU files; James J. Matles, *Them and Us* (Englewood Cliffs, N.J.: Prentice-Hall, 1974), p. 200; Philip Taft, "The Association of Catholic Trade Unionists," *Industrial and Labor Relations Review*, January, 1949, p. 218; George Kelly, *The ACTU and Its Critics* (New York: ACTU, 1946) p. 2; *Labor Leader* 1, nos. 27 and 29, 2, no. 1, 3, no. 5, 5, no. 5, 6, no. 2, 10, no. 6, 12, no. 11.

12. "Report of the National Director," May 30–June 2, 1940, pp. 1–5; *ACTU: A Catholic Apostolate for Labor*, p. 7; "The ACTU," p. 2; *Labor Leader* 1, no. 1, 2, no. 13, 3, nos. 17 and 3, 4, nos. 3 and 17.

13. *Labor Leader* 1, no. 1.

14. *Michigan Labor Leader* 2, no. 14, 4, no. 22, 5, no. 1; *Labor Leader* 1, nos. 25 and 30, 3, no. 12.

15. *Labor Leader* 1, no. 1, 4, no. 9, 4, no. 10, 12, no. 4.

16. Interview with George Donahue, July 22, 1974; Weinberg, "Priests, Workers and Communists," pp. 53–54; *The Hearst Strike* (Chicago: ACTU, undated), pp. 1–4; *Labor Leader* 1, no. 1, 4, nos. 9 and 10, 11, no. 13, 12, nos. 1 and 3; *Michigan Labor Leader* 1, no. 7, 3, no. 23.

17. *Daily Worker*, March 27, 1950, p. 1; *Labor Leader* 11, no. 13; interview with George Donahue, July 22, 1974; Weinberg, "Priests, Workers and Communists," pp. 53–54.

18. George Morris, "Vatican Conspiracy in the American Trade Union Movement," *Political Affairs*, June 1950, p. 33; Charles Madison, *American Labor Leaders* (New York: Harper's, 1950), p. 327; "Constitution of the ACTU," ACTU files, pp. 1–2; "Articles of Federation," ACTU files, pp. 3–7; Michael Harrington, "Catholics in the Labor Movement," *Labor History*, Fall 1960, p. 253; *Labor Leader* clerical subscription list, ACTU files; *Labor Leader* 1, nos. 1, 13, 19, 21, and 30, 3, no. 6; *Michigan Labor Leader* 1, nos. 1, 2, and 8, 6, no. 18; Chapter Report, San Francisco ACTU, February, 1950, p. 2.

19. Commons, *History of Labour*, 2: 453; Foner, *History of the Labor Movement*, 3:166; Saposs, "Catholic Church and the Labor Movement," pp. 294–97; Fox, *Peter E. Dietz*, p. 27.

20. Matles, *Them and Us*, p. 200; Weinberg, "Priests, Workers and Communists," pp. 50–51; Kampelman, *The Communist Party vs. the CIO*, p. 47.

21. Jack Barbash, *Unions and Union Leadership* (New York: Harper's, 1959), pp. 216–18; *Michigan Labor Leader* 1, no. 1, 2, no. 6; *Labor Leader* 1, nos. 21, and 30, 12, no. 13.

22. "Constitution of the ACTU," ACTU files; "Articles of Federation," 1940, ACTU files, "Report of the National Director," May 30–June 2, 1941; *Labor Leader* 3, nos. 15, 17, and 18.

23. "Articles of Federation," ACTU files; Resolutions: "On Communism, Nazism and Fascism," "On Labor Unity," "On Organizing the Unorganized," "On National Defense," Detroit ACTU Collection; *Labor Leader* 3, nos. 15, 17, and 18, *Michigan Labor Leader* 2, no. 14.

24. As chapters increased in number the ACTU dropped the stipulation that chapters be coextensive with the diocese. Since some dioceses contained more than one metropolitan area a municipal organization proved more convenient. "Committee Structure," December, 1938, Detroit ACTU Collection; *Michigan Labor Leader* 1, no. 3; *Labor Leader* 1, no. 1; "Constitution of the ACTU," ACTU files, pp. 1–4.

25. Doherty to Harry Read, October 14, 1939; Joseph Line to Doherty, February 16, 1946; Doherty to Line, April 9, 1946, all Detroit ACTU Collection; Taft, "The ACTU," p. 211; "Report of the National Director," May 30–June 2, 1941, ACTU files, p. 3; Read to Doherty, October 10, 1940, Detroit ACTU Collection.

26. *Labor Leader* 1, no. 2.

27. *Labor Leader* 1, nos. 2, 4, and 7. The author of the statement on private property, Tim O'Brien, was the only Actist who described himself as a "Christian Socialist."

28. *Labor Leader* 1, no. 5.

29. *Labor Leader* 1, no. 1.

30. *Labor Leader* 1, nos. 1 and 2.

31. *Labor Leader* 1, nos. 3, 7, and 8. The ACTU's assistance to the RU during the Whelan Drug strike inaugurated a relationship that was to last until the split in that union during 1949. Several Actists were to serve as organizers, local and national officers with the RU. *Labor Leader* 4, no. 9.

32. *Labor Leader* 1, no. 2.

33. *Labor Leader* nos. 2 and 20.

34. *Labor Leader* 1, nos. 8, 2, 14, 20, and 22.

35. *Labor Leader* 1, nos. 14 and 22.

36. *Labor Leader* 1, nos. 1, 2, 5, no. 6, and 7. The very first leaflet which the ACTU distributed rebuffed a communist offer of a united front against Consolidated Edison layoffs. "No United Fronts," ACTU files.

37. *Labor Leader* 1, no. 10.

38. "The ACTU, A Catholic Apostolate for Labor," p. 6; *Labor Leader* 1, nos. 1, 4, 8, 10, 12, and 16.

39. *Labor Leader* 1, nos. 1, 2, 5, 19, and 22, 3, no. 18, 1, nos. 5 and 22.

40. *Labor Leader* 1, no. 20.

4 † The Dilemma of Progressive Actists: Social Justice or Anti-Communism

The ACTU's first year paralleled the period of greatest excitement and experimentation in the young CIO, and the Actists worked on a number of hard-fought strikes and organizing campaigns during 1937 and 1938 which promoted the same militance and enthusiasm among their own membership.[1] In this heady atmosphere the ACTU had offered support for workers' ownership of the means of production and opposition to capitalism, and had developed a "progressive" direction in strategy and tactics. While the ACTU's formal positions included support for employer-employee cooperation and a "straight down the middle" posture for the American labor movement, experience suggested that most employers were unwilling to cooperate with unions and that there was very little middle ground between the CIO and its radical supporters, on the one hand, and the AFL and the conservatives, on the other.[2] Similarly, though the ACTU was constitutionally committed to opposition to communism, the Actists had found that attacks on the communists helped employers in their strategy of red-baiting the CIO and unionism generally.[3] In a "united front" union organizing drive, active anti-communism proved to be a very poor tactic.

These lessons were brought home most dramatically in the ACTU's campaign in support of CIO organizing in Jersey City. The Jersey City experience was particularly significant in that the vast majority of the Catholic clergy of the city, as well as the AFL, joined the forces in opposition to CIO organizing. Since the AFL, the Church, cooperative employers, and anti-Communism were crucial to the ACTU's "straight down the middle" approach for American

75

labor, the Jersey City campaign tended to undercut this position. In its stead a tentative position began to emerge whose essential components were opposition to red-baiting, suspicion of AFL and Church conservatives, hostility to employers, commitment to united-front tactics in union work, and a semi-socialist stance on economic questions. The first priority, within this perspective, was opposition to employers and the organization of unions, rather than hostility to radicalism. This "progressive" position, however, had emerged eclectically. It had not been formally agreed on and its proponents were largely confined to original members of the ACTU, lay persons, and some ACTU leaders. Other members of the organization, especially clerical members, might be expected to oppose a direction so inconsistent with the tenets of the Church and with previous Catholic activity in the unions. This division emerged during the Gerson affair of March 1938 and its outcome was to shape the ACTU's direction for the remainder of the organization's existence.

Simon Gerson was a communist journalist. He was a regular contributor to the *Daily Worker*, an active member of the New York chapter of the CIO Newspaper Guild, and a fixture around City Hall, which was his *Daily Worker* assignment. Gerson was regarded as humorous, intelligent, good at his work, and dedicated. The Actists who knew him could not help but like him and respect him.[4] But he was a committed communist and has remained one.[5]

Gerson's party was a significant political force in 1938, particularly in New York City, where a large proportion of Communist party membership has always lived. The German-Soviet Non-Aggression Pact was still a year away and the Popular Front was in its heyday. The CP was playing a significant role in the organization of the CIO, had been a major factor in the fight for unemployment insurance and had further established its influence through a wide network of popular organizations in which it played a leading part.[6]

The strength of the organized left and the personal qualities of Simon Gerson converged in the winter of 1938 to elevate him to a relatively prestigious political appointment. Manhattan Borough President Stanley Isaacs, a liberal Republican, selected him as his administrative assistant. The appointment caused a squall of protest from employers and the press. The *Brooklyn Daily Eagle* and the Brooklyn Chamber of Commerce, for example, were quite beside themselves at this public "boring from within." A major campaign developed to force Isaacs to fire Gerson and pressure soon mounted for the ACTU to join this campaign.[7] Conservative Actists began to demand public ACTU opposition to Gerson's appointment.

The first event in the ACTU's movement toward a position on the Gerson appointment was a forum in February 1938 on the rights of labor at the Crown Heights School of Catholic Workmen, one of three ACTU-affiliated schools in the New York City area.[8] The school's February open forum had featured a talk by attorney George Brennan on "Collective Bargaining and the Wagner Act." The forum series was part of the ACTU's campaign to promote union organization in Brooklyn, which had also involved support for strikes at the *Brooklyn Daily Eagle*, the Todd Shipyards, and the Eagle Pencil Company, among others.[9] Despite this intention, however, the March forum soon became embroiled in heated discussion of the Gerson appointment. Ultimately a resolution protesting Gerson's appointment was presented by Actist Joseph Walsh of the AFL Pressman's Union.[10]

Speaking for opponents of the protest, George Donahue, a longshoreman and editor of the *Labor Leader*, argued that "attacks on communism by Catholics would remain ineffective until Catholics took more positive action toward curing social injustice in our present economic system." He cited Cardinal Mundelein's warnings against an "alliance with the wrong side" under the cover of anti-communism. Mundelein, the liberal cardinal of Chicago, had argued that "selfish employers of labor have flattered the Church by calling it the great conservative force and then called upon it to act as a police force while they paid a pittance to those who worked for them." Donahue seconded this position against employers who "cry out against Communism and themselves practice social injustice." He implored the meeting, rather than protest Gerson's appointment, to take some action against "these employers as well as the reactionary attitude of portions of the Catholic press and the terrible indifference and apathy of Catholic men and women toward union organization."[11]

John Cort, secretary of the ACTU and one of the original

members, quickly took up this suggestion and proposed that a committee draw up a resolution "urging Catholic employers to recognize labor's rights and Catholic workers to take advantage of those rights upheld by the Popes and protected by the Wagner Act." This was accepted unanimously by the meeting and Cort was asked to chair the committee. The attempt to outflank the protest against Gerson's appointment did not succeed, however. Walsh's resolution that the Crown Heights labor forum protest the appointment was duly passed over the opposition.[12]

Cort and Donahue did not refer, in this debate, to the ACTU's experience in Jersey City with their likely allies in such an anti-communist front. Nor did they take a forcible position against red-baiting as a tactic which "should be disavowed by all progressive trade unionists" as the ACTU had previously done. They argued instead, in an attempt to defuse the issue without bad feeling, that positive action on behalf of "social justice" was the more effective means to combat communism and that anti-communism was a "negative" issue which would ally the ACTU with the "wrong side." The Crown Heights School of Catholic Workmen was newly established and an acrimonious debate was perhaps not the best way to assure its consolidation. The ACTU schools operated autonomously as well, and since Crown Heights was not Cort's or Donahue's home ground, there was probably a fear that a provocative position might merely solidify the proponents of the protest. A firm stand against red-baiting among strangers could lead to very unpleasant results, too, as Cort himself had learned in Jersey City.[13]

The *Labor Leader*'s coverage of the Crown Heights forum was decidedly friendly to the opponents of the Gerson protest. Rather than give prominence to the Gerson protest resolution itself, the *Labor Leader* chose to elevate Cort's secondary and almost ritual resolution to headline proportions: "Catholic Apathy and Injustice Scored at Crown Heights Labor Forum." The article itself gave Cort and Donahue the first and last word on the subject and the accompanying editorial, "Communists, Cabbages and Celery," lampooned Catholics who spent their time "hunting down bogey straw men called reds." The writer, either Donahue or Cort, lamented the epidemic of "red spots before the eyes" which was interfering with the ability of many Catholics to focus on social injustice. These "well intentioned but ill advised brethren" were advised that "pickets to protest poverty were more effective than pickets to protest Communism."[14]

This preparation worked to the advantage of the opponents of the Gerson protest resolution at the regular ACTU meeting that February in Manhattan, who were certainly aware that the *Labor Leader* had not reflected the tone of the forum nor, apparently, the views of the Brooklyn members. The fact that this was a regular downtown membership meeting meant also that many veterans of Manhattan strike work and the Jersey City campaign would be in attendance, while many of those from the neighborhood of the Crown Heights School of Catholic Workmen in Brooklyn would not.

Nonetheless, the meeting saw "heated debate" on a resolution sponsored by Michael Gunn, AFL brushmaker and ACTU Executive Board member, that the ACTU issue a protest against Gerson's appointment. The proponents of the resolution did not argue for opposition to communism. That was taken for granted. Instead, they argued a kind of "fairness doctrine." Since the ACTU had attacked capitalist abuses, trade-union corruption, and Jersey City Mayor Hague, a Catholic, "to be consistent it must now attack this abuse of popular representative government."

The most vocal opponents of the protest included John Cort, ACTU secretary and a member of the United Office and Professional Workers Union (UOPWU), Tim O'Brien, the leader of the Catholic Union of the Unemployed, and Edward Scully, an attorney and member of the Catholic Labor Defense League, the ACTU's legal arm. Cort repeated the arguments he had made at the Crown Heights forum. "Attacks on Gerson's appointment," he asserted, "were made in too many cases by men who, in Cardinal Mundelein's words, 'cry out against Communism and themselves participate in social injustice.' " Gerson's appointment represented the "inactivity of Catholics who had failed in the past to react with sufficient energy to social and industrial abuses, thus allowing Communists to take the leadership in the campaign for social justice." The answer was not a campaign against Communism but a greater effort to build a Catholic movement for social justice. This backhanded slap at red-baiting, however, was not meant to be construed as either endorsement of communism or of Gerson's appointment. The opponents of the resolution denied that "the motion to protest was being attacked on principle, but only as a matter of strategy." The ACTU was engaged in "positive action" and "need not backwater into the more negative position of joining the anti-Communist front."

O'Brien seconded the arguments for a positive program for social justice rather than anti-communism. A "constructive" program was better than "mere anti-ism," in his opinion. O'Brien brought the authority of the Bible in on the side of the opponents of protest, as well, pointing out that "the first commandment is 'Thou shalt love the Lord thy god' and not 'Thou shalt hate Communists.'" If biblical authority was not convincing to the opposition, Edward Scully offered a more mundane and procedural objection. According to him, the "democratic way of protesting" Gerson's appointment was to oust Manhattan Borough President Stanley Isaacs at the next election and not attempt to "pressure" him now. The proponents of the protest thought this a bit farfetched given the ACTU's campaign against Hague, himself an elected official.

Despite the heavy preliminary publicity for the opponents of the Gerson protest, the relatively favorable circumstances of a Manhattan ACTU membership meeting, and the weight of past ACTU attacks on "social injustice" parading as anti-communism, the motion to protest Gerson's appointment failed to pass by only three votes. This was certainly an uncomfortable margin, especially since ACTU members Joseph Zarella and Patrick Whelen were circulating a petition "demanding a special meeting to reconsider the motion" to protest Gerson's appointment. There were other reasons for apprehension among the progressives as well. Whelan, a plumber who supported the Gerson protest, took his turn at this time as "managing editor" of the *Labor Leader*, under Donahue, who was "editor," and over an "editorial board" consisting of Gunn, who supported the protest, and Cort, who opposed it. The former lineup had been Donahue as editor and the other three as the editorial board.[15]

The increased influence of the proponents of the "anti-communist front" was expressed in the editorial which accompanied the coverage of the ACTU meeting. Previous editorials in the *Labor Leader* had, in succession, attacked corruption in the AFL International Longshoremen's Association, criticized the wage-push explanation of inflation, defended the NLRB from conservative and

Catholic attacks, dismissed the red-baiting testimony of Joseph P. Ryan of the ILA to the House Un-American Activities Committee (HUAC) as a cover for his own corruption and inertia, and ridiculed Catholic anti-communism.[16] The editorial of February 28, 1938 departed sharply from this pattern. It was entitled "Communism and Democracy" and was the first full-blown editorial attack on communism which the *Labor Leader* had published. Stalin's purges, the absence of democracy in the USSR, and American "apologists" for communism received special prominence, but it was not only the Communist party which came under fire. The ACTU opposed, the editorial said, all of the "various cults of Marxism" which were no less undesirable for "cloaking themselves in the armor of democratic idealism."

The anti-communists were clearly gaining ground, despite the apparent victory of the progressives at the February ACTU meeting. Not only did this editorial represent the conservative position, but the "readers' requests" for clarification of the ACTU's position on communism which had occasioned it were obviously running against the progressives. Cort, Donahue, O'Brien, and the other progressives, fearful of being backed into a "fellow traveling" position, had agreed to an anti-communist editorial in the hopes of establishing that any internal ACTU disagreements were among anti-communists, and therefore merely tactical. But this continuing attempt to skirt and defuse the Gerson issue was unsuccessful, except in the sense that the progressives' position shifted toward that of the right wing. The progressives had argued originally that communism was merely a mistaken response to social injustice. By accepting the editorial language that it represented "class hatred, murder and pillage," the progressives were shorn of much of their argument against alliance with employers against communism. If communism was so bad, then why not welcome any allies against it? In their attempts to hold off the proponents of the protest the progressives were coming close to abandoning their position against redbaiting.

The progressives' conciliatory position, meanwhile, was not meeting with any such response from the proponents of Gerson's ouster. Their position was becoming sharper and sharper as the progressives retreated. The Reverend William J. Smith, S.J., director of the Crown Heights School of Catholic Workmen, himself sent a lengthy letter to the ACTU disputing the progressives' position. Smith was not impressed by the argument that employers' social injustice was the primary enemy, nor that communism was merely a mistaken response to social injustice which would fall into eclipse once Catholics rallied to the fight against social injustice. Decrying the progressives' "attack on Catholic employers and Catholic newspapers," he argued that there "is a world of difference between Communism and the Catholic employer who may be failing to do his Christian duty." In fact, since Catholic employers were a very small proportion of employers as a whole and since no statistical proof had been offered of their misconduct, "it would be neither prudent nor just to condemn them as a whole." More generally, he continued, the determination of "Capitalist abuses" was "a very delicate matter."

> The moral theologians, specialists in the moral aspects of economics, are finding it difficult to put their finger on just what party can be branded as the guilty one in many of these questions. Great harm can be avoided if we temper our enthusiasm and zeal for a great cause with the conservative teachings of the Church.

While in Smith's view employers, especially Catholic employers, should not be criticized indiscriminately, no such reticence was appropriate with regard to the left. Since "Communism is directed by an international ring using every possible means foul or fair to foment revolution in every country," every means and every ally had to be used in combating it. For Smith, then, even the fight for social justice had to take a back seat to the struggle against communism. Smith's position, as we shall see, proved to have considerable support within the ACTU.[17]

Reverend Smith's argument was more extreme than that of previous proponents of Gerson's ouster. The Crown Heights labor forum which had passed the Gerson protest resolution had also voted unanimously for Cort's resolution criticizing Catholic employers. No Actist had heretofore suggested that Catholic employers were not deserving of criticism. The conservatives' argument, rather, had been that both Catholic employers and communists deserved it. In contrast, the progressives had directed their attack on social injustice, on the theory that communism was merely a response to it. The Reverend Smith, however, was willing to absolve employers at least partially from criticism, especially if they were willing to fight communism. "Social injustice," in his view, became a technical matter subject to the interpretation of experts and beyond the reach of the ACTU membership. Communism, on the other hand, was an unmitigated evil about which moral theologians had no doubts. Communism, therefore, was the clearer target and the first point for attack. Since employers, especially Catholic employers, were guilty of lesser sins, they should be welcomed into the ranks of the anti-communist front. And since the progressives had not raised the issue of the politically conservative and devisive function of anti-communism, Smith could discuss anti-communism as though it were merely a matter of moral opposition to a vague and monolithic conspiracy, rather than a practical question of how to relate to the left-wing in the fight against social injustice.[18]

Smith's letter, a critique of which might have been credible even to proponents of Gerson's ouster, received a very brief and defensive editorial comment instead. Catholic employers' "philosophy of rugged individualism and their lack of social leadership in the field of business [is] justly deserving of criticism," argued the editorial. On the question of opposition to communism, however, the editorial stated that "it is our contention that attempts at positive application of the social teaching of the Church must precede or at least coincide with our attacks against Communism." From opposition to red-baiting as an attempt to divide the "solid united body of labor," the progressives had first retreated to a position accepting the necessity for active opposition to communism but not until Catholics were united against social injustice, that is, no alliance with unjust employers against communism. Now they appeared willing to accept anti-communist activities which coincided with opposition to social injustice. The progressives had virtually embraced the earlier position of the proponents of the protest against Gerson, while the conservatives had moved even further to the right.[19]

The special ACTU session on Gerson for which members Zarella and Whelan had petitioned was duly held in the first week of March 1938 and the result was a crushing two-to-one defeat for the progressives. The ACTU was thereby committed to a public protest of Gerson's appointment and to working with business and conservative anti-communists to achieve his ouster. ACTU member Stephan Johnson characterized the resolution as a legitimate protest

against "abuse of power" and defended the necessity of such
" 'negative action' against injustice in every form." The progressives' retreat developed into a rout at this meeting. Donahue
withdrew his opposition to the resolution since it "appealed to
[Borough President] Isaacs' goodwill and intelligence and did not
take the form of a bludgeon demand from another minority pressure
group." The implication, of course, was that Donahue's earlier
opposition concerned the style of the resolution, and not the position
it reflected. Cort went so far as to deny that he had opposed the
passage of a resolution of protest at the first ACTU meeting on the
subject. He had only opposed a resolution in the name of the Crown
Heights School, he now said, because it "had not established itself
as thoroughly pro-labor and anti-racketeer." The only resistance
offered was in the form of a flanking resolution by ACTU members
Delaney and Carleton along the lines of the *Labor Leader*'s editorial
reply to the Reverend Smith. This resolution would have "protested
Gerson's appointment and also the un-Christian spirit of many who
protested." This was about as far as the progressives could go and
have any position left at all, and perhaps it was merely an attempt at
honorable surrender. In any case, the conservative faction was
adamant. The compromise resolution was soundly defeated.[20]

After the adoption of the Gerson protest resolution the progressive
position was essentially removed from contention in the ACTU. A
Labor Leader editorial following the passage of the Gerson protest
did renew the argument that "the character of the groups demanding
Gerson's ouster" and the inadvisability of "joining a pressure group
movement" made the wisdom of the action suspect. The meeting
which had earlier rejected the motion was applauded for refusing to
"join the parade, although the martial music did seem enticing to a
goodly number," and the editorial writer called on the ACTU to
cultivate "intellectual courage and honesty" in order to resist being
stampeded, "even at the risk of being denounced as 'Reds.' " For
its part the *Labor Leader* held to the "peculiar conviction that if
something is right it deserves support even if the *Daily Worker* and
J. Pierpont Morgan also support it."[21]

Rather than a renewal of the battle, however, this editorial might
better be seen as a summing up for the record. Now that the
progressives had been defeated, and especially since they had

virtually adopted the ground of their opponents, a last recapitulation of their earlier position was harmless enough. In addition, even though the progressive position was no longer ACTU policy, editorial staff changes after the Gerson resolution favored erstwhile "progressives." Michael Gunn, who had favored the protest, left the *Labor Leader* editorial board and Cort, who had opposed it, became assistant editor over Whelan, a proponent who had been second in command. But, again, rather than indicating renewed struggle on the issues surrounding the Gerson appointment, these changes seem to reflect the timely surrender of the progressives and a unified ACTU position increasingly inclined toward active anti-communism.[22]

The shape and rapidity of consolidation of this new conservative direction is attested by a number of significant events in the month following the passage of the Gerson protest. Cort, the former progressive, published an apology to the Reverend Smith and to the Crown Heights School of Catholic Workmen for his statement that the school had not "established itself as thoroughly pro-labor." No criticism had been implied, he said. He had merely meant that the school "hadn't established itself in the public mind and eye" and congratulated the school and the Reverend Smith on their good work. The progressives' imputation that Catholic supporters of the "anti-communist" front were less than energetic in the fight for social justice, the last position held to in defeat, was thus formally repudiated and the progressive position abandoned.[23]

The new, conservative direction is also revealed in the considerably increased space devoted to attacks on the Communist party in the March 1938 *Labor Leader*. One editorial, entitled "Murder and Plunder," was a rejection of an offer from the *Daily Worker* for common cause in a campaign against Consolidated Edison layoffs. There was irony in this in that the very first ACTU leaflet, soon after the founding of the organization, had been a reply to a similar Communist offer involving Consolidated Edison. The editors perhaps meant to indicate that the ACTU was now returning to the path symbolized by that early leaflet. The ACTU had worked very hard to build a movement against Consolidated Edison layoffs and had endorsed public ownership of the utility. If a united front with the left had value anywhere, it would have had value in a battle with Con Ed, a "private" public utility which had laid off thousands of predominantly Catholic workers. Instead, the ACTU rejected the offer of a united front and reaffirmed their opposition to the communists. The ACTU had joined a quite different united front.[24]

This same March 14, 1938, issue of the *Labor Leader* contained a letter from the Reverend Charles Owen Rice, the director of the Catholic Radical Alliance of Pittsburgh, congratulating the ACTU on its protest against Gerson's appointment. According to Rice, those who might think that such action threatened the civil liberties of Communists did not understand that

> a Communist is not like other men. When you say a Communist should not hold public office you say that a man who is sworn to use any means in his power to overthrow a state and put a monstrous caricature in its place should not be given the tremendous aid of public office in carrying out his plan.

The communists, thought Rice, simply could not be treated "as a normal American party." Rice's compliments to the ACTU were not occasioned by the group's year-long effort on behalf of unionization, but rather by the active anti-communism of the Gerson protest. Rice sympathized with this direction and, once convinced that the ACTU was firmly committed to anti-communism, he began contacting people in Pittsburgh who might be interested in forming an ACTU chapter.[25]

Rice's group, however, did not have the honor of becoming the second ACTU chapter. That distinction went to a Boston group organized in March 1938. Cyril O'Brien of the CIO Industrial Insurance Agents' Union was the president. Jane Marra of the International Ladies' Garment Workers' Union served as vice-president. The executive board included Van Vaerenwyck of the AFL Retail Store Employees and Mary McSweeny of the Boston Teachers' Club. Catherine Ahern served as treasure and Clement O'Brien, as educational director. And in July the Detroit ACTU was founded. This group included members of the UAW, the Newspaper Guild, and the Steel Workers Organizing Committee. The president was Paul Weber, president also of the Detroit Newspaper Guild, and the secretary was Paul Saint-Marie, a member of the Ford River Rouge UAW local, number 600. The Pittsburgh group finally organized in September. The thirty members endorsed the policies of the parent New York group and elected the Reverend Rice as chairman. All three new chapters immediately inaugurated classes on the social encyclicals and were very soon operating full-fledged labor schools.[26]

It may have been merely coincidental that this burst of ACTU organizing came on the heels of the Gerson decision. But it seems more likely that the ACTU's new focus on anti-communism and more conservative direction generally were providing new sources of support. This is suggested by the fact that the largely Jewish ILGWU and Amalgamated Clothing Workers (both of which had experienced considerable infighting over the issue of communism) were early supporters of the Boston ACTU. It is borne out also by the subsequent careers of the officers of these chapters. Cyril O'Brien went on to lead an anti-communist grouping in the CIO Industrial Insurance Agents' Union. Paul Weber led the anti-communists in the Detroit Newspaper Guild and as a national Guild convention delegate and resolutions committee member. He continued this struggle as national secretary of the Newspaper Guild in 1946. Paul Saint-Marie became chairman of UAW local 600, the largest local in the world, in opposition to the strong left-wing contingent in the River Rouge plant. Father Rice was to lead the anti-communists in Pittsburgh, particularly in their struggle in UE local 601, the largest UE local.[27].

The ACTU swiftly began to put its new stress on anti-communism into practice. An instance of this was the work of ACTU supporters in UAW local 156 in Flint, Michigan. Carl F. Thrasher, newly elected secretary of this local, had "conducted a program of infiltration [into the communist-supported Unity Caucus] by conservative Catholics for several months prior to the election," with the support of Homer Martin, the conservative UAW president. This group ultimately split from the Unity Caucus and ran independently, throwing the election to the opposition and securing the election of some of their own people. This incident was the first occasion of ACTU intra-union factional fighting against the left and it swiftly became a model of how such work might be conducted. The Actists were losing no time in implementing an anti-communist program of action.[28]

The consolidation of the conservative direction within the ACTU is also evident in a much-altered relationship with both the AFL and the right wing of the Catholic clergy. Disenchantment with the role of these two groups in the organizing efforts of the CIO in New York City and Jersey City had a good deal to do with the ACTU's short-lived progressive direction. The conservative restoration brought about a new relationship with these groups.

The ACTU began, for example, to offer measured support for the suggestions of AFL and conservative CIO spokesmen that the CIO rejoin the AFL, under AFL terms. President Homer Martin of the UAW, who led the opposition to the Unity Caucus supported by the Communist party, was quoted prominently by the *Labor Leader* as seeking "the resumption of peace negotiations between the AFL and CIO." Abraham Hershkowitz of the CIO Amalgamated Clothing Workers indicated that "both unions, craft and industrial, can be banded together in the framework of the AFL." The ACTU continued for some time to oppose particular AFL leaders and locals when it felt that the leaders were corrupt or that CIO organizations offered better representation, but a new sympathy for the craft organization, born of the need for allies against the left, was apparent. The ACTU was working with the Martin forces in Flint and the Amalgamated leadership in Boston, and later in Troy, and shared their feeling that the AFL provided the best insurance against radicalism if forces internal to the CIO could not defeat it.[29]

The ACTU also continued to offer criticism of clerics and Catholic spokesmen who were hostile to union organization or the Wagner Act, but a new regard for the right wing of the Church was apparent in the aftermath of the Gerson decision. This was in marked contrast to the ACTU's previous notion of its allies among the clergy. Liberal Cardinal Mundelein's statements on the dangers of anti-communism had been a major source of ACTU inspiration prior to the Gerson decision. Among other clerics who had received favorable coverage were the Reverend Joseph Moody, who had spoken at several of the ACTU's Consolidated Edison layoff meetings, the Reverend Thomas Conerty, who sat on the Citizens' Committee of the *Brooklyn Daily Eagle* strike, and Fathers Edward Swanstrom, William Kelly, and Bertram Weaver, who had all been involved in strike-support activity. The cleric most closely associated with the ACTU was the organization's chaplain, Father John Monaghan. Monaghan, who was active in many strike-related activities, was director of the ACTU-affiliated Fordham Labor School, and had on one occasion suggested that "the workers could take over big business and run it for the benefit of the community." While he had not taken an active role in the debates, he had apparently opposed the Gerson protest. These churchmen were all active in strikes and were either silent on the question of communism or cautioned against the dangers of red-baiting.[30]

As with the lay ACTU members, the Gerson decision brought no purge of clerical supporters. The clerical progressives were apparently as ready as the lay progressives to abandon their position and take up the anticommunist campaign. Quotations from right-wing clerics, however, especially on communism, became much more prominent after the Gerson protest. Monsignor Fulton J. Sheen, for example, began to be regularly quoted in the *Labor Leader*. On one occasion, taking the direction of the Reverend Smith of the Crown Heights School of Catholic Workmen, he lamented the fact that there was "greater hatred of capitalism than love of social justice" among many Catholic union activists. On another occasion the *Labor Leader* cited Sheen on the danger of "class hatred" and the need to consider the employer as a person. Always present in ACTU ideology, even in the period of intensive strike-support efforts, this theme of class harmony began to edge out the themes of social injustice and "capitalist abuses." The note of class harmony was sounded again, for example, in a front-page *Labor Leader* article on Archbishop Mooney. As a solution to prevailing inequities, the archbishop suggested the creation of agencies of "industrial conciliation and discussion" since the interests of capital and labor were "essentially in harmony."[31]

As more conservative clergy began to be won to support of the organization, the ACTU began to offer less criticism of this wing of the Church. While an occasional parish priest would be brought to task for anti-union propaganda, as was Coughlin's magazine *Social Justice* for an attack on the National Labor Relations Board (NLRB), there was no recurrence of the scathing criticism of the clergy of Jersey City for their support of Hague's "fascism."[32] Indeed, the ACTU now undertook to defend the authority of the clergy against all

comers, particularly the left. One editorial argued that the clergy
were "appointed by God" and therefore beyond criticism.[33] The
ACTU's position had effectively converged with that of the more
conservative churchmen: both now espoused class harmony, mediation, avoidance of strikes, and nonviolence. And, for both, anti-
communism had become the first priority.

The outcome of the debate over Simon Gerson's appointment was
a rather swift, if far from complete, reorientation in the ACTU's
perspective and activity. The impending ACTU convention and
constitution, new chapters and supporters, and intra-union factional
fighting against the left all pointed toward consolidation of this new
conservative direction. How had this come about? If experience in
Jersey City and New York City had had a radicalizing effect on the
ACTU, if the Actists had been moving toward a virtually socialist
stance in print and an increasingly left-of-center practice, hostile to
employers, the right wing, the AFL, and red-baiting, how had they
been pointed back on the conservative track so easily and so
quickly?

The answer is that even the progressive faction was more
conservative than either their practice or their more radical statements would suggest. While elements in their background and
experience pushed them in a more radical direction, these were in
constant conflict with conservative background and ideology. The
conservative faction faced no such internal ambiguities, since the
full weight of Church doctrine and clerical authority was on their
side, and was thus able to play on those among the progressives,
forcing their retreat and ultimate capitulation. Since the progressives were unwilling to entertain a break with the Catholic labor
tradition and the Church their defeat was virtually assured. A closer
look at both the progressives and their conservative opponents may
shed some light on this crucial event in the ACTU's history.

A number of influences had operated in a radicalizing way on the
progressives in the ACTU. These included strike-support activity;
bad experiences with the AFL, conservative clergymen, or
employers; unskilled industrial work, lower-echelon office work, or
unemployment, and apparently college. The progressives were all
Irish and male as well, though this did not distinguish them from the
Gerson protest supporters.

Those members of the ACTU who had been most active in

strike-support work were invariably opponents of the Gerson protest, at least initially. Cort had been heavily involved in the major strike at the *Brooklyn Daily Eagle,* the Jersey City organizing drive, and the campaign against Con Ed layoffs. He and Donahue, the senior officers of the ACTU, bore the brunt of strike-support efforts at many of the other strikes which the ACTU assisted as well, including the Elmhurst Transit Line and the Krug Bakery Chain strikes. Edward Scully, another progressive, was an attorney with the Catholic Labor Defense League, which defended ACTU pamphleters in Jersey City and workers fired for union activity. In many of these strikes the employers, whether Catholic, Protestant, or Jewish, did not hesitate to fire union activists, resist NLRB decisions, deny recognition, and refuse offers of mediation. These experiences, then, left the progressives suspicious of employers' anti-communism and of their willingness to reform unjust practices voluntarily.

A number of progressives had had bad experiences with AFL unions. Scully and Donahue, for example, had both worked as teamsters and as checkers in the ILA. Donahue's refusal to "go along" with corruption in ILA local 346 and his open opposition to ILA President Joseph P. Ryan had led to a "frame up" against him. *Labor Leader* support had helped him to quash the charges. The episode no doubt soured Donahue considerably on the ILA, if not on the AFL as a whole.

The progressives' work experience and education distinguished them, also, from the ACTU membership as a whole. Many more of them were college-educated than the membership generally, and they were either white-collar employees or professionals or un-skilled and semiskilled workers. Skilled craftsmen were not repre-sented. Cort was an office worker and a member of the UOPWU; Tim O'Brien, another progressive, was unemployed and served as secretary of the Catholic Union of the Unemployed. Lawrence De-laney was a working journalist and News Guild member. Cort was a Harvard graduate, and Scully was an attorney.

The progressives' suspicion of employers and the AFL extended, also, to the more conservative clergy. Cort, Donahue, and Scully had all been involved in the Jersey City campaign and had reacted angrily to the Jersey City clergy's support for Hague and opposition to CIO organization.[34]

The background and experience of the supporters of the Gerson protest were in some respects markedly different. Only one of them, Michael Gunn, had been involved in ACTU strike-support activity. He had worked on the strike at the *Brooklyn Daily Eagle*. In addition, none of them was college-educated and, of those whose union membership was available, all were members of elite AFL craft unions. Whelan, for example, was a plumber, Walsh was a printing pressman, and Gunn was a brushmaker. The Reverend Smith, of course, was not a union member. None of them, apparently, was unemployed. Of the active proponents of the anti-communist front not one had been involved in the CIO-ACTU campaign in Jersey City. [35]

A combination of experiential and background factors, then, identified ACTU progressives. Unskilled and badly paid jobs, corrupt unions and unemployment appear to have been radicalizing factors, as was personal experience of employer or clerical hostility to unions. Many of the progressives, however, in comparison to their opponents and to ACTU members at large, were highly educated and several were journalists, lawyers, or social workers. Apparently, experience of the class system, combined with an academic training which encouraged reflection on that experience, favored a progressive position. Well-paid jobs, high skills, and secure craft-union membership, on the other hand, encouraged a conservative position, as did inexperience in strikes or organizing drives, and either clerical status *or* lower educational attainment among the identifiable conservatives.

The conservatives, of course, enjoyed the knowledge that their position was in full accord with the teachings of their Church and with the past practice of Catholics in the American labor movement. Catholic ideology and tradition were emphatic in supporting private property, employer-employee cooperation, and the AFL. They were equally unequivocal in opposition to class conflict, socialism, and communism. The progressives, however, could find no precedent for their position in the sixty-year history of organized Catholic activity in the labor movement. There was no Catholic authority for demands that workers own the means of production. Neither was there precedent for opposition to the AFL, employers, or the clergy. There was certainly no Catholic justification for common cause with radicals against Churchmen and employers or for toleration of communism. Catholics who attempted to organize, as Catholics, in support of these objectives would certainly face the prospect of excommunication. The further development of the progressive direction of the ACTU, it must have been apparent, would have had to take place outside the fold of the Church.

The progressives were not able or willing to undertake any such break with their faith. Indeed, even the activities and positions of the progressives demonstrate this underlying commitment to the essentials of Catholic labor dogma. The strikes which the progressives had supported, while hard-fought in themselves, had often been terminated through mediation efforts by the ACTU or an affiliated Churchman. The *Brooklyn Daily Eagle* strike, the Elmhurst Transit Strike, and the strike of the Schraeger Cigar Stores were all mediated through the ACTU. The Whelan Dry Goods Company dispute was mediated by Jules S. Freund of the New York State Mediation Board at the ACTU's invitation. Since collective-bargaining procedures in 1937 were, to say the least, uncertain, mediation itself did not necessarily imply weakness and concession on the part of the workers. Nonetheless, for the progressives to promote mediation as the major route to settlement reflected their belief in a fundamental class harmony. This is particularly so since the ACTU itself did much of the mediating. Participation in mediation suggested that even the ACTU's progressives tended to regard the organization as an agency of class harmony more than as a partisan and advocate of the workers.[36]

Indeed, class harmony was a constant theme in the *Labor Leader* before as well as after the Gerson decision. A statement on the editorial page in one early issue argued that the employer was a "slave of economic disorder" no less than the worker. The solution was union participation with "employers of good will" in "industrial cooperation." The lead article of February 16, 1938, under the headline "Labor Peace Plan Outlined," indicated that "amicable discussions in which representatives of employers and workers will sit down together and calmly attempt to work out the problems of industry and of labor provide the ultimate solution to the nation's industrial strife." In the same issue an NLRB decision was applauded as faithful to the spirit of the social encyclicals: "to foster and promote harmony between the various ranks of society." Thus, from the beginning the ACTU progressives held to the essentials of the Church doctrine of class harmony.[37]

Study of the apparently radical ideology of the first year of the ACTU discloses the same underlying conservatism. While some of the radical expressions were clearly socialist in inspiration, ("the means of production must be owned in common by all the workers in that industry"), many more were grounded in the social encyclicals or romantic medievalism, with a strain of American utopianism. The frequent calls for "workers' control of the tools of production" for instance, sometimes meant expropriation, but more often indicated restoration of artisanal production methods. In the same vein the early ACTU called for support for "back to the land movements" and endorsed the "spread of handicraft workshops." So, while the "alienation" of the worker was an issue for the progressive Actists, their own program for its elimination included both radical and literally reactionary elements drawn from the papal encyclicals and their commentators.[38]

The progressives' commitment to the Church was the most important factor in the conservative resolution of this ambiguity in their activity and ideas. The ACTU was an official Catholic organization which operated under the general supervision of the bishops and within the framework of Church doctrine. The members of the ACTU, progressives no less than conservatives, took their faith seriously. Their disposition would naturally be to avoid a break with the Church and the renegade status of the left-wing Catholic. This was both a matter of positive inclination and of enforced discipline. The threat of excommunication was a real one for Catholics who strayed too far to the left. Indeed, the Actists were to wield the threat themselves as their anti-communist position became consolidated. Had the progressives pressed their position against the conservatives during the Gerson debate they would have been open to charges of "renegade" and to possible excommunication. The prospect of a split with the church was perhaps the most significant factor in the progressives' retreat and adoption of the conservative position.

The religious faith of the progressive Actists was related, also, to their position on communism, the crucial issue in the Gerson debates. The impetus for the Church's social encyclicals had been the gains of the socialist movement and their main content was a polemic against the left. The most recent social encyclical, at the time of the Gerson decision, was *Divine Redemptoris* of 1937, which singled out the communists as the foremost enemy of the faith and the primary source of "evil social theses," though it eschewed any endorsement of reformist socialism. If "opposition to socialism" had been the "fundamental issue", from the point of view of the Church, in the period of 1900–1918, opposition to communism was seen as even more imperative in the 1930s. While the Church's positions on trade-union structure or state intervention might change, anti-socialism and especially anti-communism were constant and primary duties for Catholics in the labor movement. The faith of the progressives therefore bound them to an anti-communist position, despite their belief, as unionists, that red-baiting was a major weapon of employers in dividing and defeating the workers and deflecting the fight for social justice. [39]

At the same time the progressives *were* anti-communists themselves. Even at its most radical the ACTU under the progressive ascendency was far from a "Catholic communist" organization. In an early 1938 editorial attack on ILA President Joseph P. Ryan for anti-communist testimony before the House Un-American Activities Committee (HUAC), the *Labor Leader* explained that "no group of unionists is more vehemently opposed to Communist influence in the ranks of labor than our own ACTU." Though the left-wing ILWU and NMU were admitted to be democratic, free of corruption and militant in pursuit of workers' interests, the Actists felt that, "if Bridges and Curran are Communists then we unhesitatingly say that they should be eliminated from labor leadership." Communists might secure economic gains for workers, they admitted, but only in order to win them to a program which "has proved disastrous to civilization, organized religion and labor unionism itself." Pius XI's warning on the importance of reaching those "seduced by Communist doctrines" was quoted approvingly also during the period of progressive ascendency. Despite the occasional mild socialism, then, there could be no doubt that the progressives had serious differences with the communists over long-range goals. [40]

There are anti-communists and there are anti-communists, however. What seemed, initially, to distinguish the progressives from the conservatives in the ACTU was that the progressives, though opposed to communists, were unwilling to be drawn into an active campaign against them. They had reasoned that unjust employers used red-baiting in an attempt to divide workers, defeat strikes, and prevent the winning of social justice. For workers to use such tactics themselves, in the view of the progressives, was suicidal: it meant joining with conservative employers against other workers and would certainly lead to more broken strikes and less social justice. The progressive position, then, tended to make opposition to communism secondary to opposition to the common enemy—the employer.

The dilemma of the progressives, and of the ACTU as a whole, was that Church doctrine did not permit any such view of communism. In the view of the Church, communism was more than an error, it was an evil. No compromise on opposition to communism was possible, no alliance with communists, or even with socialists, except perhaps to defeat the communists, was permissible. The Reverend Smith merely paraphrased the popes when he argued that opposition to communism was the first duty of Catholic workers and must take precedence even over the fight for social justice itself. This theological view of communism ruled out a political decision to distinguish between areas of disagreement with the left, largely long-range goals, and areas of possible agreement and common work, which included many practical union issues and some political issues. In the view of the Church, then, the tendency of the progressives was a heresy. [41]

The progressives knew that this was so. The position of the Church on communism was clear. For that very reason the progressives' position was unclear. They had never clarified the difference between disagreeing with communists and fighting them, and they did not take up the challenge of the Gerson protest in those terms. To have articulated a position explicitly hostile to red-baiting would have been to place themselves in opposition to the fundamental tenet of Catholic work in the labor movement. The progressives' commitment to the Church, their piety, their own deep anti-communism, and their fear of being red-baited themselves held them back from such a step.

The fundamental weakness of the progressive position, then, was that it contended with the whole weight of Church doctrine and past

Catholic labor action. The attempt to develop a Catholic position and practice favoring solidarity of all workers, class consciousness, militancy, and socialism, and in opposition to employers, red-baiting, and the conservatives in the AFL and the Church, all within the framework of the Catholic Church, was all but impossible. Despite the radicalism of much of the early ACTU ideology and strike-support work and its apparent consolidation during the Jersey City contest, the progressives themselves shared most of the conservative premises of their opponents. When the conservatives forced the issue in the Gerson protest debate, the progressives faced a choice between retreating from their position, and remaining within the bounds of official Catholic labor action, or of developing their position further outside the Church. Their faith and their fundamental conservatism joined to lead them back into the fold.

NOTES

1. The *Brooklyn Daily Eagle* strike had involved several ACTU members in support activities which lasted for eleven months before the Newspaper Guild was recognized. *Labor Leader* 1, no. 1.

2. "Stand of the ACTU," ACTU files, p. 1.

3. "ACTU Constitution," ACTU files, p. 2.

4. Interview with George Donahue, July 22, 1974.

5. Gerson is now an editor of the *Daily World*, the successor to the *Daily Worker*.

6. Among the organizations in which the Communist party played an important role were the American Student Union, the American League for Peace and Democracy, the National Negro Congress, the American League Against War and Fascism, the American Youth for Democracy, the Workmen's Circles, and the International Labor Defense. Though communist membership was never more than 100,000, the party was able to exert considerable influence over these organizations, many of the local, state, and regional CIO organizations, twelve to fifteen of the international CIO unions, locals in many other unions, and organizations of the Farmer Labor party, Labor's Non-Partisan League, and The American Labor party (ALP). In New York City this infrastructure was even more extensive and the Communist party was able to elect two members of the City Council on the ALP ticket. New York Congressman Vito Marcantonio was also close to the party. On communist strength see Kampelman, *The Communist Party vs. the CIO*, pp. 13, 43–45, 98, 114; Walter Galenson, *The CIO Challenge to the AFL*, (Cambridge, Mass.: Harvard, 1960) pp. 239, 265, 320; Bernstein, *The Turbulent Years*, p. 783; Bernard Karsh and Phillips L. Garman, "The Impact of the Political Left," in Milton Derber and Edwin Young, eds., *Labor and the New Deal* (Madison, Wisc.: University of Wisconsin, 1961), pp. 87–97.

7. The ACTU had just emerged from a long campaign in support of the CIO Newspaper Guild

against the *Brooklyn Daily Eagle* and would very soon square off with the Chamber of Commerce over its suggestion that relief recipients be disenfranchised. *Labor Leader* 1, nos. 1, 8, and 11.

8. The Crown Heights school had been established only two months before. It used the facilities of the Brooklyn Catholic Preparatory School to offer a free evening program of instruction for unionists in parliamentary law, public speaking, correct speech, labor history, labor relations, the workers' rights and duties, and apologetics, an examination of Catholic labor doctrine. The faculty included John D. Moore of the New York State Labor Relations Board and members of the Brooklyn Prep staff. The director of the labor school was the Reverend William J. Smith, S.J. "Crown Heights School of Catholic Workmen," brochure, pp. 1–4, ACTU files.

9. *Labor Leader* 1, no. 2.

10. "Support the Newspaper Guild," "Catholics Support Shipyard Workers," leaflets, ACTU files; *Labor Leader* 1, nos. 1 and 8.

11. *Labor Leader* 1, nos. 2 and 8.

12. *Labor Leader* 1, no. 8.

13. Cort would be red-baited again, in Slottville, New York for his support of the Textile Workers Organizing Committee in its drive to unionize Atlantic Mills. Cort's major opponent in this incident, in May 1938, was the local parish priest. *Labor Leader* 1, nos. 13, 21, and 22.

14. *Labor Leader* 1, nos. 8 and 9.

15. Interview with George Donahue, July 22, 1974; *Labor Leader* 1, nos. 8 and 9.

16. The *Labor Leader* editors, in their comments on Joseph Ryan, had indicated that they were "suspicious of the motives of some red-baiting individuals" though they themselves opposed communism. *Labor Leader* 1, nos. 4, 5, 6, 7, and 8.

17. Interview with George Donahue, July 22, 1974; *Labor Leader* 1, no. 9.

18. *Labor Leader* 1, nos. 8 and 9.

19. Ibid., 1, no. 9.

20. Ibid., 1, no. 10.

21. Ibid.

22. Ibid., 1, no. 11.

23. Ibid.

24. "No United Fronts," ACTU leaflet, ACTU files; *Labor Leader* 1, nos. 1, 10, and 11.

25. Rice proved to be a very capable organizer. In a few years he was able to build the ACTU chapter into a significant force in Pittsburgh unionism. He organized a network of ACTU labor schools and became a leader of the anti-communist opposition in UE local 601, the largest local in the union. *Labor Leader* 2, no. 1. Rice later reevaluated his role. He was "involved" in the fight against the UE leadership, he said, but on reflection he had concluded that the UE had been "democratic" and "efficient" and that his opposition had been misplaced. Rice, "Ecumenism in Labor," *Pittsburgh Catholic*, June 9, 1966: *Labor Leader* 1, no. 11.

26. "Constitution of the Detroit ACTU," p. 1, Detroit ACTU Collection; *Michigan Labor Leader* 1, no. 1, 2, no. 14; Lecture outlines, brochures of Detroit Workers School, ACTU Collection; *Labor Leader* 1, nos. 22 and 35. It became the pattern for new chapters to organize a labor school as virtually their first activity. These schools were extremely important in the diffusion of Catholic social theory and in recruiting for ACTU chapters and affiliated union caucuses. By the late 1940s one friendly observer reported that 7,500 unionists were

graduated annually from labor schools operated by the ACTU, the diocesan authorities, or the two in conjunction. A large proportion of them were local union officers. Weinberg, "Priests, Workers and Communists," p. 52.

27. *Michigan Labor Leader* 3, no. 23, 4, no. 19; *Labor Leader* 1, no. 39, 9, no. 19, 11, no. 13. On factional fighting in the ILGWU and the Amalgamated, see Bernstein, *The Lean Years*, pp. 85, 137–38; Berstein, *The Turbulent Years*, p. 405; Galenson, *The CIO Challenge to the AFL*, p. 320.

28. *Labor Leader* 1, nos. 10 and 12.

29. *Labor Leader* 1, nos. 11 and 12.

30. *Labor Leader* 1, nos. 1, 2, and 8, vol. 1, no. 10.

31. *Labor Leader* 1, nos. 11, 14, and 31.

32. The Detroit ACTU generally opposed Coughlin's influence, which was considerable among UAW members. They were not reticent, however, to work with the UAW Coughlinites against the communists. One of the priests who worked with the ACTU, Edward Lodge Curran, was a Coughlinite, but he seems to have been a minor figure. *Michigan Labor Leader* 1, no. 6; *Labor Leader* 1, no. 13.

33. This was in reply to a letter to the editor which complained that the ACTU was "top heavy with priests." *Labor Leader* 1, no. 24.

34. Cort, "Ten Years of ACTU," pp. 143–44; Monaghan, "ACTU," pp. 1–6; Weinberg, "Priests, Workers and Communists," pp. 49–56; *Michigan Labor Leader* 2, no. 14; *Labor Leader* 1, nos. 1, 3, 9, 10, 22, and 38; interview with George Donahue, July 22, 1974.

35. Cort, "Ten Years of ACTU," pp. 143–44; Monaghan, "ACTU," pp. 1–6; Weinberg, "Priests, Workers and Communists," pp. 49–56; *Michigan Labor Leader* 2, no. 14; *Labor Leader* 1, nos. 1 and 8, 2, no. 11; interview with George Donahue, July 22, 1974.

36. The ACTU even advertised its services as a mediating agency on several occasions. *Labor Leader* 1, nos. 1, 6, and 18, 3, no. 6.

37. *Labor Leader* 1, nos. 4 and 6.

38. See the discussion of Catholic social doctrine in chapter 2. *Labor Leader* 1, no. 5.

39. Camp, *Papal Ideology*, p. 102.

40. The idea that there could be a "Catholic communist," a "mythical stupidity" in the view of the ACTU, was obviously dangerous, since it raised the possibility of radical influence within the Church itself and provided religious cover for the socialists and communists, who were seen as the worst enemies of Christianity. Accordingly that notion was attacked with special vehemence by the ACTU. The *Michigan Labor Leader* answered a reader's query on this point with a flat, "No one can be at the same time a sincere Catholic and a true socialist." The *Labor Leader* described such "Catholic communists" as "renegades" to their Church. *Michigan Labor Leader* 2, no. 6; *Labor Leader* 1, no. 21.

41. See chapters 2 and 5 for discussion of the Catholic position on socialism and communism. Also Camp, *Papal Ideology*, pp. 50–60, 102, 112, 115, 116, 129; Saposs, "Catholic Church and the Labor Movement," pp. 225–30; Gregor Siefer, *The Church and Industrial Society* (London: Darton, Longman, Todd, 1964), pp. 54, 73; Fox, *Peter E. Dietz*, pp. 18, 22–42; Karson, *American Labor Unions and Politics*, pp. 212–85.

5 † The Church and the ACTU

The members of the ACTU were labor-movement activists, as their self-descriptive acronyn, Actist, suggests. But the direction of their activity was determined by the Church whose members they were and by the social ideology promulgated by the hierarchy. The influence of the Church hierarchy is evident in the structure of the organization and its activities, while the ACTU's periodicals, positions, and educational efforts demonstrate the dominant role of Catholic social ideology. The judgment of one sympathetic contemporary, that the ACTU was "trained and directed by the Catholic Church," may be overly strong as a statement of the ACTU's relationship to the Church, but the evidence leaves no doubt that the organization was subject to considerable clerical supervision and participation and that Catholic social ideology outweighed all other influences in shaping the Actists' world view.[1]

"STRAIGHT DOWN THE MIDDLE"

On January 3, 1938, the first issue of the *Labor Leader*, the ACTU's national newspaper, stated that the function of the new Catholic labor newspaper was to provide labor news and comment that was politically "straight down the middle." A statement of principles, "the Stand of the Association of Catholic Trade Unionists," indicated that "the ACTU stood for sound trade unionism built on Christian principles." The "Stand" urged all Catholics to join "*bona fide* unions" in their field of employment, with the proviso that "no Catholic can remain in a union that is run along Marxist or unChristian lines." But Catholics should first attempt to unite with other disaffected workers to win control in such unions. The members of the ACTU, it was affirmed, stood for a "Christian reconstruction of the social order" in line with the encyclicals *Rerum*

Novarum (1891) and *Quadragesimo Anno* (1931) and the Bishops'
Statement on Reconstruction of 1919.

A specific summary of some of the principles of these texts was
provided in the form of "the Rights and Duties of the Worker." The
worker had a right to job security, an income of "reasonable and
frugal comfort," decent hours and conditions of work, some profit
sharing after a "just return to capital," "just prices" as a consumer,
and collective bargaining. In order to assure these rights, the worker
had a corollary right to strike and peacefully picket. In return, the
worker had the duty to perform an "honest day's work," to join only a
"bona fide union," to strike only for just cause and only after
exhausting other means of settlement, to refrain from violence
against the employer, strikebreakers, or private property, and to
abide honestly by all agreements. The worker, furthermore, had the
right and the duty to participate in guilds for the self-regulation of
industry or in more limited schemes of co-management, where these
existed.[2]

Three other overarching propositions complete an introduction to
the ideology of the ACTU. These are private property, class
harmony, and opposition to all forms of radicalism, socialism, and
communism. The ACTU accepted and defended the institution of
private property in the means of production as the basis of economic
activity. References to a guild structure of industry and to producers'
cooperatives sometimes confused supporters as to the ACTU's
position on collective ownership.[3] But, apart from support for
municipalization of Con Edison, the ACTU consistently argued
against collective ownership of industry.[4] The only exceptions to this
were the previously cited expressions of support for more sweeping
collectivization prior to the Gerson decision. With the defeat and
recanting of the progressives, however, no further mention was made
of socialization of the means of production. On the contrary, the
ACTU declared that "such plans are usually impractical," and
responded to confused interpretations of its guild program by
affirming its commitment to the "legitimacy of the profit motive" and
to private property.[5]

A second general premise of the ACTU was that the interests of
capital and labor were "essentially in harmony."[6] Class-conflict
theories and class politics had no valid place in the American labor

movement, according to the Actists. The bitterness and intractability they inspired worked against the achievement of peaceful agreements, promoted unnecessary strife, and made the building of a harmonious Christian social order more difficult. Therefore, the ACTU was "out to tear down the barricades of class war in America."[7] Once the Christian teachings on economic justice were fully understood, there would be no insuperable barrier to peaceful solution of all industrial disputes. The plan for a guild structure of industry, representing both workers and employers in the planning and direction of economic life, would end all class animosity and result in a just and harmonious social order.

The third general proposition in the ideology of the ACTU, the most constant in the life of the organization, was that socialism, in whatever form, and especially communism, were erroneous in their analysis and dangerous in their prescriptions and activities.[8] The membership pledge and the ACTU's convention resolutions, as well as editorials and columns in virtually every issue of the *Labor Leader* and the *Michigan Labor Leader* regularly reminded ACTU supporters of their duty to combat radicalism.[9] After the defeat of the progressives in the ACTU, this position became absolute and unbending. No compromise was to be made with the left and anything the left supported was suspect to the ACTU.[10] Nor could any alliance be made with radicals, except perhaps to defeat other radicals. Thus Catholics who accepted the leadership of socialists in their unions were "renegades."[11] In general anti-radicalism became the single most prominent theme in the ACTU's ideology.[12]

The ACTU's ideology was a Catholic ideology. It was derived from the encyclicals *Rerum Novarum* (1891) and *Quadragesimo Anno* (1931), from the Bishops' Program of 1919, from Catholic commentary and interpretation of the encyclicals, especially that of Monsignor John A. Ryan, and from the current pronouncements of the Church hierarchy. *Rerum Novarum*, in particular, they held to be "labor's magna carta" and the inspiration for New Deal labor legislation.[13] Passages from the encyclicals and the Bishops' Program were common in the *Labor Leader* and the ACTU membership was pledged to "abide by all the teachings and practices of my Catholic faith including those expressed in the social encyclicals."[14]

The idea for the ACTU itself had come from a study group on the encyclicals comprising most of the founding members of the organization, and the study and promotion of the encyclicals remained an important function of the group. As John Cort saw it, the ACTU had been relieved of the duty of developing an organizational program since "in the labor encyclicals of Leo XIII and Pius XI there was a program that would not only solve the problems of the American labor movement, but bring order out of chaos in American industry."[15] That program included just such organizations as the ACTU: "Side by side with the trade unions [nonsectarian, non-socialist unions] there must always be associations which aim at giving their members a thorough religious and moral training, that these in turn may impart to the unions to which they belong the upright spirit which should direct their entire conduct."[16]

Thus, the ACTU drew not only its most fundamental ideology, but its very organizational rationale, from the labor encyclicals of the popes. The organization's "Christian Social Apostolate" involved educating Catholic workers in the social teaching of their Church and attempting to shape the labor movement and social policy generally within the framework of these teachings. Since a scant majority of union membership in the United States was Catholic, this commitment to Church dogma presented problems.[17] In the view of the ACTU, however, there was no real contradiction between the beliefs of non-Catholic workers and the social teachings of the Catholic Church. Since the latter did not involve religious questions and were merely a systematic ethical approach to social questions, they provided a "commonsense" solution that all might follow, regardless of faith.[18]

The ACTU, then, was Catholic in its ideology as well as in its religious commitment. Only practicing Catholics whose good faith was attested by their priest could join the organization, and the chaplain could challenge even these. Members were bound to observe the rituals of their faith and to attend the nocturnal adoration-society meetings, retreats, communion breakfasts, and other ACTU observances which formed an important part of the organization's activities. The chapters themselves were under the religious supervision of their chaplains and bishops. Just as the Actists respected the rituals of their faith, so too did they take their inspiration in secular tasks from the Church.[19] There were problems as well as strengths that followed from this fact.

Their Catholic faith provided the Actists with a certain clarity of purpose and a defined agenda for their organization. Since the encyclicals offered a theory and a program, the ACTU's only task was to apply these to conditions in the United States. This was by no means so simple as it might seem, however. The "Americanization" of the guild plan for industry proved quite elusive, for example.[20] But received Church doctrine enabled the ACTU to avoid some of the theoretical disputes which plagued other organizations. On a more emotional level, common membership in the Church and common observance of its rites provided the ACTU membership with a unity and a sense of collective purpose which would otherwise have been difficult to achieve.

As "social apostles" the Actists felt a continuity with the whole history and tradition of the Catholic Church. This enhanced their sense of the dignity and importance of their organization and its activities. This identification with the Church also gave authority to what the ACTU had to say to other communicants. This was particularly important in the case of those Catholic workers who were indifferent to unions, afraid of them, or believed them to be "communist." A Catholic frame of reference for union agitation was of obvious utility in winning the support of these workers. As the official, papal-mandated Catholic organizations in the American labor movement, the ACTU, in a sense, could claim all Catholic workers as its constituency. While its small membership in relation to the Catholic portion of the working class made this largely a moral claim, it was no less significant for that. To many workers, non-Catholic and Catholic alike, and to many Churchmen and union officials, the ACTU was the voice of Catholic workers.[21] This was especially so for Catholic union officials concerned to maintain their good standing in the faith.[22] Catholicism, then, provided the ACTU with an ideology, with certain organizational strengths, and with a wider constituency and field of influence for that ideology than it would otherwise have enjoyed.

One of the weaknesses which followed from the official Catholic status of the ACTU was a tendency to see union and political problems in exclusively ethical and theological, rather than economic or class terms. This was evident in the ACTU's absolute prohibition on violence in strikes, whatever the provocation.[23] More significantly, Catholic morality was also the major source for the insistence on class harmony, as against class conflict, and the mediation efforts and co-management plans which followed from it. Catholic theology and ethics contributed to the ACTU's increasing inflexibility on the anti-communist issue as well. The absolute anathema on communism and socialism made it nearly impossible to consider areas of common agreement with radicals, while maintaining differences. While a secular approach might have apprehended the dangers of union splitting and of the cross-class alliances with employers implicit in anti-communism, a theological definition of communism as "evil" tended to override any such objections.

Another organizational weakness which derived from the official Catholic status of the ACTU was the explicit sectarian limitation on its constituency and membership. A prospective member had to be a practicing Catholic whose good faith was attested by his parish priest and by the chaplain of the ACTU chapter involved.[24] Protestants, Jews, and the irreligious, including nonpracticing Catholics, were excluded from membership. The problems with the sectarian definition of potential members, however, were outweighed by the strengths gained from the Catholic connection in coherence of program, unity, and purpose. The significance of the sectarian problem was in its effect on the ACTU's relationship with non-Catholic forces in the unions and those who, while nominally Catholic, did not identify themselves as such in their union roles. Important among the latter were Catholic union officials who were obliged to maintain a nonsectarian public position.

The ACTU attempted to overcome this problem, in part, by defining its Catholic-derived ideology and program as a "common-sense" program, without religious overtones. But this was only a partial solution and could hardly satisfy the left, or many in the center. The guild program in particular was often viewed with suspicion as a feudal or Fascist program at worst and impossible at best.[25] The ACTU did not allay this suspicion by referring to the program as the "Pope's Plan." The prominent role of the ACTU's clerical members, too, inspired further criticism and forced some otherwise sympathetic Catholic union officials to keep their distance.

The sectarian character of the ACTU did tend to limit its influence on the labor movement as a whole insofar as its positive program was concerned. The official Catholic connection afforded the ACTU's opponents the opportunity to criticize them as "outsiders," "sectarians," and "papal agents."[26] Since *Rerum Novarum* did call for Catholic unions, "dual unionism" was another common charge, despite the ACTU's denial of any intention to split Catholics from the existing unions.[27] These attacks certainly alienated some non-Catholic workers, especially those who were already hostile to Catholicism or to the Irish, and made it difficult for union officials who depended on the support of these workers to work with the ACTU.

In order actually to influence the direction of industrial unionism the ACTU found it necessary to pursue issues which minimized their Catholic orientation and opened connections with non-Catholic unionists. During 1937, the first year of ACTU activity, the issues of corruption and inertia on the part of union leaders and "organizing the unorganized" had served this purpose.[28] These issues were of self-evident importance to all supporters of unionism, including, as we have seen, the left wing. Corrupt union leaders such as Joseph P. Ryan of the ILA or the local leaders of Teamsters local 802 were often Catholics.[29] They could not very easily attack the ACTU members as "papal agents." The fact that the ACTU did criticize Catholics, among them Mayor Hague, also tended to undercut the sectarian charges against them among non-Catholics.

These issues, however, were in large measure played out by 1939. Once the CIO unions were established and staffed, outside assistance in running strikes and building support became considerably less important. The role of the ACTU in mediation efforts was lessened, also, by the activities of the NLRB. Indeed, a number of ACTU members shifted the focus of their activity to membership on the labor-relations boards or staff positions with the unions they had often helped to build.[30] It appears also that the ACTU became less interested in "organizing the unorganized" once its efforts in that direction had served to win them a base of support.

In the case of union corruption and leadership inactivity, the ACTU's retreat from the fray is somewhat more complicated. The ACTU's campaign against corrupt union leaders had led to some convictions and election defeats in 1938–40 and in many cases the offending AFL unions had lost representation elections to CIO unions.[31] Despite these victories, however, many corrupt AFL officials remained entrenched and many unionists continued to suffer from honest but inactive or ineffective leaders.[32] The declining ACTU interest in combatting union corruption and inertia, then, cannot be explained by the eradication of these problems.

These issues had become an embarrassment to the ACTU for two reasons. In the case of local 802 of the Teamsters the ACTU's campaign against corruption had led to a number of convictions which the ACTU considered well deserved. On the other hand, a number of union members whom the ACTU considered innocent of any misconduct were also convicted and local 802 was placed under a court-appointed receiver.[33] The ACTU concluded that, while corruption could not be tolerated by union members, it should not furnish an excuse for employers and the courts to weaken unions. This court action against a union local paralleled a campaign by the Liberty League and other employer groups against "corruption" in the unions and on behalf of a definition of union "unfair labor practices" similar to that ultimately embodied in the Taft-Hartley Act. In this situation the ACTU understandably became somewhat hesitant about public campaigns against corruption in the unions.

The second reason the ACTU chose to soft-pedal the corruption issue and the fight against inactive union leadership was that these issues were rebounding to the advantage of radicals in the labor movement. Even before the Gerson affair the *Labor Leader* had indicated that one of its major reasons for fighting corruption was that such misconduct gave the communists an opening in the unions as "rank-and-file" opponents of corruption.[34] Some of the most bitter fighting against corrupt and employer-tied union leaders had, indeed, been waged by the communists and, consequently, many local union members saw the left as the only coherent alternative to the racketeers and supported them for local office.[35] Thus the corruption issue tended to cut two ways.

The ACTU had emulated the leftists in its attacks on corruption and had won considerable support through these campaigns. At the same time, when there were no ACTU contacts in a local, the stress on corruption tended to the advantage of the left wing. This was apparently acceptable prior to the Gerson affair. But when anti-communism emerged as the major ACTU issue, these "spillover" benefits to the left became unacceptable. Indeed, the Actists' position changed so drastically that the *Labor Leader* announced it would support the union leaders it had previously attacked as corrupt and do-nothing when they were opposed by radicals. Corruption in the Brooklyn ILA was so bad in the summer of 1940 that rank-and-file opposition members were being murdered by gangsters. Nonetheless, the *Labor Leader* commented editorially that the real problem was not gangsterism but the fact that the ILA opposition was being "taken over by Communists."[36] By 1945 the Brooklyn locals had thrown out President Ryan's supporters, and elected a communist, William Warren, the first breakthrough for the opposition. The ACTU, however, thought Warren was worse than Ryan and urged the opposition to throw the communists out.[37] This was fully in line with the ACTU's general rightward movement subsequent to the Gerson decision. Since corrupt union leaders and the employers who profited from their inaction were to be welcomed into the "anti-communist front," it was inconsistent to continue to mount attacks on them which benefited the left.

Thus the two issues which had protected the ACTU from charges of sectarianism and had furnished links to non-Catholic workers were unavailable after the first years of organizational activity. The issue which replaced them was anti-communism. The anti-communist issue had a great many advantages as an alternative to inertia and corruption among the union leadership and "organizing the unorganized." While the left could provide leadership on these issues, it obviously could not coopt anti-communism. Though the ACTU's commitment to anti-communism was more fundamental than tactical, it was an added advantage that this issue was "nonsectarian." It provided, that is, a basis for coalition with Protestant, Jewish, and secular workers. In addition, anti-communism provided a way out of the paradoxical impasse represented by the success of the CIO. Once the unions were organized, the issue on the agenda then became: What was the labor movement to be and do?

Insofar as their program did not parallel what the New Deal was already doing, the ACTU's answer to this question was the guild or corporate organization of American economic and social life. But this program, developed as it was by clerical theoreticians, did not win much support outside of the Catholic community. Indeed, most Catholic workers were indifferent to it and most Catholic union officials were evasive at best.[38] At the same time, this issue tended to rekindle the charges of "sectarianism," papal conspiracy, and fascism. In fact, it was the major source of such attacks.[39]

The anti-communist issue avoided these problems and provided explicit (and implicit) answers to the question of the shape and direction of the labor movement. Since there was no contradiction between the views of the Church on communism and those of non-Catholic anti-communists, anti-communism tended to undercut "sectarian" criticism of the ACTU. Turning the fire on the communists as outsiders, totalitarians, and agents of a foreign power also helped to deflect such criticism of the ACTU.[40] Most important strategically, perhaps, anti-communism was an issue which might unite Catholic, Protestant, Jewish, and nonreligious workers, and thus provide the ACTU with a solution to its sectarian dilemma. Many union officials who found their conservative brand of business unionism under attack by the left, as well as aspirants to union office seeking to unseat left-wing leaders, could be expected to work with the ACTU against the communists, if not on behalf of the "Pope's Plan."[41] Thus anti-communism, firmly based in Catholic social doctrine and in past Catholic activities in the labor movement, also served as a solution to some of the weaknesses and limitations of a purely Catholic organization seeking a wider influence in the labor movement.

THE CLERICAL CONNECTION

Though doctrine was very important in the life of the Actists, clerical participation in and supervision of the ACTU had a conservative impact on the ACTU's views and activities beyond the indirect effect of the clerics' Catholic ideology. As we have seen, the clerical role was an important one. ACTU members accepted the legitimate authority of the Church hierarchy in all questions, specifically the teachings on unionism and radicalism.[42] The membership pledge bound an Actist to work for the program embodied in the social encyclicals.[43] The ACTU's chaplains were important officers in the organization, holding half the seats in the highest ACTU body. The chaplain's determination of a prospective member's good standing in the faith was a precondition to ACTU membership. Furthermore, the approval of the diocesan authorities was constitutionally necessary before an ACTU chapter could be formed, and then the organization operated under the general supervision of the bishop. Thus the program, the membership, and the activities of the ACTU were under rather close clerical control. [44]

As a Catholic organization directed toward winning Catholic workers to support unionism, the ACTU depended heavily on the influence of Church authorities and lower clerics with rank-and-file workers. The ACTU's main line of argument for support of unionization was that it was one's "duty" as a Catholic. [45] The major sources cited for this duty were the social encyclicals, the Bishops' Program of 1919, and the statements of individual archbishops, bishops, and priests. Three priests, Monaghan, O'Connor, and Rice, wrote regular columns in the *Labor Leader* and a large amount of news space was devoted to the statements, speeches, or writings of Churchmen. Biographies of Pope Pius XI, Monsignor John A. Ryan, and Bishop Francis Haas appeared in a series entitled "Labor Profiles," and eulogies to deceased clerics, including Cardinal Patrick Hayes of New York, were common. [46] Pictures of Churchmen in the *Labor Leader* seemed to outnumber all others, and in one issue, photographs and statements from virtually the entire American hierarchy appeared, commending the ACTU's work and urging union membership. [47]

The prominence given to the pro-union statements of clerics in the *Labor Leader* had a double purpose. On the one hand, they represented an attempt to convince Catholic workers disillusioned with the conservatism of the Church that the hierarchy was indeed pro-union. Winning the errant back to the fold was a goal of some importance to the ACTU, particularly when these Catholics had been recruited to radicalism. [48] At the same time, the clerical promotion of unionism was designed to convince Catholics who were indifferent or hostile to unions that the Church supported unionization and social justice.

The ACTU's dependence on the authority of the clergy was not confined to the printed page. Priests played a prominent role, as has been noted, in many of the early strike-support and mediation efforts of the organization. Chaplain John Monaghan was involved in several strike-support campaigns, as were the Reverend Edward Swanstrom, William Kelly, and Joseph Moody. ACTU members Charles Owen Rice and John P. Boland sat on the labor-relations boards of Pennsylvania and New York respectively.[49] These clerics and many others spoke before groups of workers considering unionization, union meetings and conventions, Holy Name societies, Catholic alumni and womens' associations. Clerics thus formed an important and active section of the ACTU membership.[50]

Another arena in which priests played a prominent role was that of the ACTU's labor schools, which will be discussed at greater length in chapters 6 and 7. The first of these schools was organized in 1937 at Fordham University in New York under the direction of the Reverend John Monaghan.[51] By 1946 there were seventy such ACTU-affiliated labor schools.[52] The instructors in all cases were predominantly clerics and most of these were Jesuits. The Fordham school staff consisted of faculty from Fordham with the addition of the Reverend Monaghan and the Reverend John P. Boland, chairman of the New York Labor Relations Board.[53] The Crown Heights School staff included the Reverend John D. Moore of the New York Labor Relations Board and several members of the Brooklyn Prep faculty.[54] The schools taught a curriculum of Catholic social doctrine, labor history, ethics, parliamentary procedure, public speaking, and union leadership.[55] They, together with the diocesan labor schools, graduated 7,500 students yearly in the late 1940s, many of whom became local and international union officers.[56] The labor schools were an extremely important component of the ACTU's effort to influence unionists and potential union leaders, and here clerics predominated.

ACTU clerics articulated ideology and program; they held many offices in the organization; they wrote polemics on behalf of unionism; they helped organize labor support activities; and they staffed ACTU labor schools. This clerical prominence within the ACTU provided a conservative influence on the organization. The ideology developed by the Churchmen was itself conservative in its impact. Apart from this, however, in their role as clergymen they tended to strengthen the passivity of Catholic workers, to work against the erstwhile progressive within the ACTU, and to buttress conservative positions in the day-to-day work of the ACTU.

Such conservatism among the clergy extended on occasion to anti-unionism, though this was obviously not the case with the ACTU's members and supporters.[57] The ACTU's own efforts to promote the CIO and "social justice" were consistently countered by the efforts of many parish priests and other clerics more highly placed. The Actists were forced on several occasions during strike-support activities to counter anti-union propaganda in the sermons and parish letters of local priests.[58] During the Jersey City campaign the entire Catholic establishment in the city had publicly argued that the CIO and the Communist party were equivalent.[59]

Despite the mixed record of Churchmen, the ACTU defended the authority of the clergy uncompromisingly. When members and readers of the *Labor Leader* complained that the organization appeared to be controlled by the Church, or that it was "top heavy with priests," the criticism was countered with the assertion that the clergy "were appointed by God" and thus beyond criticism.[60] The ACTU's dilemma here was that of a Catholic organization which depended on clerical approval and support for its own legitimacy and was thus obliged to defend the priesthood even when many of its members were hostile to some of the ACTU's most cherished goals. Since the members of the ACTU agreed with the conservative program of the clergy in most respects, however, this was not so great a contradiction as it might seem.

The ACTU's defense of the clergy tended to increase the authority of a generally conservative group and to strengthen traditional authoritarian relationships within the Church. This posed a significant problem for the ACTU's work within the unions. A major target of the ACTU was the apathy and passivity of Catholic workers and their perceived ignorance of and inexperience with democratic forms. These were held by the Actists to be the main sources of racketeer, do-nothing, or left-wing leadership in many unions.[61] The ACTU often lamented that communist leadership could be overthrown easily if only Catholic workers would become active within their unions.[62] The conservatism of the clergy and the authoritarian relationships within the Church, however, encouraged this passivity, and contributed to fear or indifference to unions and inexperience with democratic forms. Thus the ACTU's adamant defense of the clergy strengthened the very behavior syndrome which made it so difficult to organize Catholic workers and, once organized, to spur them to an active involvement in their unions.

This would have occurred even had the ACTU's active clergy been radicals themselves, because of the spillover authority accruing to the larger number of conservative parish priests. Most of those clergy who sympathized with or were active in the ACTU, however, were themselves conservative in important respects. Indeed, the ACTU's position on the Gerson protest, its stress on mediation, its anti-communism, and its treatment of the Spanish Civil War were all influenced in a conservative direction by the organization's clerical supporters.

The Gerson protest debate was first raised at a forum of the ACTU Crown Heights School of Catholic Workmen. The school staff were Jesuit clergy and the leading proponent of the protest was the Reverend William J. Smith, S.J., director of the school. The Reverend Smith, it will be recalled, articulated the most conservative position during the debate that followed. He argued that communism was an unmitigated evil and that opposition to it should be the first priority of the ACTU. Even anti-union employers might be welcomed into the anti-communist front, in the Reverend Smith's opinion, and this issue ought to take precedence over the fight for unionism and social justice itself. His position became the basis for the ACTU's anti-Gerson protest resolution. [63]

Just as the original ACTU commitment to a public campaign against communism had clerical sources, so too did its continuation and its virulence. The Reverend Smith stoked the fires with pamphlets such as "American or Communist? You Can't be Both!"[64] The Reverend Charles Owen Rice's major concern was the anti-communist issue and it furnished the basis for his organization of an ACTU chapter in Pittsburgh. [65] While Chaplain Monaghan's regular contributions to the *Labor Leader* were largely explanations of the credo of the "Rights and Duties of the Worker," the columns of other clerics were almost entirely devoted to excoriating the communists. The column "Don Capellano," written by Rice, followed this pattern. The Reverend Neil O'Conner's column "Real Issues" was also largely devoted to red-baiting. [66]

Clerical supporters also influenced the ACTU's particular stress on mediation of strikes, and the idea of class harmony which underpinned it. The Reverend Smith had argued that the definition of "capitalist abuses" was "a very delicate matter."[67] The guilty party in a given industrial dispute, in his opinion, had to be determined on the merits of the case. Since such a determination demanded a "neutral" arbitrator, mediation was his solution. Mediation was, indeed, the ACTU's preferred alternative to the "misery and strife of a strike" and its clerical supporters almost invariably did the mediating.[68] The strikers and the particular clergymen involved have been indicated previously. It will suffice to say here that nearly every strike the ACTU supported was terminated by mediation. The promotion of class harmony, as against class conflict, through mediation was a constant theme of the ACTU's clerical supporters. Similarly, quotations from Monsignor Fulton J. Sheen and from other clerics routinely appeared in the *Labor Leader* suggesting that the employer should be considered as a brother and not an enemy and that the interests of the classes were "essentially in harmony."[69]

The heavy emphasis on mediation on the part of the ACTU's clerical supporters led to ambiguity as to the ACTU's function in a strike. Was it an advocate and partisan of the workers involved or was it an "impartial" mediating body? This ambivalence was never totally resolved in the direction of mediation and the ACTU certainly did offer partisan support for the workers in most of the strikes it assisted. Nonetheless, the constant reiteration of class harmony as theory and mediation as practice led to a discernible shift from workers' advocate in the direction of a multiclass and "impartial" group standing outside the labor movement. That the ACTU came to be so regarded by many workers is attested by the volume of requests for mediation, rather than strike-support assistance, which the *Labor Leader* received.[70]

Clerical participation in mediation tended to blunt class perspective and downplay militancy among the workers involved in favor of interclass harmony and compromise. It also tended to reaffirm the workers' sense of their inability to carry on and conduct their own struggles. Through their role as mediators and "experts" the clergy tended to transfer the control and authority they had within the

ACTU, and within the Church, to groups of striking workers. Thus workers who were passive, afraid, or inexperienced with strikes or negotiations tended to remain so while their clerical supporters carried on the bulk of the negotiating and organizing. Thus the extensive clerical influence within the ACTU tended to undercut the very qualities of self-confidence, self-reliance, experience, and aggressiveness which the ACTU was attempting to promote among Catholic workers. Finally, the preponderant interest of the clergy in class harmony may well have led them to be satisfied in settling a strike for something less than the workers themselves would have found adequate.[71]

The issue of the Spanish Civil War demonstrates the conservative influence of the ACTU's clerical supporters in more general terms, and in most dramatic fashion, since the ACTU's support for Franco divided them from most of the labor movement and from radical as well as liberal opinion generally.[72] The ACTU held that the loyalists, or republicans, could not be supported because they were hostile to religion and accepted the aid of communists. Franco's nationalists, on the other hand, had the full support of the Catholic Church.[73] The ACTU, however, supported unionism, progressive taxation, and regulation of monopoly, all of which were violently opposed by the Spanish nationalists, and the Actists were constitutionally opposed to Fascism. No independent workers' organizations existed in nationalist Spain and "social justice" was hardly the watchword of the nationalists or their Italian and German allies. The working class of Spain in its entirety supported the Republic and the left.[74] Nevertheless, the ACTU's support for the Church, and the influence of its own clerics, led it to a position of support for those forces in Spain which were the dedicated enemies of unionism and of the progressive legislation of the Republic.

This position was particularly important in that Spain was a touchstone of political sentiment in the late 1930s. The ACTU's support for Franco put it in the conservative camp on one of the foremost international issues of the period. If international issues are often a "purer" indication of political sympathies than domestic ones, since one does not have to live with their practical implications, then the ACTU's position on Spain was most revealing. Support for Franco also increased suspicion of the Catholic program of corporativism since Franco, like Mussolini, claimed without contradiction from the Vatican to be following such a program.[75]

The ACTU's Catholicism, then, brought both strengths and weaknesses to the organization. A common religious faith and doctrine provided unity, coherence, and a sense of purpose within the organization. Official Catholic status also provided, to some degree, a ready-made constituency with a susceptibility to the ACTU's religiously framed arguments for unionism and social justice. Clerical participation and aid meant that the Actists could count on support from some portion of the powerful Church establishment and the traditional authority of these Churchmen also provided strength and direction to particular workers' struggles with which the ACTU was involved.

The Catholic connection of the ACTU, however, limited its impact on non-Catholic workers and opened the organization to charges of outside direction, clerical domination, "dual unionism," and sectarianism. The Actists' response to this problem was to seek issues of broader appeal. Initially the ACTU stressed the issues of corruption in the unions, inactive union leadership, and "organizing the unorganized," but a number of factors led them to abandon these in favor of anti-communism. Catholicism also contributed a tendency to a moral and theological, rather than a political and instrumental view of many union issues, including violence and communism. The clergy were also responsible for the priority given to class harmony and mediation, which, in some degree, tended to eclipse the ACTU's partisan commitment to working class interests. Clerical participation in the organization's work and direction intensified these problems and also tended to reinforce the inexperience and passivity of Catholic workers.

THE ACTU AND CATHOLIC SOCIAL DOCTRINE

The Catholic labor activists of the ACTU were constitutionally and programatically committed to the social encyclicals *Rerum Novarum* (1891) and *Quadragesimo Anno* (1931), and to the Bishops' Program of 1919 and the writings of Monsignor John A. Ryan as the most authoritative American adaptation of these texts.[76] Thus they fell heir to the practical limitations and the conservative content of these doctrines discussed in chapter 2. How did this ideology affect ACTU positions on significant issues in the labor movement? How did the doctrinal commitment to class harmony and cooperation, social hierarchy, private property, and anti-radicalism influence their efforts to build a strong working-class movement for "social justice"? The third section of this chapter attempts to answer these questions through a consideration of the ACTU's position on the issues of industrial unionism, labor unity, strikes and mediation, violence and militance, union democracy and corruption, dual unionism, radicalism, and independent political action by labor.

Originally, the ACTU had been critical of private property in industry. Indeed, on a number of occasions in 1938 the ACTU had printed articles and poems which endorsed collective ownership of industry as the only solution to workers' status as "slaves" of production. In January 1938 ACTU officers John Cort and George Donahue unsuccessfully sought the endorsement of the Catholic Conference on Industrial Problems for a "Catholic condemnation of capitalism." The following month the Catholic League of the Unemployed, a subsidiary organization of the ACTU, announced its opposition to "excessive" private ownership. But with the Gerson debates and the conservative consolidation that followed, the mainstream Catholic position of support for private property was reaffirmed.

The ACTU endorsed small-scale property holdings as the best insurance against social upheaval, but agreed with Ryan that, whatever the injustice or danger in its distribution, private property had to be defended. The reason for this was the familiar one of Catholic doctrine: property was a "natural right" and represented the reward of labor. Thus ACTU member the Reverend Charles Owen Rice made "the right of ownership of private property" a major item in his argument against socialism. While the ACTU stressed the "social duty of wealth," this voluntary duty was premised upon the validity and continuation of the private ownership of industry. Even state intervention to redistribute income was justified, not so much as a matter of justice as a means of preventing property from "rushing to its own destruction." Since neither Pope Leo XIII nor Pius XI had "condemned" capitalism itself, the *Labor Leader* informed its readers, neither would the ACTU. Indeed, the organization affirmed the "legitimacy of the profit motive." Thus the unorthodox position on private property which the ACTU had held during the progressive ascendency gave way to a more characteristic and conservative view of the institution consistent with the doctrine of the Church. From 1938 onwards the ACTU was to offer no criticism of private property in the means of production. The "abuses" of property rather than the institution itself were the proper target for reform according to the Actists. [77]

In the case of "just prices, profits, and wages," the ACTU had no initial heresy to overcome. From the beginning the organization followed the encyclicals and Monsignor John A. Ryan on these subjects. "The worker has a right to a just price for the goods he buys," wrote Chaplain John Monaghan of the ACTU, in one of a series of explanations of the "Rights and Duties" of the worker appearing in the *Labor Leader*. The just-price doctrine was the subject of a number of such summaries in the *Labor Leader* over the years. The ACTU shared in the dilemma of Catholic just-price authorities, however, for no indication was ever given as to how such prices were to be made a reality other than through voluntary "stewardship" on the part of corporations or of cooperative purchasing societies of workers. The just-profits doctrine was hedged by these and other difficulties in the ACTU formulation, no less than in that of Monsignor Ryan. While contemporary executive salaries and a six-percent profit rate seemed "too high" to the ACTU, no rigorous mechanism for determining what they should be was developed. The actual just-profit rate would have to "be determined by experience." Despite their lack of precision, the doctrines of just prices and profits served as the major ideological basis for the ACTU's frequent condemnations of monopoly, "sticky" prices, excess profits, and maldistribution of income. [78]

The living- or just-wage doctrine was especially important to the ACTU since it was the main ideological rationale for union organizing and the kernel of the idea of social justice in the Catholic perspective. As a consequence it occupied a prominent place in the original "Stand of the ACTU," a statement of principles, and in a later summary of the "Principles of a Christian Social Order in a Democratic Society," adapted from the National Catholic Social Action Conference. The concept of the living wage was the most prominent motif, after unionization itself, in the ACTU publicity and educational efforts. The doctrine was regularly summarized and defended in the *Labor Leader* and it served as the major yardstick in determining whether strikes and legislation were worthy of support.[79]

The ACTU's explanation of the living-wage doctrine paralleled the weaknesses of the original formulations in the encyclicals and the works of Ryan. The Actists repeated the definition of Pope Leo XIII that a living wage should guarantee an income of "reasonable and frugal comfort," despite its imprecision. The ACTU's endorsement of an "increased wage in view of increased family burdens" and of the reverse sliding-scale idea that the living wage varied according to "the standard suitable to a man's station in life" increased the complexities and contradictions of the doctrine. Just what constituted a living wage was no clearer in the ACTU's account than it had been in Ryan's. It was "difficult to say exactly what such a wage should be in dollars and cents," according to the ACTU, but something on the order of $1,500 to $2,500 was probably necessary in 1936, adjusted for family size and whether one was a "mechanic, clerk, teacher or President." Despite this extreme fuzziness and the pronounced tendency to an austere definition of "reasonable comfort," the living-wage doctrine was the major ideological weapon available to the ACTU in its critique of prevailing wage standards and brief for unionization.[80]

Employer-worker cooperation figured as the primary means by which reform was to be secured and social justice institutionalized in Catholic doctrine. The ACTU fully accepted this perspective. The original "Stand of the ACTU" indicated that workers had a right to profit sharing and a duty to participate in "guilds for the self-regulation of industry." As has been indicated, these passages served as the basis for an ACTU endorsement of collective ownership of industry during the first year of the organization's existence. This apparent socialism was abandoned with the Gerson decision. After 1938, the ACTU-approved position was that "outright government ownership and operation [of industry] is neither necessary nor desirable." The conservative consolidation that followed the Gerson decision threw even the rather mild and Catholic-sanctioned solution of producers' cooperatives into disfavor. Confusion continued, however, and as late as 1942 the *Labor Leader* editors had to remind the readership that firms "owned and operated by the workers themselves as opposed to the usual set-up of stockholders, management and workers" were "impractical."[81]

If outright cooperative enterprise was too radical for the ACTU, other forms of "reciprocity" continued to be touted as the answer to social injustice and class conflict. Profit sharing was one of the forms advocated by Ryan and the ACTU also endorsed it. The problem of "rights" versus voluntary action continued to be a sticky one, however, and at various times the ACTU held that "labor, which is the primary source of all wealth (after God) has a definite right" to profit sharing, and, to the contrary, that labor did not have a right to "control over the distribution of profit."[82]

If the ACTU was confused on profit sharing, it was no less certain that some form of employer-worker cooperation was the solution to social problems. The Bishops' Program of 1919 was repeatedly quoted to this effect and such interclass cooperation was a regular subject of articles, editorials, and theoretical pieces. One article, entitled "Labor Peace Plan Outlined," indicated that "amicable discussions in which representatives of employers and workers will sit down together and attempt to work out the problems of industry and labor, provide the ultimate solution to industrial strife."[83]

The ACTU did not go as far as Ryan had in endorsing the Standard Oil company union as an example of such "amicable discussions," "labor peace" and cooperation. While at least one of the ACTU labor-school instructors favored company unions, the ACTU in general opposed them. For practical examples of the cooperation they had in mind the ACTU preferred to cite the NRA. Though labor was represented on only 59 of 442 NRA industry boards, the *Labor Leader* editorially argued that a similar structure which gave labor "equal representation with capital" would be the kernel of "self-regulation and self-government of our economy."[84] Thus, while various forms of cooperation, profit sharing and co-management might pave the way, the ACTU's ultimate program was always the corporative order or "new guild system." Termed at different times the "Guild Plan," the "Pope's Plan" and the "Social" or "Industrial Peace Plan," this was the ultimate program to which the ACTU sought to win its constituency and the union movement as a whole. Such a corporative economy, controlled by "capital and labor acting in co-operation under the conviction that their interests are essentially in harmony," would herald a "decent social order."[85]

The ACTU was thus within the mainstream of Catholic social doctrine in its views on private property, "just" profits and prices, the living wage, and the various forms of reciprocity, including the corporative program. The Actists, therefore, inherited the weaknesses, problems of application, and fundamental conservatism of these doctrines. Private property was sacrosanct and thus major reforms in its distribution or control, even those addressed by Catholic doctrine, were undercut. No specific determination could be made of excess profits or prices and therefore no real price or profit control was possible. The living wage could not be precisely determined and had no relation to productivity. In addition, the just-wage doctrine was defined in mere subsistence terms and varied in relation to family size and "social station." The living-wage idea was thus shorn of most of its critical utility and reduced to the status of a slogan.[86]

The combination of the weaknesses of price and profit doctrine, the commitment to private property, and an impractical, limited, and austere doctrine of living wages added up to a very slight threat to the "social injustice" embodied in a system of concentrated power and property and large-scale deprivation and dependency. Employers would probably not have found it difficult to live with a national policy based on these doctrines. The critical edge of Catholic social ideology was further blunted by its dependence on ethical reform and voluntary action by employers to implement even the modest reforms which were contemplated. This requirement ruled out collectivization, cooperative enterprise, or serious profit sharing and co-management.[87]

The ACTU was left with the National Recovery Administration, albeit with increased labor representation, as its best example of the reciprocity to be embodied in the "guild economy." This was not likely to be a very attractive version of utopia to workers, who found that voluntary business action under the "National Run Around" consisted of price gouging, production and employment cutbacks, increasing profits, and pay cuts. If these were the only sort of voluntary business "reforms" to be expected, then "class harmony" and "reciprocity" were elusive indeed. Voluntarism was only one of many problems with the corporative program, however. The guild system also placed a great deal of stress on social status, hierarchy, authority, and economic as opposed to political representation, and it assumed the continuation of private property. With these additions the doctrines of reciprocity and corporativism emerge as genuinely conservative.

The ACTU, then, was in the difficult position of attempting to organize a movement for "social justice" around an ideology which was fundamentally conservative. How did this ideology affect the ACTU's position on issues within the unions? An investigation of the ACTU's response to the issues of industrial unionism, labor unity, strikes versus mediation, violence, union democracy and corruption, dual unionism, radicalism, and independent political action by labor will offer some answers to this question.

Industrial unionism and the CIO were strongly supported by the ACTU. Most of their organizing and strike-support work involved industrial, white-collar, service, and transport workers ignored by the AFL, and most of their propaganda was directed to these workers. While the ACTU argued the case for unionism in general and promoted membership in all *"bona fide* unions," the CIO was its particular focus. In contests for representation the ACTU usually supported the CIO affiliate over AFL or "independent" unions. The campaign in Jersey City in 1938 was described as an "ACTU-CIO" effort and had even involved the opposition of the AFL. Similar campaigns in New York City, Elizabeth (New Jersey), and Troy (New York) were also CIO affairs. The ACTU shared the general belief in the CIO that, if the unskilled industrial work force was to be organized, it would have to be through industrial unions and outside the framework of the AFL. Since the ACTU had been founded in the midst of the CIO organizing drives for the express purpose of influencing and encouraging the organization of the unskilled, the stress on industrial unionism and the CIO was natural enough. [88]

At the same time the ACTU consistently opposed the permanent organization of the CIO as a separate union federation and regularly promoted "labor unity" of the AFL and the CIO. The first issue of the *Labor Leader* had indicated ACTU support for a "peace conference" of the two federations and editorials in this vein appeared in both the *Labor Leader* and the *Michigan Labor Leader* throughout the life of the organization. One editorial, entitled "Fratricide," termed the intention of the CIO to "form a permanent separate body" a "grave mistake." Another alleged that this CIO "threat" would "undo all [labor] has struggled so hard to gain." The arguments for unity by AFL spokesmen such as Dan Tobin of the Teamsters were prominently reported, as were similar pleas from right-wing CIO leaders such as Homer Martin of the UAW. The weight of the Church hierarchy was thrown into the unity campaign through such recurrent headlines as "Bishops Urge Unity in the Ranks of Labor." Disunity meant separate counsel on labor and social legislation. It also encouraged divide-and-conquer tactics by employers and waste of effort in jurisdictional disputes between competing unions, argued the Actists. This was certainly an accurate analysis. Most union partisans, including those in the CIO, agreed with the ACTU on the disadvantages of a divided labor movement. Indeed, all unionists endorsed unity in some form. The important question was that of the politics of unification. [89]

In fact, unification was a highly charged political question within the trade-union movement, which was consistently opposed by the CIO and the left wing and favored by the AFL and the right wing. The CIO's position was that "there can be no compromise with its fundamental purpose and aim of organizing workers into powerful industrial unions, nor with its obligation to fully protect the rights and interests of all its members and affiliated organizations," while the AFL unity proposals called for dismemberment of the CIO unions among competing craft unions. The AFL had always opposed industrial organization and discounted the unskilled workers. The CIO unions had been expelled from the AFL for persisting in organizing efforts in the mass-production industries. The great strikes in these industries and the enormous gains in union membership in the late 1930s and early 1940s, to AFL unions as well as to those in the CIO, were CIO-inspired, -organized, and -led. Unemployment insurance, minimum-wage legislation, and the Social Security Act all owed more to CIO support than to the AFL, which had actually opposed them. From the CIO's point of view, unification of the two labor federations under AFL leadership would threaten all these gains. Apart from the dissolution of the industrial unions, "labor unity" on the AFL's terms would undercut broad social and political initiatives in favor of conservative business unionism. The AFL's regular unity proposals were seen as a means to increase AFL per capita fees and to head off the possibility that a younger, more radical, and industrially based CIO would soon overshadow the AFL. Consequently the CIO opposed and ignored these belated offers of unity.[90]

The praise accorded AFL unity proposals by the ACTU and their criticism of CIO reluctance to "unify" under AFL terms are therefore somewhat puzzling. Why should an organization working within the CIO and favoring industrial unionism support a plan whose result would be the submerging of the CIO within the AFL, an end to industrial organizing, and generally a more quiescent, apolitical, and conservative labor movement? A possible explanation for this position may be found in the long-term Catholic influence in the AFL, documented by Marc Karson, and in the strength of the radicals in the CIO. After a long struggle within the AFL, in which Catholics had played a major role, the socialists had been vanquished and a politically conservative business unionism had been established which was entirely satisfactory to contemporary Catholic labor strategists. The AFL was Catholic in its majority, it eschewed class conflict, it practiced class harmony and cooperation with employers, it resembled a guild in structure and mentality, and opposed most social legislation, as well as any political role for labor. Despite the AFL's approximation of the Catholic union idea, however, it left unrepresented the masses of industrial workers.[91]

The subsequent rise of the CIO unions made a Catholic, conservative presence in these unions imperative. The CIO was heavily influenced by radicals, had fewer traditions to restrain it, and was based on a potentially radical base of industrial workers.[92] It seemed likely that the CIO would out-organize the AFL, and it was possible that it would take a radical direction. The conservative solution was to reunify the two organizations under AFL dominance, thus assuring the generally conservative stance of American labor. The ACTU's support for the AFL unity proposals, then, placed it in the conservative camp on a significant question within the CIO. Since a major element in the ACTU's concern for unity was that a separate CIO was "playing into the hands" of the communists, it is apparent that anti-communism, once again, had the effect of promoting a conservative stance within the ACTU.

The ACTU's search for unity in the labor movement (excluding, of course, the radicals) was a corollary of their search for unity in society as a whole. Class harmony was perhaps the single most important theme in Catholic social theory. As conservatives and as Catholics, the Actists sought to minimize conflict and contradiction between the classes, if not quite deny them altogether. In this vein, one *Labor Leader* editorial reminded the readership that the employer, no less than the worker, is a "slave of the economic disorder." The proper solution was for workers to join with "employers of good will" in "industrial co-operation." An immediate expression of this spirit, as discussed earlier, was mediation as a solution to possible or actual strikes. Nearly all the strikes in which the ACTU was involved were settled through mediation. Most of the mediators were clerical members or friends of the ACTU and several of them were on the New York, Maryland, and Pennsylvania labor relations boards. The ACTU's stress on mediation reached the point where the *Labor Leader* quoted approvingly a characterization of the ACTU by Michael Widman, an assistant national director of the CIO, as an "impartial organization" whose purpose was to mediate between employers and workers. The ACTU acted on this definition by advertising its services as a mediating agency in the *Labor Leader* and elsewhere.[93]

In addition to the effects discussed previously, the ACTU's stress on mediation promoted a muted opposition to the strike weapon itself. This was implicit in the promotion of mediation as the preferable solution, but was sometimes made explicit as well. Thus the ACTU argued against an impending railroad strike because of the "misery and strife" which would ensue. A pronounced regard for class harmony also led to a total prohibition on wildcat strikes, especially those led by radicals, as inconsistent with the workers' duty to "abide by all agreements."[94]

The ideas of class harmony and voluntary "spiritual reform," and the ethical orientation of Catholic social theory combined in the ACTU's prohibition on violence in the labor movement. Since the classes were in fundamental harmony and voluntary action was assumed to provide a solution to all social problems, violence was neither necessary nor moral. Leo XIII, in *Rerum Novarum* (1891), had cautioned that "religion teaches the laboring man and the workman . . . never to injure capital, nor to outrage the person of an employer; never to employ violence in representing his own case, nor to engage in riot and disorder." This was likewise the position of Ryan, and the ACTU concurred: "The interests of a class must yield before the interest and rights of the community," which would be threatened by violence. As an alternative to violence and class conflict the ACTU approved the statement of Nelson Rockefeller, that "proper leadership on both sides" would result in friendly capital-labor relationships free of violence.[95]

Violence in a strike, according to the Actists, would only precipitate police or vigilante counterviolence and outrage public opinion. The moral standing of the workers would be undercut. They would be linked with radicals and communists in the public eye and demoralization would follow. In addition, violence would imperil mediation, alienate strikebreakers from unionism, and serve as a justification for anti-labor legislation.[96]

While violence was thus usually seen as ineffective, the Actists admitted that, in some cases (such as the intimidation of strike-breakers), it might *seem* an effective tactic or even (as in the case of defense against employer violence) a justifiable one. Even in such cases as these, the ACTU believed that violence was absolutely intolerable. The well-being and peace of society in general, believed the Actists, took precedence over any gain which workers might achieve through the use of violence, even in self-defense.[97]

As a consequence of this position, the ACTU regularly con-demned outbreaks of violence during strikes, including those of Akron rubber workers and New York City taxidrivers in 1938. On a number of occasions it threatened to withdraw support from strikes in which violence occurred. Such a threat resulted in a reluctant policy of nonviolence by strike leaders at the American Razor Company in 1938. When one incredulous reader wrote to ask if violence might not be justified, however reluctantly, if workers had exhausted all peaceful means and stood to lose their jobs to strikebreakers, the *Labor Leader* editors responded with a flat "no."[98]

The ACTU's promotion of nonviolence was a selective one, however, since the organization supported preparedness and the American role in World War II and the Cold War to follow. It was the labor movement, in particular, which was to refrain from violence.

Therefore, while the ACTU's hostility to violence was based largely on Catholic ethics, it was not a strictly pacifist position.[99] At the same time, despite the practical case made against violence, it was not wholly an instrumental position, since violence was admitted to be effective in some cases. What then was the reason for the uncompromising commitment to labor nonviolence?

At the heart of the ACTU prohibition on violence was the fear of promoting revolutionary sentiment. If violence could be contained, it would be easier to argue against the "Marxist fabrication that always—now and forever—there must be conflict between labor and capital." On the other hand, with violence and counterviolence, "the workers' resentment is increased, the class war spirit grows." This was bad enough in itself, from the point of view of the Actists, but in addition such militance "will be taken advantage of by Marxist leaders." It was just such occasions of violence and Marxist intervention that inspired the ACTU's most vigorous warnings against violence in strikes. A combination of ethical hostility to violence, fear of some of its practical effects, and hostility to its class war and revolutionary implications that led the ACTU unequivocally to oppose force for the labor movement, despite the experience of many unionists that it was often unavoidable in any successful struggle for workers' interests.[100]

The most consistent theme in the ACTU's ideology, however, was opposition to radicalism. This hostility to radicalism was fed both directly and indirectly from the whole corpus of Catholic social doctrine and the tradition of Catholic social action. The foremost social encyclicals, *Rerum Novarum* (1891) and *Quadragesimo Anno* (1931), were themselves reactions to radical doctrine and organization. These encyclicals consisted largely of attacks on socialism and communism, and the program of Catholic social policies they developed were generally reactive to "erroneous" socialist views. Materialism, atheism, class consciousness and conflict, violence, denial of authority, hierarchy, and the institution of private property and private profit, extreme democracy and equality, totalitarianism, and statism were among the major items in the recurrent papal condemnations of socialism and communism. The papacy and the national hierarchies prohibited Catholic cooperation or membership in the left-wing parties and unions, dissolved left-wing Catholic organizations such as the worker-priests of France, which had "absorbed Marxist doctrines," and excommunicated individuals who worked with the left. For long periods there were standing general excommunications against members of the left-wing organizations in Italy and France, which were held by the ACTU to apply to the United States as well.[101]

In Europe the Church had organized Christian unions and parties as working-class alternatives to the left. In the United States, however, mixed faiths undercut this strategy. At the same time, there were no mass socialist unions, though the left was strong within the existing unions and class warfare open enough to "plainly disturb" the popes. The proper Catholic response in such a situation, according to Pope Pius XI in *Quadragesimo Anno* (1931), was to join with other conservatives in the existing "neutral" unions so as to "combat with united purpose and strength the massed ranks of revolutionaries." As further insurance against the radicalization of Catholic unionists, however, Leo XIII advised the organization of separate and parallel "societies of workers and artisans which, instituted under the guidance of religion, would be able to make all of their members content with their lot and resigned to labor."[102]

The ACTU and the earlier Militia of Christ for Social Service traced their origins to such passages as these. Opposition to radicalism was their *raison d'être*, whatever other concerns they might express. As one CIO official put it, "In early AFL, this Catholic thrust was against socialism and Socialist Party strength in the unions. Similarly, the ACTU devoted itself to fighting Communist influence, in CIO especially." From 1900 to 1920 the Militia of Christ, supported by the hierarchy, parish priests, the Knights of Columbus, the German Catholic Verein, and former-socialist Catholic converts, had been the cutting edge of a successful campaign to minimize socialist influence among Catholic AFL members. While the AFL remained, for the most part, a secure bastion of conservative unionism, the rise of the CIO prompted a renewed Catholic effort against radicalism. The ACTU, founded to "tear down the barricades of class war in America", was the main organizational expression of that effort.[103]

From the beginning the ACTU was committed to hostility to radicalism. Though the progressives had been opposed to making anti-communism the organizational focus of the ACTU, they too adhered to the fundamental anti-radicalism of the Church. When the progressives' hostility to red-baiting and their mild socialism came under attack, they were quick to abandon their position and rejoin the conservatives in a thoroughgoing and unambiguous opposition to all forms of radicalism, socialism, and communism. The ACTU membership pledge demanded active opposition to communism and an important convention resolution of 1940 stated that "the efforts of all Actists should be directed toward exposing those who espouse all forms of Communism, Marxism, Nazism or Fascism or who in practice agree with all of their policies." The anti-Fascism of the ACTU, apart from the war years, remained latent at best. The *Labor Leader* carried only a few hostile references to Fascism and only one editorial, condemning anti-Semitism, which touched on the subject. [104]

On the other hand, the ACTU's main ideological luminary, Monsignor John A. Ryan, found many "good features" in the Fascist system and the organization itself supported a corporative society and sympathized with the Fascists in Spain. It would seem that Nazism and Fascism were included in the resolution as much for the bad connotation they brought to communism as for any other reason. Opposition to radicalism was certainly the sole practical effect of the resolution. [105]

The ACTU's hostility to radicalism was not directed solely against the Communist party. "All forms" of Marxism as well as all those who agreed with Marxist policies were to be opposed. A *Labor Leader* editorial of August 1942, entitled "Socialism as an Error," offered "an opinion on Socialism and all those splinter groups such as Social Democrats, Socialist Workers, etc." that was uniformly negative despite the hostility of both these latter groups to the Communist party. Another editorial defined Marxism as "class hatred, murder and pillage." Assumed fellow travelers fared nearly as badly as actual Marxists. Thus the ACTU opposed a City College faculty appointment for Bertrand Russell, an "atheist" whose criticisms of the Soviet Union were apparently too mild for the ACTU. Catholic "fellow travelers," who might have some appeal among the faithful, received the sharpest criticism as un-Christian "renegades." It was a "mythical stupidity" that a "true Catholic can at the same time be a

Communist." Pope Pius XI himself had "placed the vast campaign of the Church against World Communism" and thus Catholics must resist the communists' "outstretched hand." Even the celebration of May Day was held to be an error for those who "are opposed to the class struggle theory," as was the ACTU. The ACTU's opposition to Marxism, then, was more fundamental than tactical, nor were Communists the only target for attack. The ACTU stress on social harmony and industrial peace paralleled that of other Church authorities in tolerating no form of class politics.[106]

The Communist party, as the largest and most influential grouping, did receive far more critical attention from the ACTU than the smaller socialist groups. A *Labor Leader* column by the Reverend Neil O'Connor, entitled "Socialism, the Father of Modern Communism, Offspring More Dangerous Than its Parent," singled out the communists as the main enemy of "true reform," a theme which was echoed in articles, editorials, and columns in the ACTU periodicals and in the statements of the organization. The program of the communists was held to be "disastrous to civilization, organized religion and labor unionism itself." Anti-communist editorials with titles such as "Communists Mis-Use Union Machinery" or "Justice? Murder and Plunder" appeared in the *Labor Leader* almost weekly, with especial frequency after 1945. The Reverend O'Connor's column, as well as three others, "Don Capellano," written by Rice, "Views on the News" and "Comment," were almost wholly devoted to excoriating the communists.[107]

Some readers apparently did not share the ACTU's view that the "reds" were the main enemy of "true reform." Several were moved to protest *Labor Leader* red-baiting or the amount of space devoted to it. One writer accused the *Labor Leader* of "using up a great deal of valuable space that might be devoted to some real union views." The editors apologized for the amount of anti-communist material, but explained that they would "be shirking from duty if we failed to report their activities and comment on them."[108]

On one occasion the editors defended their low opinion of communists as the fruit of experience: "The ACTU has worked side by side with Communists in both AFL and CIO unions, and it has seen by long and painful experience that their tactics and their final objectives run directly counter to any decent idea of democracy or religion." But when challenged by a reader to offer instances of any such united-front associations, the editors begged off with the comment that "these things cannot be published in detail." In fact, the ACTU had rebuffed all such efforts at direct alliance from the very first. The ACTU's opposition to radicalism, as this reader suggested, was rather an *a priori* religious and political commitment, derived from the encyclicals and transmitted through decades of Catholic anti-radical activity.[109]

Communist party activities within the unions were the major focus of the ACTU anti-communist campaign. "Exposés" of alleged communist leadership of particular unions were a favorite topic and any possible misstep on the part of radical led unions could set off a storm in the pages of the *Labor Leader*. The United Electrical Workers, the Newspaper Guild, the West and East Coast longshoremen and New York locals of the printers, painters, fur workers, transit workers, office and professional workers, technical workers, and engineers were all among the targets of such ACTU criticism. Michael Quill of the Transit Workers Union, the most important of those anomalous Catholic radicals who so outraged the ACTU, was attacked weekly for years. While the ACTU often expressed respect and even envy of communist discipline and zeal on behalf of their union memberships, no amount of hard work could exempt a "communist" union leader from the general anathema. The ACTU, for example, admitted that the left wing CIO longshoremen and seamen were remarkably free of corruption, complacency, or authoritarianism, but concluded, nevertheless, that "if Bridges and Curran are Communists, then we unhesitatingly say they should be eliminated."[110]

Critics of the communists often objected to some particular policy or general position of the party. In the case of the ACTU, however, complaints were registered about everything the communists did and many things they did not do. Contradictory positions were ascribed to the Communist party and then condemned with equal energy. Communist "atheism" or pretenses to religious toleration, economic militancy, or "supine submission" to employers, readiness to lead wildcat strikes during wartime or refusal to support them were all equally criticized by the ACTU.[111]

The ACTU went to the brink of nonsupport in several strikes led by communists and often condemned wildcats led by radicals while supporting those led by conservatives. One communist-led wildcat during the war was supported by President Murray of the CIO, but attacked nonetheless by the ACTU. A Transit Workers' wildcat in New York City was grudgingly defended, but the radical strike leadership was attacked in the same breath. The same treatment was accorded to a Western Union strike involving the communist-led CIO Communications Workers Union.[112]

In jurisdictional disputes the ACTU regularly supported the conservative over the radical-led unions, whatever the other particulars of the case, even if this meant an endorsement of an AFL over a CIO affiliate. One local of the Transit Workers Union, under ACTU leadership, quit the CIO for "independent" status, then AFL affiliation, on the grounds of radical domination of the CIO Transit Union.[113] In the case of the federal government's deportation proceedings against Harry Bridges, the left-wing longshoremen's leader, the ACTU did not quite explicitly support the government, but it did attack the New York City CIO Council for denouncing the proceedings.

The lack of support for unions led by radicals was often more extreme, however. When the Navy commandeered the Merchant Marine in the spring of 1942 it also dismissed 1,000 "un-American" seamen, members of the left-wing National Maritime Union. Had any other union been involved, it seems certain that this would have been considered a violently anti-union measure. Indeed, this action was taken under legislation which the ACTU had attacked as likely to lead to "dictatorship" over labor. In this case, however, the ACTU heartily approved the purge and commended the Navy for the "realism" it had shown. Similarly, the ACTU defended the Reverend Charles Owen Rice, an ACTU member who served on the Pennsylvania State Labor Relations Board, for upholding the action of an employer who had fired a union activist who was a communist.[114]

The ACTU naturally focused on communist activity in the unions, but they fought the CP in other arenas as well. The international news in the *Labor Leader* consisted almost entirely of reports on the activities and defeats of the left. The ACTU regularly attacked the campaign to support Republican Spain and union resolutions indicating such support were taken as prima facie evidence of communist control. The Actists criticized CIO President Murray for publicly condemning Franco, as well as for opposing the postwar British intervention in Greece. The group also opposed a program of the left-wing National Maritime Union to educate grade-school children about unionism. When the Americans for Democratic Action was formed, the ACTU endorsed it and attacked the Progressive Citizens of America, a competing organization which included communist participation. Even the call for a second front during World War II met with ACTU hostility as communist-inspired. Finally, the ACTU rejected attempts by the Communist party in speeches and leaflets to initiate a united front with the Actists in opposition to Consolidated Edison layoffs or anti-labor legislation, despite the Actists' commitment to "labor unity."[115]

The ACTU's unrelenting, extreme, and early anti-communism placed them, as it were, in the vanguard of CIO anti-radicalism. While Lewis and Murray might recognize the importance of the left in the coalition that had built the CIO, and thus refrain from public attacks on the Communist party, no such compunctions influenced the ACTU. This sort of united front was nothing less than a surrender to the communists' "boring from within" in the eyes of the Actists. Such "pussyfooting" was to be exposed and condemned, and thus constant pressure emanated from the ACTU from 1940 onward for a CIO break with the communists.[116] The 1946 CIO Convention resolution "resenting and rejecting the efforts of the Communist Party or other political parties and their adherents to interfere in the CIO" represented a victory for this anti-communism position, but the ACTU found it far "too mild."[117] The ACTU had always held an anti-communist position far to the right of any other faction in the CIO. This position had no counterpart except among AFL leaders such as Woll, Frey, or Ryan and in the person of Homer Martin, the Ford Motor Company's candidate for UAW president.

The ACTU was thus within the conservative tradition of Catholic social ideology and a fitting heir to the mantle of such organizations as the Militia of Christ in its practical expression of these ideas. The organization was based upon the social encyclicals of the popes and their commentators and drew its inspiration from decades of conservative Catholic action in the United States and European labor movements. The Actists defended private property in the means of production in spite of complaints over its distribution and "abuses." Their critique of social injustice operated through the doctrines of just wages, prices, and profits. Since these doctrines were in considerable measure archaic, conservative, and admittedly impossible to administer, the ACTU's version of social justice was a limited one and tended to a justification of the status quo.

The organization was committed to reciprocity as the major means of social amelioration. The commitment to property and voluntarism, however, undercut the more sweeping expressions of this doctrine such as cooperative enterprise. Instead, the ACTU promoted the guild system. The guild system itself incorporated hierarchy, authority, and acceptance of social station as its leading ideas. The industrial-council program guaranteed private property and contained much that was hostile to democracy, equality, and political participation. More immediately, the ACTU pressed for class harmony and cooperation through mediation, a policy which tended to undercut the strike, dilute the ACTU's commitment to workers' interests, and promote "expertise" and employer-worker collaboration. Such a policy inhibited workers' independent initiative and limited their opportunity to gain experience in labor struggles. At the same time, the ACTU's Catholic vision of social and industrial harmony obscured rather than clarified the conflicts between capital and labor.

The ACTU opposed all expressions of class consciousness within the labor movement and sought to deny the reality of class conflict. The Actists opposed violence under any conditions for the unions, though not for their opponents, out of fear of promoting just such class conflict. Underlying and reinforcing all these positions was the ACTU's fundamental hostility to "all forms" of radicalism and especially the Communist party. The logic of this position was to oppose whatever the radicals supported and the result was to push the ACTU to even more conservative positions.

The ACTU was an orthodox Catholic action organization which derived its organizational rationale from the Church's call for societies to guide labor in a moderate direction. The organization promoted the conservative brand of labor unity, CIO subordination to the AFL, in the tradition of the earlier Catholic effort in the AFL to combine conservative forces in order to defeat incipient radicalism and assure the continuation of pure and simple unionism. Their commitment to a fundamentally conservative labor ideology was reinforced by a parallel commitment to the Church as a religious and social institution. The extensive clerical participation and control over the organization assured the consistency of this conservative position and prevented the recurrence of even such still-born opposition as that of the ACTU progressives. The priority given to class harmony and anti-radical themes owed much to the influence of the organization's clerical supporters.

NOTES

1. Clayton Fountain, *Union Guy* (New York: Viking, 1949), p. 194.

2. *Labor Leader* 1, no. 1.

3. Commenting on readers' assumptions that "producers' cooperatives" referred only to "those companies that are owned and operated by the workers themselves," the *Labor Leader* editors wrote that "such plans are usually impractical." *Labor Leader* 5, no. 7.

4. On February 26, 1940, for example, the *Labor Leader* quoted approvingly from a pastoral letter of the American bishops, which the ACTU had reprinted, as follows: "It is not intended that labor should assume responsibility for the direction of business beyond its own competency or legitimate interest nor has labor a right to demand dominating control over the distribution of profit." *Labor Leader* 3, no. 3.

5. *Labor Leader* 1, no. 21, 5, no. 7; "Errors of Individualism," Detroit ACTU Worker School lecture outline, p. 1.

6. *Labor Leader* 1, no. 21.

7. Cort, "Catholics in the Labor Movement," p. 34.

8. See, for example, editorials in *Labor Leader* 1, nos. 41 and 34, and Ryan, *A Better Economic Order*, pp. 126–46.

9. See, for example, ACTU Convention Resolution, "Communists in Union Office," 1941, p. 1; *Labor Leader* 1, nos. 1, 7, and 11, 3, no. 17, 4, no. 1, 5, no. 19, 7, no. 15; *Michigan Labor Leader*, 1, nos. 2, and 4, 2, no. 7, 3, no. 10, 5, no. 1.

10. *Labor Leader* 1, nos. 23, 28, and 38, 8, no. 1, 9, no. 7, 5, no. 14, 10, no. 1.

11. *Labor Leader* 1, no. 21; *Michigan Labor Leader*, 2, no. 8, 3, no. 5.

12. See, for example, *Labor Leader* 1, no. 24, in which five of ten articles are concerned with opposition to radicalism.

13. *Labor Leader* 1, no. 20.

14. The New York ACTU Constitution, for example, indicated that the purpose of the organization was to "make Catholic social principles an effective force for sound unionism and industrial relations," ACTU files, p. 1; See also *Labor Leader* 1, nos. 1, 24, and 45.

15. Cort, "Catholics in Trade Unions," p. 34.

16. Pius XI, quoted from the encyclical *Quadragesimo Anno* in the ACTU "Articles of Federation," ACTU files, p. 2.

17. Though no real statistics exist on the question of the percentage of Catholics among union members, most students believe that between one-third and one-half of union members are Catholic in heritage. See, for example, Foner, *History of the Labour Movement*, 3:112; Ware, *Labor in Modern Industrial Society*, p. 35; DeCaux, *Labor Radical*, p. 393; Perlman, *Theory of the Labor Movement*, p. 169; Karson, *American Labor Unions and Politics*, p. 221.

18. This argument reflected the ACTU's apprehension over charges that they were "sectarian" outsiders meddling in trade-union affairs or religious "splitters." See George Morris, "Spotlight on the ACTU," *Political Affairs*, March 1947, pp. 252–63; also *Labor Leader* 1, no. 35; *Daily Worker*, February 23, 1950.

19. "Constitution of the ACTU," ACTU files, pp. 1, 2, 4, 6.

20. The Guild Plan was ultimately endorsed by Murray, several CIO unions, and the CIO Executive Council, but it was never to figure very prominently as an issue.

21. Charles Madison reports that the ACTU was believed to be "backed by the Church" and thus a semiofficial spokesman for Catholics. DeCaux supports him on this count. The official Catholic status of the ACTU made their opposition a serious matter for union officials. The officers of the American Communications Association (CIO) complained in January of 1947 that ACTU opposition was tantamount to a threat of excommunication of those Catholics who supported the union administration. The hierarchy, of course, did support the ACTU and their constant endorsements carried weight among the religious. Archbishop Edward Mooney of Detroit, for example, told the audience at a Detroit ACTU rally in 1940 that "the ACTU *is* Catholic action in the social field." Madison, *American Labor Leaders*, p. 327; DeCaux, *Labor Radical*, 393; *Michigan Labor Leader* 2, no. 9; *Labor Leader* 10, no. 2, 11, no. 3.

22. Since more than half the AFL leadership and a similar proportion of CIO officers were Catholics, the ACTU enjoyed considerable leverage in this respect.

23. *Labor Leader* 4, no. 4; John Cort, "Labor and Violence," *Commonweal*, November 10, 1939, pp. 68–70.

24. "Articles of Federation," ACTU files, p. 2. "Associate membership" in union conferences was, however, open to non-Catholics.

25. George Morris, political writer for the CP, thought it was a Fascist program. Others thought it would split the labor movement along religious lines and hence opposed it. Morris, "Spotlight on the ACTU," pp. 252–63; see also "Labor Leaders Rebuff ACTU," *Daily Worker*, July 28, 1947, "When Red-Baiting Failed" (editorial), *Daily Worker*, September 12, 1947, "List Fifteen Renegades From Waterfront CP," *Daily Worker*, April 5, 1948.

26. See Morris, "Spotlight on the ACTU," and James Matles, *The Members Run This Union* (UE publication, no. 94, 1947). Such criticism sometimes came even from allies of the ACTU. See Carey's letter to the ACTU, May 16, 1940, ACTU files.

27. *The ACTU, A Catholic Apostolate for Labor*, ACTU files, p. 3; *Labor Leader* 10, no. 4.

28. *Labor Leader* 1, no. 1. See discussion in chapter 4.

29. Ryan was the prince of the gangster unionists. He was widely believed to earn a commission on every waterfront hiring and, consequently, under his regime New York was the last major port in the world to abolish the "shape-up." He was the only union leader to hold the position of President for Life. Malcolm Johnson, *Crime on the Labor Front* (New York: McGraw-Hill, 1950), p. 152.

30. Interview with George Donahue, July 24, 1974. More than a dozen ACTU priests ultimately served on state or city labor relations boards, while scores of lay ACTU members became local and national officers of the CIO and AFL unions.

31. This was the case in the election victory of the CIO United Office Workers over the AFL Insurance Agents' Association at John Hancock in Boston in October of 1938. See *Labor Leader* 1, no. 39.

32. On criminal activity in New York City unions see Johnson, *Crime on the Labor Front*, Bernstein, *The Turbulent Years*, pp. 123–25.

33. *Labor Leader* 4, no. 6, 5, no. 4, 1, nos. 22 and 23.

34. Ibid., 1, no. 22.

35. This had been the case in many of the garment locals, the ILA, and the Hotel and Restaurant Union. See Bernstein, *The Turbulent Years*, pp. 123–25.

36. *Labor Leader* 3, no. 15.

37. Ibid., 8, no. 17.

38. Lewis rejected the council plan. Murray favored it as did the leadership of the Retail Union and the News Guild, among whom were several Actists. *Labor Leader* 11, nos. 7 and 20, 1, no. 21. No movement beyond the ranks of the ACTU, however, ever materialized on behalf of the Pope's Plan.

39. The ACTU references to the corporate or guild program as the "Pope's Plan" did not assuage these critics and the similarities between the Council Plan and Italian and Spanish "corporativism" promoted considerable criticism of "clerical fascism."

40. Such criticisms were often made by ACTU opponents in the CIO. See, for example, Matles, *The Members Run This Union*.

41. Jim Carey was among the latter group. Despite his criticism of the ACTU, he was willing to work with them against the left wing in the UE. Though a Catholic, he was not so ready to promote "corporativism."

42. *Labor Leader* 1, no. 24. The ACTU's Constitution itself had to be approved by Cardinal Hayes. Monaghan, "The ACTU," ACTU files, p. 26.

43. *Labor Leader* 13, no. 18.

44. Ibid., 3, no. 18.

45. Ibid., 3, no. 18.

46. See, for example, *Labor Leader* 1, no. 25, 2, no. 4, 1, no. 36.

47. Ibid., 10, no. 6.

48. On one occasion the editors of the *Labor Leader* expressed their apprehension at the fact that "American Communists are very obviously trying to lure social minded Catholics into the ranks of the CP" and argued that this "outstretched hand must be ignored by all Catholics" lest they assist in the formation of an "unAmerican and unChristian state." *Labor Leader* 1, no. 28. When argument was ineffective, the ACTU sometimes threatened such "renegades" with excommunication. *Labor Leader* 1, no. 21, 7, no. 15, 8, no. 1.

49. *Labor Leader* 1, nos. 1, 7, 19, and 32, 2, no. 1, 4, no. 2.

50. See the following issues of the *Labor Leader* for instances of clerical speeches before union and Catholic bodies: *Labor Leader* 1, nos. 1, 21, and 30, 2, no. 15, 3, no. 5, 7, no. 19, 9, no. 7.

51. *Labor Leader* 1, no. 1.

52. Ibid., 9, no. 1, 10, no. 4.

53. Ibid., 10, no. 4.

54. Ibid., 1, no. 2. The Reverend William J. Smith, S. J., Director of the Crown Heights Labor School, figured prominently in the debate over the Gerson appointment.

55. Detroit Workers' School course outlines and information bulletins, Detroit ACTU Collection.

56. Kampelman, *The Communist Party vs. the CIO*, p. 153.

57. William Collins, an instructor at the Westchester Labor School, however, was an advocate of company unions. *Labor Leader* 1, no. 21.

58. A Textile Workers' Organizing Committee campaign in Slottsville, New York, during May of 1938 was undercut by one such priest's charges that the CIO was a communist organization. Cort was forced to confront this priest in a public debate on the question. *Labor Leader* 1, no. 21.

59. *Labor Leader* 1, no. 20.

60. Ibid., 1, no. 24.

61. "If Catholics were to join the union movement in a wholehearted fashion, then the problem of radicalism would be quickly solved," argued the *Labor Leader* editors in issue 1, no. 33. See also editorials in 1, nos. 22, and 37.

62. *Labor Leader* 1, no. 33.

63. Ibid., 1, nos. 8 and 9.

64. Reverend William Smith, *American or Communist? You Can't Be Both* (Brooklyn: Catholic Truth Society, 1938), p. 24.

65. Rice remained the leader of the Pittsburgh ACTU and a leader of the anti-communist forces in the UE into the early 1950s.

66. *Labor Leader* 1, no. 41.

67. Ibid., 1, no. 9.

68. Ibid., 1, no. 16.

69. See, for example, *Labor Leader* 1, nos. 11, 14, 19, and 31.

70. ACTU log of requests for assistance, 1942, ACTU files; *Labor Leader* 5, no. 3.

71. Some or all of these problems were undoubtedly involved in the recurrent complaints received from members and *Labor Leader* readers as to the large clerical role in the ACTU. See, for example, the letters to the editor in *Labor Leader* 1, nos. 3 and 24.

72. Even Murray, who was the personification of "center" opinion in the CIO, opposed the Nationalists. The ACTU, on the other hand, actively opposed union resolutions in favor of or contributions to the Republicans. See *Labor Leader* 2, no. 2, 1, no. 30; *Michigan Labor Leader* 2, no. 11.

73. Hugh Thomas, *The Spanish Civil War* (New York: Harper's, 1961), p. 182.

74. See Thomas's account of the rebellion in *The Spanish Civil War*, pp. 117–98.

75. *Labor Leader* 1, no. 30.

76. Camp, *Papal Ideology*, p. 37. See the ACTU's "Statement of Principles," "Articles of Federation," the Constitutions of the New York and Detroit ACTU, "ACTU" by Monaghan and *What Is the ACTU?*, ACTU files and Detroit ACTU collection.

77. *The ACTU, A Catholic Apostolate for Labor*, pp. 11–12; *Questions and Answers About the ACTU* (Detroit: ACTU, 1941), p. 34; Detroit ACTU Collection; "Errors of Collectivism," Detroit Workers School lecture outline, p. 13, Detroit ACTU Collection; *Michigan Labor Leader* 2, nos. 4 and 19; *Labor Leader* 1, nos. 1, 6, 7, 9, and 21, 2, no. 17, 5, no. 7; W. K. Kelsey to *Detroit News*, letter, Detroit ACTU Collection; Weinberg, "Priests, Workers and Communists," pp. 52–53.

78. *Labor Leader* 1, nos. 8, and 13, 3, no. 12.

79. "Stand of the ACTU," pp. 2–3, ACTU files; *Labor Leader* 1, nos. 1, 21, and 38. See also Norman C. McKenna, *The Catholic and his Union* (New York: Paulist Press, 1948), pp. 5–7.

80. Kelly, *The ACTU and Its Critics*, pp. 7–9, *Labor Leader* 1, no. 5, 3, no. 4.

81. Carl P. Hensler, "Industrial Cooperation," address to ACTU rally, April 4, 1938, p. 3, ACTU files; Cort, "Labor and Violence," p. 70; *Labor Leader* 1, nos. 1 and 14, 5, no. 7.

82. Morris, "Spotlight on the ACTU," pp. 252–55; *Labor Leader* 1, no. 8, 3, nos. 3. and 7.

83. *Labor Leader* 1, no. 6, 4, no. 14; Cort believed it was only a matter of time before "labor takes its rightful place in partnership with capital," "Catholics in Trade Unions," p. 36.

84. *Labor Leader* 1, no. 6, 4, no. 14.

85. Though President Murray and the officers of the Utility Workers' Union and the Newspaper Guild were to endorse the plan, the ACTU was in general unable to spur much enthusiasm for corporativism in the American labor movement. See Philip Murray, *Organized Labor and Production* (New York: Harper's, 1946); *Labor Leader* 1, nos. 21, 40, and 45.

86. Ryan, *A Living Wage*, p. 31; Ryan, *Social Reconstruction*, p. 230; *Labor Leader* 1, nos. 1 and 12, 3, no. 4.

87. Ryan, *Social Reconstruction*, pp. 194, 237–38; Ryan, *A Better Economic Order*, p. 174.

88. In their discussion of the conflict between the CIO United Retail Union and the AFL Retail Clerks Union at Reeves Department Stores in New York during May of 1938, the *Labor Leader* editors establish their clear preference for the CIO affiliate. See *Labor Leader* 1, nos. 14, 18, 20, and 25.

89. *Labor Leader* 1, nos. 1, 16, 22, 39, and 40, 9, no. 15; *Michigan Labor Leader* 1, no. 4.

90. For a discussion of the abortive AFL-CIO unity negotiations, see Bernstein, *The Turbulent Years*, pp. 505, 694–702 and Galenson, *The CIO Challenge to the AFL*, pp. 242–43. On the CIO's responsibility for membership gains to both federations in the 1930s and 1940s, see Bernstein, *The Turbulent Years*, p. 685. On AFL opposition to minimum wages, unemployment insurance, and Social Security, see Bernstein, *The Lean Years*, p. 504, *The Turbulent Years*, p. 26.

91. See Karson, *American Labor Unions and Politics*, pp. 212–85. See also Foner, *History of the Labor Movement*, 3:111–35; Fox, *Peter E. Dietz*.

92. On radical strength in the CIO unions, see Kampelman, *The Communist Party vs. the CIO*, p. 45; Bernstein, *The Lean Years*, p. 783.

93. *Labor Leader* 1, nos. 1, 3, 4, 15, and 8, 3, no. 6; *ACTU: A Catholic Apostulate For Labor*, ACTU files, p. 6. *Michigan Labor Leader* 1, no. 5, 2, no. 9. The long-term effects of this marked stress on mediation are illustrated in the subsequent careers of several Actists. George Donahue, former *Labor Leader* editor, now operates a labor-relations consulting firm in New York and Peter Sheehan is the labor-relations director of the Washington, D.C., Transit Authority. Several others remained active as professional mediators. Interview with George Donahue, July 22, 1974.

94. *Labor Leader* 1, nos. 16 and 38, 8, no. 1.

95. Pope Leo XIII, *Rerum Novarum*, quoted in Cort, "Labor and Violence," pp. 69–70; Ryan, *A Better Economic Order*, p. 138; Labor Leader 1, no. 3.

96. Cort, "Labor and Violence," p. 69; *Labor Leader* 1, no. 15.

97. *Labor Leader* 1, nos. 3 and 4.

98. Interview with George Donahue, July 22, 1974; Cort, "Catholics in Trade Unions," p. 70; *Labor Leader* 1, nos. 4, 22, and 26, 10, no. 6.

99. Tim O'Brien, chairman of the Catholic Union of the Unemployed, was the only Actist holding an absolute pacifist position. Interview with George Donahue, July 22, 1974.

100. Cort, "Catholics in Trade Unions," p. 34; *Labor Leader* 1, no. 22.

101. Camp, *Papal Ideology*, pp. 30, 62–69, 93, 102, 113, 116, 129; Foner, *History of the Labor Movement*, pp. 112, 114; *Labor Leader* 12, no. 13.

102. Camp, *Papal Ideology*, pp. 112, 116, 126.

103. DeCaux, *Labor Radical*, p. 393; Cort, "Catholics in the Trade Unions," p. 34; *Labor Leader* 2, no. 18. The ACTU's purpose was generally understood to be combat against the communists. See Kampelman, *The Communist Party vs the CIO*, p. 153; Fountain, *Union Guy*, p. 194; Madison, *American Labor Leaders*, p. 327; Jack Barbash, *Labor's Grass Roots* (New York: Harper's, 1961), p. 180.

104. *Labor Leader* 1, no. 43, 13, no. 18; Resolution: "On Communism, Fascism and Nazism," 1940 Convention, ACTU files.

105. Ryan, *A Better Economic Order*, pp. 124–25; *Labor Leader* 1, no. 30.

106. Richard Deverall, "Socialism—The Road to Slavery," pp. 1–2, Detroit ACTU Collection; *Michigan Labor Leader* 1, nos. 2, 3, 4, and 8, 2, no. 2; *Labor Leader* 1, nos. 9, 16, 18, 21, and 30, 3, no. 6, 5, no. 14; the Detroit ACTU organized celebrations in honor of the Virgin Mary on May first as an alternative to left-wing May Day observances. *Michigan Labor Leader* 2, no. 8.

107. George Morris, "Vatican Conspiracy in the American Trade Union Movement," *Daily Worker*, February 23, 1950, p. 6; *Labor Leader* 1, nos. 7, 11, and 41, 8, no. 7, 9, no. 8; *Michigan Labor Leader* 1, nos. 2, 4, and 8, 2, nos. 2, 8, and 12, 3, no. 10, 5, no. 1.

108. One reader attacked what he viewed as "scandal mongering" and "futile baiting" which only "widens the breach between Catholics and Communists." *Labor Leader* 1, no. 30; also see *Labor Leader* 2, no. 14, 3, no. 14.

109. *Labor Leader* 1, nos. 1, 23, 25, and 28.

110. Voice of America broadcast, May 18, 1949, transcript, p. 7; Detroit ACTU Collection; "Why Wreck a Great Union?," leaflet of New York ACTU TWU conference; ACTU open letter to *New York Sun*, February 20, 1947; *Labor Leader* 1, no. 7, 2, nos. 13, and 18, 3, nos. 7, 9, 12, and 17, 4, nos. 7, 14, 5, no. 3, 6, no. 19, 8, no. 14, 9, no. 7.

111. *Labor Leader* 1, no. 38, 4, no. 14, 6, no. 14.

112. Ibid., 1, no. 38, 8, no. 1, 9, no. 7.

113. Twelve of the leaders of this former local of the TWU were graduates of the ACTU's Xavier Labor School and members of the ACTU TWU conference. Weinberg, "Priests, Workers and Communists," p. 53.

114. *Labor Leader* 4, no. 2, 5, nos. 1 and 7.

115. *Labor Leader* 1, no. 1, 2, no. 2, 5, no. 14, 8, no. 1, 9, no. 7, 10, no. 1.

116. See, for example, *Michigan Labor Leader*, 1, no. 4; *Labor Leader* 1, no. 34, 9, nos. 14 and 20. A resolution calling on the CIO to "bar from union office members of the Communist Party or consistent followers of Communist Party policy" was first passed at the ACTU's 1941 National Council meeting in Pittsburgh, "Resolution on Communists in Union Office," ACTU files.

117. *Proceedings of the Eighth Constitutional Convention of the CIO*, November 8–22, 1946, pp. 111–13; *Labor Leader* 9, no. 20.

6 † The ACTU, "The Providential Answer of the Church to Communism"

During 1937 the ACTU moved somewhat to the left in its organizing and educational work in New York City, Jersey City, and elsewhere. This radicalism coexisted uneasily with the conservative tradition of Catholic labor action and with the constitutional commitment of the organization to a "straight-down-the-middle" position. The victory of conservative ACTU members and their clerical supporters in the Gerson affair, however, reconsolidated the conservative position within the ACTU. From 1938 to 1945 the ACTU expanded its organization throughout the country and became an important influence within several CIO unions. The Actists promoted conservative ideology and practice in these unions and consistently sought to expand the anti-communist coalition in the CIO. The ACTU's activity in these years was increasingly successful and by 1945 a solid basis had been developed, in considerable measure because of the ACTU itself, for the anti-communist drive of the postwar period and the victory of conservative union principles and leadership.

EXPANSION AND ANTI-COMMUNISM, 1938–1941

The defeat of the progressive Actists in March of 1938 inaugurated a period of ACTU expansion and the beginnings of activity designed to isolate and defeat the communists within the unions. By September 1938 three new ACTU chapters had been organized, in Detroit, Boston, and Pittsburgh.[1] The Boston group included members of the United Office and Professional Workers' Union, the Industrial Insurance Agents' Union, the Furniture Workers' Union, and the ILGWU, all CIO, the Retail Store Employees' Union, AFL, and the independent Boston Teachers' Club and Harvard Employees' Association.[2] The president was Cyril O'Brien, one of the leaders of the successful drive for union recognition at the John Hancock Insurance Corporation, who was later to play an important role in anti-communist faction fighting in the Industrial Insurance Agents' Union.[3] The "inspiration for the growth of the [ACTU] work in Pittsburgh" was the Reverend Charles Owen Rice, who served on the Pennsylvania State Labor Relations Board and became one of the most active figures in the fight against communist influence in Pittsburgh-area unions, particularly the UE.[4] The Detroit chapter president was Paul Weber, who was also the president of the Detroit local of the News Guild and a perennial anti-communist convention delegate.[5] The Detroit chapter also included members of the Steel Workers' Organizing Committee (SWOC) and the UAW.[6] The Reverend Sebastian E. Erbacher, president of Duns Scotus College, served as chaplain.[7] In November of 1938 two more chapters were added to the ACTU roster. A meeting at the Knights of Columbus hall in Bayonne, New Jersey named George Campbell the provisional chairman of the Bayonne ACTU.[8] In San Francisco, 102 members of AFL, CIO, and Railway unions formed a chapter. Gus Gaynor of the Independent Brotherhood of Railroad Clerks was installed as chairman.[9]

This burst of organizational expansion, following on the heels of the conservative ideological consolidation within the ACTU, was paralleled by activity on other fronts. A Speakers' Bureau, directed by Norman McKenna, was organized to coordinate the extensive activity of ACTU speakers in promoting the Catholic labor perspective before union meetings and conventions, Holy Name societies, Knights of Columbus chapters, and other Catholic organizations.[10] Another subsidiary organization of the ACTU formed at this time was the Catholic Union of the Unemployed (CUU), whose chairman was Tim O'Brien, the one ACTU member of identify himself as a "Christian socialist."[11]

The CUU had been organized in February 1938 and promoted handicraft and back-to-the-land solutions to unemployment. It was strongly opposed to the "industrialization of farms" and recommended measures to resuscitate the family farm much on the order of those of the Bishops' Program for Reconstruction of 1919.[12] The CUU was also involved in efforts to unionize WPA workers in New York City. None of these efforts was very successful, despite the obvious need for organization among the unemployed, who constituted twenty percent of the work force in 1935.[13] This failure was no doubt partly the result of the utopian perspective of the CUU, which was more heavily influenced by the romantic agrarianism of the *Catholic Worker* organization than was the rest of the ACTU.[14] Another factor in the lack of success of the CUU was the tremendous growth of the left-wing unemployed organizations, which had begun organizing efforts in 1931. These formations had in considerable degree preempted organization among the unemployed.[15] Since the ACTU refused to join mass organizations dominated by the left, their own efforts tended to be minimal and outside the mainstream of unemployed organizing. This fact was not lost on the ACTU. Indeed, the CUU viewed its own organizing among the unemployed as a means to combat the preexisting left-wing formations, quite as much as a vehicle for the unemployed.

The one organizing drive which the CUU attempted substantiates this interpretation. In April 1938 O'Brien spoke before a group of Catholics in Troy, New York. He argued that "the time is ripe for a Troy branch of the ACTU." Right-wing local leaders of the Amalgamated Clothing Workers were ready to "cooperate with Catholics in union and unemployment action" because of "dissatisfaction with the activities of our left-wing friends."[16] O'Brien and another ACTU member, Jim Schneid, spent a week in Troy attempting to organize such a group, though nothing came of their efforts. Just as the first occasion of ACTU activity within rank-and-file caucuses in the unions, that of UAW local 156 in Flint, was directed against the left, so too was this first unsuccessful venture in unemployed organizing.[17] The Troy effort was significant as well in that it was the first, if abortive, instance of cooperation between right-wing Jewish unionists and ACTU members against the left. The hoped-for coalition of Protestant, Catholic, and Jewish workers against the left wing was not to be realized for some time, but the initial contacts were already being made.

Another subsidiary effort of the ACTU which commenced in 1938 was the Catholic Labor Defense League (CLDL), which provided legal defense for union organizing. This group was formed, as we have seen, in response to police and vigilante harassment of ACTU and CIO organizers in Jersey City in 1937 and 1938.[18] By the end of 1938, the CLDL had engaged the volunteer services of twenty Catholic lawyers in three cities under the direction of John Sheehan, a graduate of Manhattan College and Fordham Law School, who had worked as a teamster.[19] As was the case with both the CUU and the earliest rank-and-file caucus activity of the ACTU, the CLDL was partly a response to existing left-wing efforts. The radical-led International Legal Defense had made legal assistance available to workers since 1925.[20] The bulk of its activities were directed to employer-employee conflicts. While the CLDL announced that it intended "to do for the underprivileged in a Christian way what the Marxist groups were trying to in furtherance of their brand of revolution," its own concentration was largely on cases of intra-union disputes.[21] Defense of unionists against corrupt, right-wing leaders in the ILA and the Teamsters was a staple of the early CLDL and paralleled the work of ACTU-supported rank-and-file members to "clean up" these unions.[22]

The anti-corruption focus of the ACTU, however, began very quickly to give way to the fight against communism.[23] While the CLDL continued into the 1940s to defend union members harassed by corrupt union leaders such as Joseph Ryan of the ILA or John O'Rourke of Teamsters local 807, such activity slackened when the ACTU realized that the fight against corruption tended to help the left-wing opponents of the Ryans and O'Rourkes.[24] The ACTU's explicit preference in such cases was for Ryan over his rank-and-file, but left-wing opponents.[25] Consequently, the CLDL's major cases after 1938 involved ACTU-affiliated union members who opposed the communist leadership of various locals or international unions. In the main, the CLDL became the legal arm of ACTU-supported anti-communist struggles in the unions.[26]

Another major expansion of ACTU activity after 1938 was in labor education. The first ACTU Workers' School had been organized at Fordham University under the direction of ACTU chaplain the Reverend John Monaghan in 1937.[27] The curriculum consisted of labor history, labor ethics, Catholic social doctrine, parliamentary procedure, and public speaking.[28] The Faculty included the Reverend John P. Boland, chairman of the New York State Labor Relations Board, the Reverend Monaghan, and Professor James Downing of Fordham.[29] Sessions were held on weekday afternoons and evenings and attendance was both free and open to all unionists, Catholic and non-Catholic alike.[30] The first graduating class at the Fordham Workers' School numbered 343.[31]

During 1938 three more ACTU affiliated labor schools were organized. One was the Crown Heights School of Catholic Workmen, located in Brooklyn and directed by the Reverend William J. Smith, which graduated 150 students in 1938.[32] The other two schools were the Tarrytown Workers' School, conducted at St. Theresa School in North Tarrytown, and St. Athanisias Labor School in the Bronx.[33] Separate trade-union schools were also organized for Teamster and ILA members.[34] In addition to these formal schools, the ACTU offered lecture series and parish forums on union topics and current events and ran a study group on the social encyclicals during 1938.[35] One such forum held at Our Lady of Refuge Church in the Bronx in September 1938 was attended by 1,000 unionists who heard ACTU members explain the closed shop and suggest "methods of combatting Communist anti-union tactics."[36] Several ACTU members were also active in the educational programs of international unions. Robert Smith, for example, served as an instructor with the ILGWU educational department.[37]

The organization of such schools and educational programs was an extremely important part of the ACTU work. The first activity of most of the new ACTU chapters was to organize local equivalents of the ACTU schools in New York City, and educational directors were always among the officers of the chapters. Where they could not sustain a chapter school alone, the ACTU units usually worked with diocesan authorities to establish labor schools.[38] The schools were extensively advertised through the *Labor Leader* and the equivalent papers of other chapters such as the *Michigan Labor Leader* and through parish papers and sermons.

The importance of these schools was enhanced by the relative vacuum in which they operated. As with the CLDL, the CUU, and the rank and file ACTU union conferences, the labor schools were, in part, a response to Marxist initiatives. The Jefferson School, Commonwealth College, Brookwood Labor College, and similar left wing schools, some dating from the early 1920s, had a near monopoly on formal labor education during most of the 1930s. Few unions, either AFL or CIO, carried on educational programs for the rank and file or local leadership. College programs were exceedingly rare. A unionist seeking formal training in union procedures or labor history therefore could obtain it only from Marxist-oriented schools.

From the ACTU's point of view, this was an intolerable situation, especially since left wing education often went hand in hand with the recruiting of students, including Catholics, to radical caucuses in the unions. The ACTU shared the conclusion of Catholic labor activist Richard Deverall, who, impressed by his experience at Commonwealth College, held that similar efforts by Catholics on behalf of "Christian education of the workers" would be "one of our most intelligent answers to atheistic Communism."[39] Indeed, education was viewed as the single most important weapon in the fight against communism and the value of education was usually portrayed by the ACTU in just such instrumental terms. The cartoons which the *Labor Leader* ran stressing the importance of union education, for example, commonly took the form of ignorant "Joe McUnion" being bested by "Isidor Communist," who studied his Marxism and his parliamentary procedure.[40]

The ACTU schools, then, filled a gap which other conservatives within the unions were not prepared to fill. In 1938 more than 500 unionists graduated from a year's course of study in the ACTU's New York City labor schools alone. By 1938 ACTU-affiliated labor schools were graduating 7,500 students yearly at over 100 schools throughout the country. This was the only instruction in the theory and practice of unionism that most of them would encounter.[41] Many of these students were, or soon became, stewards or local union officers. Eighty-one of the 343 students who attended the Fordham School in 1938, for example, were local union officers. The ACTU's impact on the unions through the labor schools, then, was quite significant.

The schools taught practical skills in negotiating, running a meeting, and public speaking coupled with instruction in Catholic social doctrine. The faculty at the labor schools were predominantly Jesuit high school and college instructors and the ideological tone of the schools was quite conservative. One instructor was a defender of company unions, and the Reverend William J. Smith, Director of the Crown Heights School of Catholic Workmen, originated the ACTU position that the fight against communism must take precedence among Catholic activists over the fight for social justice itself.[42]

The ACTU schools promoted the general diffusion of Catholic-conservative ideas on union policy and social issues. But perhaps even more important, the schools functioned as a vehicle for the recruitment of unionists to the anti-communist struggle within the unions. Edward Squitieri of the Utility Workers' Union was recruited in this way. Squitieri and Martin Wersing organized local 1212 of the UWU and subsequently became local officers and opponents of the left wing caucus in the union. UAW members who "had been faithful students at the ACTU school at Fordham University" and at the Tarrytown School became the leaders in a fight to oust left wing leaders in the North Tarrytown GM plant's UAW local and ultimately replaced them as local officers. Similarly, an ACTU "waterfront labor school" for NMU members soon led to an ACTU-supported caucus and bulletin, *The Rank and File Pilot,* both instrumental in defeating Jack Lawrenson, the left wing incumbent in the pilots' subsection of the NMU.[43]

The harvest of cadre from the labor schools, however, had only just begun in 1938. Another immediate source of contacts and recruits was the strike-support work of the ACTU. In April 1938 Chaplain John Monaghan mediated the settlement of a dispute at 2-B Yarn Mills and Montgomery Dye Company in West New York, New Jersey, while John Cort assisted workers in a textile strike at the Atlantic Mills in Slottsville, New York, the following month. Cort was forced during this strike to defend the Textile Workers' Organizing Committee, CIO, against charges of "communism" by the local parish priest. In June Monaghan spoke in support of a Business Machines and Office Appliance Mechanics' local of the UE in New York City. This month also saw the beginning of support activity for UE local 1224 members at the New York City-based Eagle Pencil Company who had struck in response to a ten-percent wage reduction. The ACTU urged a boycott of the company's products.[44]

A recognition strike in July by local 231 of the CIO United Razor Workers' Union against the American Razor Company, manufacturers of "Gem" razor blades, called forth a major ACTU response. Members picketed and contributed money while John Cort and Chaplain William Brennan addressed several union rallies. This strike was significant, as noted earlier, in that it illustrated the influence the ACTU could exert against those union policies which it opposed. The company secured strikebreakers in an attempt to defeat the job action and at one of the strike meetings a union officer suggested that violence against them might be appropriate. John Cort reminded the meeting that a "fundamental principle of the ACTU" was rejection of violence and "urged the strikers to outlaw violence if they wanted the continued support and cooperation of the organization." On a motion of Joseph Flynn, another ACTU member, the local then voted to oppose "the use of violence as a strike tactic." In August this strike was settled to the satisfaction of the strikers, who voted thanks to the ACTU for its support. The Eagle Pencil strike was also successfully mediated in that month as was a dispute at the *Long Island Daily Press*. [45]

During the remainder of 1938 the ACTU joined a number of other strike-support efforts. Cort spoke at a strike meeting of workers at the Allen A Knitgoods Company in Bennington, Vermont. The Reverend William Brennan and other Actists worked on a strike by the UE at the Aerovox Company in New York City. ACTU member John Cadden led a successful organizing and recognition fight by the CIO United Retail Workers at A & P and Reeves stores in New York City. The ACTU would continue to be prominent in the organizing efforts of the Retail Workers. ACTU members George Donahue and Martin Kyne became international organizer and vice-president, respectively, of this union.

ACTU members were leaders of other organizing campaigns as well. The recruiting efforts of local 111 of the CIO Utility Workers' Organizing Committee (UWOC) were headed by ACTU member Martin Wersing. Vice-President Bob Bennet of the ACTU led a successful strike of members of the AFL Paper Handlers and Stationery Union against the Guide System and Supply Company which resulted in higher wages, overtime pay, paid holidays, and vacations. This was a significant incident since it was the first time the ACTU supported an AFL over a CIO union in a recognition contest. This soon became policy whenever the CIO unit was held to be communist-dominated. [46]

Mediation had been the ACTU's preferred procedure for the conclusion of industrial disputes since its first strike-support activity in 1937, and it was the means of settlement in most of these strikes. The important strikes at Aerovox, the Montgomery Dye Company, the *Long Island Daily Press,* the Eagle Pencil Company, and the American Razor Company, for example, were all settled through the mediation of the Reverends William Brennan, William Kelly, Thomas Darby, and John Monaghan. Thus the ACTU's own role continued to be suspended somewhere between partisan of the workers and neutral arbiter.

Three of the strikes and one organizing drive which the ACTU supported in 1938 were conducted by locals of the UE. These included locals at the Morgenthaler Company in Brooklyn, the Eagle Pencil Company, Aerovox, and a city-wide UE Business Machines and Office Appliance Workers' local. No other single union was involved in more than one effort. This remarkable concentration reflected an emerging ACTU interest in the UE, which was the largest of the left wing CIO unions, an interest which was to lead to the ACTU's pivotal role in the anti-communist faction fighting in that union.[47] Many of the other unions with which the ACTU was involved in 1938 were also to become battlegrounds in the conservative–radical struggle.

The ACTU was also active on behalf of black workers during 1938. In January of that year the ACTU had joined in the call of the Catholic Conference on Industrial Problems for an end to racism in employment and union practices. The organization participated also in the meetings and the work of the Harlem Coordinating Committee for Negro Employment, co-chaired by Adam Clayton Powell and A. Philip Randolph, which sought through boycotts and publicity to increase the number of black workers employed at Harlem stores. Phillip Jiggets, a black ACTU vice-president who was a relief worker and member of the State, County and Municipal Workers' Union, spoke at a rally of the Coordinating Committee at Rockland Palace in Harlem. ACTU members also joined in picketing Harlem stores.[48] The ACTU itself concentrated on exposing racist employment practices and pay differentials and on organizing workers to do their utmost to eradicate racist practices from their unions as "one of the most cynical aspects of democratic American trade unionism." The Actists praised the opposition of the TWU to racist hiring practices of the IRT subway line as well as that union's distribution of a pamphlet criticising bias against black workers. [49]

The fact that black leaders often cited Irish-dominated unions as the worst practitioners of racism highlights the position of the ACTU on racial discrimination. [50] Catholicism played a significant role in this opposition to racism. While the ACTU's strong commitment to Christian ethics led them categorically to oppose militance in strikes and to favor interclass harmony over class conflict, it also promoted opposition to racial discrimination, which was viewed as plainly immoral. Catholic doctrine on the moral integrity of the worker and the Christian brotherhood of all workers supported a firm stand on behalf of racial unity which any active trade unionist, Catholic or not, could understand and support.

There was another reason for the ACTU's activity among black workers, however. The Actists feared the inroads of the Communist party in the black community. In a wartime statement endorsing President Roosevelt's Executive Order No. 8802 prohibiting discrimination in defense industries, the ACTU joined other Catholics in arguing that such antidiscrimination efforts were necessary to assure the good "morale" of black Americans since discrimination "opens the door for totalitarian agitators" and "subversive activities." The ACTU was concerned, also, with the role of the Communist party in the Harlem Coordinating Committee, but concluded that "their influence does not appear to be sufficient to prevent co-operation on the part of Catholics."[51] The ACTU, of course, hoped to use its own activity in the committee as a means of countering and limiting left-wing influence just as it did in those left-wing unions in which it was active. [52]

The ACTU's Catholicism was also a significant factor in its orientation to women workers, though with less happy results. While Catholic ethics supported an antiracist position, the Church held a conservative, traditionalist view toward women workers: a woman's place was in the home. The Bishops' Program of 1919 had argued that industrial work for women, while necessary during wartime, was a social evil which "ought to be kept within the smallest practical limits." Later Catholic authorities, including Monsignor John A. Ryan, maintained this position. Ryan believed that women's proper place was in the home, that industrial work was bad for their health and morals, and that their presence hurt the morale of male workers and undercut pay rates.[53]

The ACTU also held that women should be discouraged from working, though, like Ryan, they endorsed equal pay for equal work. Despite this support for equal pay, however, the ACTU continued to argue for a higher family wage "to be paid to male workers in order to discourage women from working." In part this position reflected the knowledge that many married, working women would not be working if their husbands earned a living wage. But it was largely based on the ideological premise that women should not work and should be in their homes raising children.[54]

In practice, the ACTU did support working women on a number of occasions. Under the headline "Girls Strike," for example, the *Labor Leader* reported on a strike of thirty Catholic women working at the Platinum Products Company on Fifth Avenue in New York City. The ACTU assisted this strike with pickets during August of 1938 and also helped organize women working in Fifth Avenue dress shops. ACTU member Katherine Walsh aided black and Irish domestic workers in Westchester County who were seeking union status. The Detroit ACTU picketed on behalf of women clerks striking the Neisner Brothers chain stores. Their demands for a forty-four–hour week, a minimum salary of $16.00 and recognition of the RU as bargaining agent were met.

Women workers were involved in other organizing drives, especially those of the Retail Workers' Union, but in proportion to their numbers in the work force, women workers received relatively slight attention from the ACTU. The membership of the ACTU reflected this fact. More than ninety percent of the members surveyed were male and most of the women members were the wives of male members, many of them "standing in" for their husbands during wartime. Though women Actists were members of the UOPW, the ACA, the News Guild, the Amalgamated, the UE, AFSME, and the Retail Workers, they were largely relegated to traditional "auxiliary" duties such as the organization of social activities. The women officers of ACTU chapters were almost inevitably the "secretary" of the chapter.[55]

While the ACTU's practice in regard to women workers and women members was considerably more responsive than its theory, the organization exhibited a traditional "male supremacist" attitude. This attitude was derived from, or at any rate confirmed by, the tenets of Catholic social doctrine, which promoted the traditional role of woman as homemaker. It is particularly arresting that the ACTU considered pay differentials between black and white workers as immoral and disgraceful, while promoting those between male and female workers as necessary and beneficial. Thus, in contrast to their position on race, which was an argument of unity of black and white, the ACTU's position on women tended to reinforce and even exacerbate the divisions between male and female workers.

The burst of ACTU organizing activity which characterized 1938 continued in the following year. A Chicago chapter was organized in spring of 1939 at a meeting chaired by the Reverend Bernard E. Burns, who served as chaplain. Harry Read of the News Guild was elected president and AFL member Joseph Hennessy became vice-president. Paul Marking was elected treasurer and Marie Antoinette served as secretary. A Chicago chapter of the CLDL was also begun, headed by Dean Fitzgerald of Loyola University Law School. The Chicago ACTU was heavily involved in the News Guild strike against the Chicago *Evening American* and *Herald and Examiner*. Harry Read, the chapter president, was the chairman of the striking News Guild unit and Actists were prominent among those picketing the Hearst newspapers. Actist Lucy Read was arrested on the picket lines and defended by A. C. Tippen, a CLDL attorney.[56]

New ACTU chapters were also organized in several other cities, including Glassport, Pennsylvania; Rochester and Corning, New York; San Pedro, California; Newark; Toledo; Cleveland; Philadelphia; and Oklahoma City and Ponca City, Oklahoma, bringing the total number of chapters to seventeen. The membership, which had reached 4,800, included seamen, fishermen, electrical workers, newspaper reporters, bus drivers, glassworkers, printers, steam fitters, auto workers, motion picture operators, steel workers, lumber workers, and fur workers, among others. Most of the officers were Irish, following the pattern of earlier chapters, but the Glassport ACTU was headed by and apparently consisted of Polish Catholics.[57]

ACTU educational work was also considerably expanded during 1939. The Pittsburgh chapter began a School for Workers at Central Catholic Boys' High School, under the Reverends Carl Hensler and Charles Owen Rice, which enrolled 100 trade unionists, many of them members of the UE. The New York chapter opened a third school, in Harlem, and an additional workers' school began in October at New Rochelle with ninety-five students. The ACTU also assisted in the organization of a workers' school in Buffalo at the invitation of Bishop Duffy. The Detroit ACTU opened twenty-five parish labor schools during the year under the supervision of the archdiocese. ACTU Chaplain Raymond Clancy directed the schools. The Detroit chapter also began publication of the *Michigan Labor Leader* and organized a speakers' bureau. ACTU–New York supplemented its earlier lay speakers' bureau with a clerical speakers' bureau. Finally, the New York and Detroit chapters secured radio time for talks on union topics, the Wagner Act, and the ACTU.[58]

ACTU union-support activity during 1939 included Chaplain Monaghan's arbitration of a dispute at the Kenmore Manufacturing Corporation in New York and ACTU–New York assistance to a successful organizing drive at Rockland Hospital. Actists who had graduated from the Fordham Workers' School brought about a merger of AFL and CIO units among A & P workers in New York City and headed the united local. ACTU priests also mediated a strike at the chain of Diamond Candle Stores in New York. The Boston chapter, like the Chicago unit, was involved in support for a News Guild dispute, this one in Lynn, Massachusetts. The ACTU was also active in the CIO United Rubber Workers' organizing drive in Connecticut and in support of a strike at Sun Drug Stores in Pittsburgh. The total number of instances of ACTU strike-support activity, however, was considerably diminished from that of 1937–38 and none of this assistance, except for the News Guild work of the new Chicago chapter, was so extensive or significant as that tendered to strikes at the Eagle Pencil Company, the *Brooklyn Daily Eagle*, or the American Razor Company during 1937 and 1938. At the same time the ACTU had expanded its number of chapters more than threefold and had more than doubled the number of affiliated workers' schools.[59]

Why then had strike- and organizing-support activity actually diminished? The answer is mainly to be found in an escalation of ACTU activity in intra-union and anti-radical disputes. At least in the case of the older chapters, an initial period of establishing contacts within the unions through educational and support activity had concluded by 1939. These cadre were now mobilized for activity within the unions and for the broader struggle against the left. [60] The commencement of this "mature" period was underlined by the ACTU's organized role and relatively massive presence at the Catholic Social Action Conference, organized by the American Federation of Catholic Societies' Department of Social Services, June 12–14, 1939, in Cleveland. ACTU delegates from San Francisco, New York, Detroit, Pittsburgh, Chicago, Cleveland, Philadelphia, Oklahoma City and Ponca City, Oklahoma, attended the congress. They participated in an ACTU caucus and distributed the "Stand of the ACTU," copies of the *Labor Leader*, and other material to the delegates. The Actists organized several of the panels held at the congress and provided the Reverends Rice, Hensler, John M. Hayes, and John P. Boland as panelists. National ACTU Chaplain Monaghan sounded the keynote of the new period of ACTU intra-union struggle at one of these sessions when he announced that "the ACTU was the providential answer of the Church to the menace of Communism."[61]

The ACTU streamlined its forces for action within the unions during 1939 by organizing a number of "conferences" of the organization. The conferences were open to all ACTU members in a given union within a chapter's area. They determined ACTU policy and strategy in the union and were regarded as the "fundamental unit" of the ACTU. In an attempt to increase the base of these conferences and promote a Jewish-Protestant-Catholic coalition against the left, these ACTU conferences provided for "auxiliary" membership for non-Catholics. Such ACTU caucuses already existed in the ILA and the Teamsters. The Teamsters' caucus alone brought nearly 3,000 unionists to a communion breakfast organized by ACTU member Dan Laughlin. New ones were now organized among Consolidated Edison workers, who were members of the UWU, and among members of the United Office and Professional Workers' Union, the Transport Workers' Union, the News Guild, and the National Maritime Union.[62]

The Con Edison ACTU conference included the leadership of local 1212 of the CIO UWU. Martin Wersing, a past ACTU president, was president of the local and Edward Squittieri, the ACTU president for 1939, was financial secretary. Actists Mary Berry and Roger Larkin were also members of local 1212. The ACTU had carried on an extensive boycott campaign against layoffs by Consolidated Edison throughout 1938 which had culminated in candlelight parades of several thousand workers and their supporters. The ACTU had extensive influence, then, among Consolidated Edison workers and especially in local 1212. Initially the ACTU discouraged affiliation with the UWU. Under ACTU leadership the local was first independent, then AFL-affiliated, then independent again before the unit finally voted to join the UWU. The ACTU's major reason for opposing UWU affiliation was that the New York UWU was too heavily influenced by the left. As in many jurisdictional disputes to come, despite its announced preference for the CIO, the ACTU here supported the AFL, or even the inherently weak "independent" status, rather than affiliation with a left wing unit of the CIO.[63]

In the case of the CIO United Office and Professional Workers' Union, this hostility to a left-wing union went even further. New York local 16 of this union, according to the ACTU, was "split by charges of red control." The ACTU-supported caucus in this local, led by Anne Gould, had therefore sought to unseat the local leadership. They failed in this and, "condemning the leadership of Local 16 for taking orders from the Communist Party," 500 of them promptly quit the UOPWU for the AFL Bookkeepers, Stenographers and Accountants. At the same time, however, other Actists were continuing work within the UOPWU. ACTU members Joseph Connel, David Fay, John Steskel, and Daniel Culhane, for example, ran for office in local 30 "on charges of Communism" six months after the local 16 secession.[64]

Secession from or raiding upon left-led CIO affiliates thus was not a general policy of the ACTU in 1939. Indeed, the ACTU usually cautioned patience to those conservative members who tired of the fight against the left within their unions.[65] Nonetheless, secession by ACTU-supported groups continued. One such split involved Joseph Curran's National Maritime Union, which was one of the ACTU's primary targets for criticism and charges of communist domination. An ACTU-supported anti-communist caucus in the Gulf Coast NMU, complaining of communist propaganda in the NMU newspaper, started its own newspaper, and withheld dues. Finally, they withdrew from the NMU entirely despite the impending NMU convention, at which they might have challenged the leadership. The ACTU's support for this split drew a letter of criticism from CIO Director John Brophy, who reminded the ACTU that the NMU dissidents had not first brought their complaints to any responsible CIO body. The ACTU replied that it honestly believed the charges of "Communist domination of this international union." While claiming generally to oppose such secessions, the ACTU ominously concluded that "factional fighting cannot always be resolved by Conventions."[66]

Despite their public opposition to splits in CIO unions, the ACTU seemed to support secession when two conditions obtained: one, the seceding unit was sufficiently large or strategically enough situated to stand on its own and, two, the left-wing leadership was so popular that opposition was not likely to be effective. In the case of the Transit Workers' Union, for example, the ACTU elected to remain within the union. Despite Mike Quill's popularity, the largely Irish Catholic membership suggested that internal opposition might, in time, be effective. At the same time, the transport companies were a formidable enemy and any divisive tactics were likely to encourage them to renew attempts to destroy the unions. A new and weak secessionist union would undoubtedly be among the first casualties of such a drive. Consequently, the ACTU both supported TWU efforts to organize the BMT subway line and sponsored a "non-sectarian, non-political, representative rank and file group" in the TWU which opposed "Communist-minded" union officers. One member of this caucus, Thomas McGuire, an executive board member of local 100, even argued for nonpayment of dues to the TWU as a weapon in the anti-communist struggle, an action which hinted of secession. He was defended against the resulting TWU charges of malfeasance by CLDL attorney John Sheehan.[67]

The history of the ACTU in 1939 was thus a history of growth and shifting focus. The major development was a decline in the ACTU's emphasis on strike support and organizing. Such efforts diminished in 1939 while activity against the left wing, including ACTU caucuses, contests for election, splits, and threatened splits increased. Rather than a new departure, however, the increase in factional activity seemed to reflect the consolidation of the membership, constituency, and experience of the older chapters toward an end which had priority since early 1938.

During 1940 the ACTU's focus on intra-union factional fighting became even more pronounced, while organizational expansion abated and pure and simple strike-support activity virtually disappeared. No new chapters were organized during the year, though the Pittsburgh chapter opened a second branch of its workers' school and the Detroit chapter assisted in the formation of an archdiocesan labor institute. The institute's director, the Reverend Raymond S. Clancy, was also the Detroit ACTU chaplain. The Newark ACTU's chaplain, the Reverend Lambert Dunne, also took on additional duties as a member of the New Jersey Labor Relations Board. The Chicago ACTU began publication of a monthly newsletter. Additional ACTU industry conferences were organized in New York among members of local 272 of the Garage Washers' and Polishers' Union and in other unions across the country. Apart from a contribution to the striking News Guild unit in Chicago, the ACTU did not engage in any strike-support work in 1940. Rather than expanding further, the ACTU during 1940 concentrated on consolidating those chapters and schools founded during 1938 and 1939 and intensified the drive against the left wing within the unions.[68]

A hardening of the ACTU's anti-communism was discernible during 1940 in their changed position on Congressional and Justice Department actions against suspected communists. For example, at the American Communications Association Convention the ACTU conference, led by William J. Shinnick, helped to defeat a "Communist Party Line" resolution criticizing the Dies Committee for anti-union and red-baiting activity. In contrast, during HUAC investigations in February of 1938 the ACTU had been "very suspicious" of the opportunistic motives of witness Joseph Ryan, president of the ILA. Ryan had offered testimony on communist influence in the CIO unions which the ACTU believed to be merely a cover for Ryan's own corruption and collusion with employers. The Actists therefore had offered no support for HUAC's activities. The

intervening ACTU commitment to active anti-communism, however, made the Dies Committee investigations rather more welcome,
despite the obvious anti-labor intentions of the committee members.
The ACTU's position on the Immigration Department's attempt to
deport Harry Bridges, the left-wing ILWU leader, showed a similar
development toward more open alliance with non-union anti-
communists. When this case was initiated, the ACTU had argued
that the "Hearst press is the only real force actively urging that
Bridges be deported." The *Labor Leader* had then approvingly
quoted John Shelley, San Francisco Labor Council president, who
argued that the reason for the deportation action was that Bridges
"has done a [good] job for labor." In 1940, however, the ACTU
condemned "Bridges and his Communist supporters" and dismissed
efforts to defend him against deportation as "Communist propaganda."[69]

Apart from general broadsides against such left-wing union
leaders as Bridges, Curran, and Quill, the ACTU continued and
extended its intra-union activities against the left during 1940.
Since the communists "are but a minute minority" in the unions, the
ACTU reasoned, anti-communists had only to "imitate their zeal"
and the radicals could easily be defeated. While others might be
sluggish in acting on this advice, no one could fault the ACTU for
lack of zeal in the anti-communist fight. Indeed, during 1940 the
organization energetically supported conservative caucuses in the
AFT, the UOPWA, the News Guild, the Garage Workers, the
Painters, the ACA, the UAW, the ILA, the TWU, and the UE.[70]

The ACTU's increasingly violent red-baiting occasionally drew
criticism from *Labor Leader* readers, even those who shared an
anti-communist perspective. One argued that such activities were a
waste of time and effort that might otherwise be spent on
strengthening and expanding the unions. The organization's initia-
tion of conservative caucuses within CIO unions also drew fire from
James B. Carey, secretary of the CIO. Carey accused the ACTU of
following a "policy of functioning as an organized opposition
'caucus' to 'bore from within' in exactly the same fashion as the
Communists operate." Carey was exactly on the mark, since ACTU
members explicitly modeled their own union activity, as well as their
educational, legal, and other efforts, on that of the communists.[71]

This anti-communist activity included, in 1940, a renewed drive to defeat the left in the Newspaper Guild. ACTU members, including Paul Weber, president of the Detroit News Guild, were active in the anti-communist caucus at the News Guild's Seattle convention in May 1940. This group secured the convention's approval of a resolution condemning communism. With this victory in hand the ACTU concluded that the "time has come for the left-wing New York Guild to clean house." Lawrence Delaney and Norman McKenna of the New York ACTU News Guild Conference were already hard at work on this clean-up. Delaney himself was the sponsor of an unsuccessful pre-convention resolution to leave the New York local uncommitted to any slate of national officers, since the strength of the left in New York meant that any endorsement would go to the left-wing slate. In July, after the convention, the Guild Conference of the ACTU in New York went "on record as condemning Communism as a menace to the Newspaper Guild." Victory in New York was not to come for some time, however. As with the TWU, ACTU members were active in support of the union, despite their opposition to the left-wing local leadership. Actists leafleted and joined picket lines, for example, during a successful drive to bring *New York Times* commercial department employees into the Guild.[72]

The ACTU continued to oppose racketeering in the unions during 1940, though such activity usually paralleled the struggle against the communists so as not to encourage gangster-victimized workers to shift left. In the AFL Painters' Union, for example, the Actists endorsed presidential candidate Philip Zausner over left wing incumbent Louis Weinstock and aided caucuses in locals 848 and 442. The first caucus was mainly concerned with racketeers in the local while the second ran on a platform of "Straight American Trade Unionism Run by Union Painters—Not by Hitler-Stalin Agents."

Racketeering was a continuing issue in two other unions with which the ACTU was involved during 1940. The Garage Washers' and Polishers' ACTU conference organized in response to lack of democracy and racketeering in local 272 and despite "strong-arm threats" by the leadership. The ACTU pledged that it was "at all times ready to give what aid it can to any such legitimate movements." Which movements against racketeer leadership were "legitimate," however, was an open question. In the case of the ACTU's involvement with the ILA, for example, criticism of the admittedly corrupt Ryan machine began to be muted, despite the murder of rank-and-file leaders, because the fight against corruption was being "taken over by Communists."[73]

Communism, rather than corruption or militance, was also the major issue, as far as the ACTU was concerned, in both the AFT and the UAW. ACTU delegates at the August convention of the UAW supported a successful resolution condemning the "brutal dictatorship and wars of aggression of the totalitarian governments of Germany, Italy, Russia and Japan." The victory of an anticommunist slate at the AFT convention in the same month inspired ACTU congratulations that the "AFT has disassociated itself from the most notorious of the militant godless." Nonetheless, the ACTU complained about the support George S. County, the new AFT president, had given the appointment of Bertrand Russell to a position at City College.[74]

Such "critical support" for centrist and liberal anti-communists was a pattern with the ACTU. While the communists themselves were the focus of their attacks, the ACTU exerted pressure on its more moderate allies to drop support for anything the communists or other leftists also supported and to disaffiliate from any organization in which they were involved. The ACTU's criticism extended to tactics and even style that appeared to them "communist." Indeed, the ACTU often practiced the strategy of maligning as "communist" those positions and actions of which it disapproved, however unlikely the connection. For example, after his speech praising Hoover and laissez-faire capitalism in June 1940, the *Labor Leader* editorially attacked John L. Lewis for "devious zigzagging" which promoted the "Communist Party line."[75]

The primary motive in this red-baiting was to isolate the communists and other radicals and frighten liberals and moderates away from any contact with them. However, since the communists were usually involved, as the ACTU admitted, "where there is necessary and vital activity," the effect of this policy was to disrupt and throw into suspicion all progressive organizations, including the unions themselves. Both the CIO and, ironically, the ACTU would become victims of this effect.[76]

The ACTU's first national convention, held in Cleveland over the weekend of August 31–September 2, 1940, confirmed the priority commitment of the organization to anti-communism. Monsignor John A. Ryan gave the keynote speech, in which he "urged the delegates to be on guard against Communist activities in their unions. While the complete exclusion of Communists from ordinary membership in unions is probably not always practicable," he continued, "they should be kept out of official positions." The ACTU's stress on intra-union battles against the left and on behalf of anti-communist candidates was thus reaffirmed while the organization's original position that communists had to be tolerated as union members in the interest of the unity of the unions was abandoned. The new ACTU stance would permit expulsion of such members if democratic methods of opposition were ineffective. The ACTU also undertook to provide for expulsion of "fellow travelers" from its own ranks either by the chapters themselves, the national director, or the national council. The convention also sought to prevent their joining with a requirement that each new member be vouchsafed by two members who had been with the ACTU for a year. The preoccupation with the communist issue was further revealed in the credentials of the new national director. Victor LoPinto, a civil engineer, had "led the fight against the 'Party Line' peace resolutions" in the Federation of Architects, Engineers, Chemists and Technicians.

Among resolutions adopted at the convention were two favoring "labor unity" and "organizing the unorganized" and one opposing "Communism, Fascism and Nazism." The latter stipulated that "the efforts of all Actists should be directed toward exposing those who espouse all forms of Communism, Marxism, Nazism, and Fascism, or who in practice agree with all of their policies" and barring them from union office. Another resolution indicated support for Roosevelt's national defense program "as long as labor's rights were safeguarded." The convention was at once a consolidation of the work of the previous three years and a significant financial drain on the apparently overextended ACTU, so much so that the *Labor Leader* was forced to suspend publication for the next four months.[77]

During 1941 the ACTU increasingly focused on the intra-union struggle with the left-wing. The organization became more favorable to AFL unions and to secessions from left-wing CIO unions and generally stepped up its propaganda campaign against the left. These issues shaped the ACTU's expansion, which was renewed during the year. Financial equilibrium was restored also and there was an increase in strike-support efforts involving several chapters, but the ACTU continued to focus on the anti-communist campaign.

New chapters were added to the rolls during January 1941 in South Bend and St. Joseph County, Indiana, and in the following month students at the diocesan labor school in Milwaukee, which the ACTU had assisted in founding, also organized an ACTU chapter. The Milwaukee chapter's membership included auto workers, steel workers, and machinists, among others. New ACTU locals were also founded in Saginaw and Bay City, Michigan, in May and in Seattle in June. The Seattle membership, all Irish, included college students, priests, attorneys, longshoremen, machinists, building-service employees, railway carmen, cemetery workers, pressmen, office workers, carpenters, letter carriers, aeronautical mechanics, and sailors.[78] The New York and Detroit chapters, meanwhile, had both increased their memberships and the number of unions represented. Detroit, for example, now had members from ninety parishes and over 100 unions.

ACTU labor-education efforts expanded considerably during 1941. In the New York City area three three new schools were added during January 1941, at St. Nicolas Church in the Bronx, Columbian High School in Manhattan, and the Knights of Columbus Hall in Yonkers. A fourth, the Xavier Labor School, was organized the following September. The Detroit chapter increased its network of parish labor schools to thirty-six, each of which held two ten-week sessions. The Pittsburgh ACTU also expanded its educational efforts, especially in districts which were "notoriously Communistic" and added its fourth local workers' school in the East Pittsburgh–Turtle Creek area. A fifth was planned for McKeesport, Pennsylvania.[79]

There was a resurgence of ACTU strike-support work, also, during 1941 in New York City, Chicago, Detroit, Pittsburgh, and San Francisco which extended the ACTU's contacts in the RU, SWOC, UWOC, and the restaurant union. These campaigns, however, were largely the initial base-building activities of newer chapters or represented activity by full-time union organizers who were members of the ACTU.

The New York ACTU played an active role in a successful fifteen-week strike at the fifty-five Whelan Drug Stores. The workers won recognition of the Retail Workers Union (RU). The ACTU was heavily involved in several other organizing drives of the RU. The New York general organizer for the RU was George Donahue, also New York ACTU president, and the Retail Workers' Coordinating Committee for New York included ACTU members Leonard Geiger and Martin Kyne, who was also international vice-president of the union. ACTU members Michael Cavannagh and James Cadden led a recognition struggle at Reeves Food Stores and Actist Angelina Leibinger organized workers at the Barricini Candy Stores. The ACTU also assisted the Retail Union in organizing Stern's Department Store in Boston, where both the Boston chapter and National Chaplain Monaghan were active. Joseph Conlon, former ACTU executive secretary, led a campaign at Montgomery Ward in Chicago as international representative of the Retail Workers. John Sheehan of the CLDL represented the union at NLRB hearings during several of these campaigns.[80]

In Detroit, ACTU Chaplain Raymond S. Clancy signed a union-shop agreement with the diocese for the CIO Cannery Workers' Union, representing gravediggers at Catholic cemeteries. The Detroit ACTU also helped to organize workers at the Currier Lumber Company and supported strikers at the Neisner Brothers retail stores. An ACTU mediation effort at Currier failed when the company fired two union members. The Actists supported the resulting strike, which secured union representation. ACTU efforts were also successful in aiding RU members at the sixteen Neisner stores. The Pittsburgh ACTU provided food, money, and picket-line support to SWOC strikers at the Hubbard Steel Company and also assisted UWOC organizing in the Pittsburgh utilities. The Philadelphia unit received thanks from the SWOC sub-regional director for help in that city. Restaurant workers in San Francisco were supported by the ACTU there, as was an organizing drive of the AFL Department Store Employees at Sears.

This campaign of strike-support activity represented a significant increase over 1940, contrary to the previous shift toward increasing

ACTU involvement in inter-union struggle. For the most part, however, these efforts were the initial campaigns of newer chapters such as San Francisco and Philadelphia, or, in the case of the Retail Union, the work of Actists who were full-time employees of the union. Major ACTU volunteer efforts continued to go into the fight within the unions. In nearly every case this fight was directed against left-wing union leadership rather than corrupt or incompetent leaders.[81]

The ACTU's struggle with the left wing during 1941 quickened in pace and became tactically sharper. The Actists began openly to support secession from left-wing unions and to favor AFL unions whose CIO counterparts were left-wing. The organization's intra-union activities during 1941 focused on the TWU, the UOPWA, and the UE, where there were ACTU conferences of long standing. These three were among the most important left wing unions with substantial Catholic memberships. The TWU, in particular, was more than eighty percent Irish, while the UOPWA and the UE, in a number of locations, contained large pluralities of Irish Catholics. The UE was the largest left-wing CIO union and the fourth largest in the union federation. The TWU, while considerably smaller, was influential because it was concentrated in New York City. Its flamboyant president, Mike Quill, was the best-known left-wing union leader after Harry Bridges, and was also the president of the New York City CIO Council. The UOPWA was about the same size as the TWU, but was a much weaker union in terms of the percentage of office workers it had organized.[82]

The ACTU's struggle within the UE was a matter of necessity since this union was the basis of left-wing strength in the CIO. The focus on the TWU was partly because of Quill's stature as a leading left-wing unionist, but the ACTU had members in this union from the beginning and the large Irish majority increased the possibility that the Actists might expand their base of support. The assault on the UOPWA was partly circumstantial—the ACTU, in New York especially, enrolled large numbers of office workers—but the weak UOPWA offered a tempting target for the conservative Actists irrespective of this fact. Indeed, CIO conservatives generally focused on the UOPWA throughout the 1940s,[83] since the more successful left-wing unions were not so easily criticized.

Though the UAW was not dominated by the left wing on the international level, the ACTU was active during 1941 in a number of locals led by the left. The UAW leadership at this time consisted of a coalition, the unity caucus, which included the left wing. The left was represented by UAW general counsel Maurice Sugar and was strong in a number of locals, including the 60,000-member Ford local 600, the largest union local in the world, at River Rouge. The UAW, given the concentrated nature of the auto industry, its impact on the economy, and its importance in armaments manufacture, was a particularly important union. The ACTU, therefore, sought to use its strength within the UAW to isolate and defeat the left.

ACTU activity within the UAW began to pay off handsomely in 1941. The conservative caucus in Plymouth local 51 in Detroit, which included several Actists, was able to defeat the left wing and elect its own slate of officers. In Milwaukee another conservative faction, led by Joe Martin and Leon Verine, ACTU chapter president, increased their strength in the Allis-Chalmers local (UAW 248). Aided by their chapter, these Actists led a successful struggle against a communist-supported strike initiative. The capstone of the 1941 campaign, however, occurred in local 600, at the River Rouge Ford plant in Detroit. After three years of activity by the ACTU conference in this left-wing local, the Actists elected Paul Saint-Marie, Detroit ACTU vice-president, to the leading position in the local—chairman of the council. He defeated a left-wing candidate, James Couser.[84]

The ACTU continued to escalate its attacks during 1941 on the left-wing leadership of the TWU in New York City, especially president Michael Quill. In a May *Labor Leader* the editors chronicled the ACTU's previous support for TWU organizing campaigns, but concluded that it could go on no longer. The union was now following the "party line" without qualification and had organized a "TWU OGPU" besides. "Quill is a discredited Communist party functionary," they added, "who must be driven from the trade union field." The reference to the "OGPU" (the Soviet secret service) was inspired by the case of Patrick Reilly, a TWU member who was suspended after a union hearing in which his allegation that the TWU had contributed money to Republican Spain was dismissed as slander. CLDL attorney John Sheehan defended Reilly in the case, which lasted into 1941. Apart from attacks on Quill and the publicity surrounding the Reilly case, the ACTU's mounting hostility to the TWU was expressed by a reversal of their support for transport workers' right to strike. The ACTU had defended this right before and had supported several strikes of the TWU. In April 1941, however, after the communist issue in the TWU had assumed significant dimensions for the ACTU, the organization concluded that "the common good of the community makes it advisable if not mandatory for these [transit] workers to waive their right to strike."[85]

One of the most significant of the ACTU's interventions in union faction fighting during 1941 involved the important Westinghouse UE local 601 in Pittsburgh. This local was the largest in the UE, with 16,500 members, and was led by the left wing. The Reverend Charles Owen Rice led the ACTU in this struggle. According to the Reverend Rice, Catholic members of the local requested his aid in "their battle against Communistic elements in the local." He agreed and helped them bring out Catholic members for a local meeting which was to consider union action in the case of a member fired by Westinghouse. Rice and the Catholic caucus considered this worker a Communist party "fellow traveler" and blocked union action to secure his reinstatement. The shop stewards council of local 601 protested against this "interference" by the Reverend Rice, but both he and the ACTU defended the action as within a priest's duty to defend Catholics from immoral influence. Subsequently, the ACTU caucus in local 601 began operation of an ACTU labor school "in the vicinity of the Westinghouse plant." In January of 1942 the caucus successfully eliminated the left-wing members of the local's executive board.[86]

The ACTU's activity within the UOPWA during 1941 was also significant. This campaign went further than any previous ACTU intervention in promoting secession and favoring AFL over CIO unions. The Actists were increasingly jettisoning CIO solidarity where the left wing was concerned, in favor of secession, dual unionism, and the AFL. In 1940 the ACTU had supported a secession in local 16 of the UOPWA while supporting a caucus within the union, and discouraging secession, in local 30. This caucus was unsuccessful in unseating the left-wing leadership, however, and the Actists then initiated a second split. "When it became apparent that Merrill and his group [the left-wing union leadership] completely dominated the union and defeated the efforts of bona-fide trade unionists to eliminate Communist influence," said the *Labor Leader*, "the ACTU advised its members within Local 30 that it could no longer support its [the local's] policies."

The AFL Insurance Agents' Union was called in by the secessionists and subsequently won an NLRB representation election among these workers at the Colonial Life Insurance Company. Thus, the ACTU's heretofore ambivalent position on secession from left-wing CIO affiliates was heading (at least in the case of the UOPWA) toward a full-scale secessionist policy whose immediate beneficiary was the AFL. The AFL, as we have seen, had originally been supported by the Church and lay predecessors of the ACTU, such as the Militia of Christ for Social Service, as a safe, conservative alternative to the Knights of Labor, the IWW, and the socialists. With left-wing influence at a peak in the CIO, the ACTU seems to have concluded that it was safest to reintegrate conservative CIO locals seceding from left-wing CIO unions with AFL units. In this way the ACTU might assure the continuation of conservative, Church-influenced leadership for these unionists and at the same time put pressure on the CIO to purge its radicals. [87]

The years 1938 through 1941 had been productive ones for the ACTU. Twenty chapters had been organized and the membership had increased to nearly 10,000. Educational efforts had been expanded considerably and thousands of unionists were now attending ACTU labor schools. Subsidiary ACTU efforts had been directed toward the unemployed, women, and blacks and a legal defense arm, the CLDL, had been organized. Newer chapters received their baptism of fire in strike-support and organizing work and thereby established a network of union supporters and contacts. [88] ACTU conferences had been organized in hundreds of union locals and ACTU members had begun to win local, state, and national union office. A national convention had been held and a more or less efficient national organization established.

An increasingly exclusive ACTU commitment to anti-communism shaped the direction of this expansion and consolidation. The national convention and the "Articles of Federation" stressed this orientation, and the labor schools too promoted anti-communism and conservative labor ideology. The schools, ACTU periodicals, and conferences served to recruit large numbers of ACTU members and supporters who were then mobilized largely for the struggle against the left wing. The ACTU's unemployed organizing, its efforts on behalf of blacks, and its legal activity were reactive also to left-wing organizing. Even the ACTU's union-support work was of less priority than anti-communism, or was made to serve this objective. The newer chapters tended to stress this activity for a year or two, in order to build a base of support, and subsequently to concentrate on the anti-communist campaign. The older chapters, by 1940, were almost exclusively concerned with the anti-communist issue. [89]

The ACTU's involvement in intra-union factional fighting began during these years and by late 1941 it constituted the most significant activity of the organization. The ACTU's network of conferences and caucuses increased many-fold and by the end of this period the Actists represented a significant force within the UE, TWU, UAW, UOPWA, RU, and the Newspaper Guild. The struggle with the left also became more bitter during these years, with the ACTU increasingly supporting conservative secession and favoring the AFL over left-wing CIO unions.

THE WARTIME YEARS

The wartime years were relatively lean ones for the ACTU. Organizational expansion virtually ceased and several chapters suspended activity. Many members left for the armed forces and the ACTU itself spent considerable effort on war work and the discussion of wartime and postwar labor policy. ACTU educational efforts, however, expanded and the discussion of postwar labor and reconstruction policy permitted a more energetic polemic on behalf of the corporative, guild, or industry-council program. Factional fighting against the left wing continued unabated. Indeed, despite the CIO leadership's commitment to a "united front" effort within the labor movement in the spirit of Grand Alliance unity, the ACTU increased its attacks on the left wing. ACTU support for AFL over left-wing CIO unions began on a mass scale. ACTU factional fighting against the left continued during 1942–45 in the TWU, UE, and other unions and expanded to the MMSW, ILWU, and ACA.[90]

The ACTU's position on U.S. entry into World War II changed considerably from 1939 to 1942. In 1939 the organization was committed to the position that "war can never result in good" and that "the greatest disservice we could do the human race would be to plunge America into the abyss [of war]." By late 1940, however, the ACTU was prepared to support "national defense" efforts, "as long as labor's rights were safeguarded." The 1940 convention had endorsed the national defense program and the 1941 convention reaffirmed this support.[91] The Actists rightly feared, however, that "national defense" arguments would be used by opponents of unions as a rationale for anti-labor legislation. Consequently the ACTU kept up a running fire on Congressional bills which seemed to threaten a wartime "labor dictatorship." They opposed the Vinson Bill, for example, which would have frozen the open shop where it existed for the duration of the war.

The ACTU had initially argued against conscription as well, unless "wealth" was also to be conscripted, as a "desperate measure" for which substitutes were available. In defense of this position, the ACTU reasoned that "sacrifices must not be expected from those who are already greatly oppressed by the ills of our own economic system." Thus the Actists pledged cooperation with the National Defense Mediation Board, but defended the right to strike and warned that the board had "practically unlimited" power in those labor disputes which it determined "threatened to burden or disrupt national defense."[92]

The ACTU's wartime program, then, stressed the preservation of labor's rights, organizations, and economic position. The Actists defended the right to strike and opposed wartime curtailment of the Wagner Act's guarantee of labor's right to organize and bargain collectively.[93] They urged the labor movement to utilize full-employment conditions to "organize the unorganized," to extend economic democracy, and to seek fuller "partnership with capital." The ACTU also supported equal treatment for blacks and women workers in war industries through the machinery of the Federal Employment Practices Committee (FEPC). Actists favored wartime rent, price, and wage controls, but argued that prices were not treated equally with wages, which were being held too low. Profits and salaries, they believed, should be controlled in the same fashion as wages. "Equal Sacrifices" remained their watchword where wartime economic policy was concerned. But it was never too early to think about the postwar period, in the view of the Actists, and they began very soon to promote the slogan "No Depression After This War." The ACTU pressed for reconstruction plans that would provide full employment and promoted the industry-council plan as a method of insuring capital-labor partnership in postwar economic life.[94]

The effect of the war on the ACTU was enormous. The attack on Pearl Harbor ended their opposition to conscription and they now lent their support to some form of regulation of labor disputes during wartime and to the "no-strike pledge," though they did defend several strikes during the war. The Actists quickly pledged their services to "the nation's united effort to achieve victory over the enemies of our country." The organization's New York office was offered to the Office of Civilian Defense and several chapters were suspended for the duration. "An ever increasing percentage of the membership of the ACTU" volunteered or were eventually drafted into the armed forces, including George Donahue, ACTU president, and John Sheehan, chairman of the CLDL.[95]

Many chapters kept up a merely nominal wartime existence and no new ones appeared from 1942 through 1945, except for an Oakland chapter, number 21, organized by the Reverend Bernard C. Cronin in June 1944. Union-support work virtually disappeared relative to the total for 1940 and 1941, which had itself represented a decrease from the peak in 1937–39. The only instances of such support activity involved organizing drives of New York City units of the Retail Workers' Union at Loft's Candy Stores in early 1943, Wanamaker's Department Store in late 1944, and a Detroit RU drive at Kerns' Department Store in late 1942. These campaigns were actually continuations of the major ACTU-assisted Retail Workers' drives of 1941, rather than new support efforts. This lack of support activity, of course, was partly the result of lessened strike activity during the war years. Organizing activity by the unions, however, stimulated by full employment, continued during the war. An all-time peak labor union membership of 14,322,000 (thirty-six percent of the nonagricultural work force) was reached in 1945. The absence of union activity, then, is not sufficient reason for the decline in ACTU assistance. A combination of membership losses to the armed forces and the continuing priority given to intra-union faction fighting by the ACTU were largely responsible for this decline. Of 120 cases of ACTU advice and aid to unionists during 1942, for example, only twenty-two involved strikes, organizing drives, or complaints against employers. The largest part of the remainder involved advice or action in intra-union affairs.[96]

Paradoxically, ACTU educational efforts expanded during the war years, while support and chapter activities declined. A Newark labor school was organized by the diocese with the assistance of Newark ACTU president James E. Nolan, in October of 1942. The same month saw the establishment of another ACTU-affiliated diocesan labor school in Waterbury, Connecticut. By October of the following year the total of Connecticut labor schools had been increased to eight. Another of the ACTU's special industry schools was also established during 1942 among members of the Brother-hood of Railway Clerks. During 1944 four more ACTU labor schools were organized. These included the Colon School of Social Action in Queens, directed by ACTU executive board member Joe Mohen, a Consolidated Edison union officer, the Holy Name Labor School in lower Manhattan, and the All Saints and Resurrection labor schools, both in Harlem.[97]

This expansion continued into 1945 with the addition of five more schools. The Bronx district added two more labor schools in February and two others were organized, at Incarnation High School in Manhattan and in Rockland County. A Rhode Island "roving labor school" was established in October under the direction of an "old friend of the ACTU," the Reverend Edmund J. Brock. Both the new and the more established schools continued to enroll substantial numbers of students during the war. The Rhode Island School instructed more than 450 unionists in sessions at Providence, Woonsocket, and Pawtucket, while the older New Rochelle Labor School graduated 173 students in the spring of 1943.

This remarkable expansion of ACTU educational activity, in the face of decline on other fronts, owed a good deal to the support and sponsorship of the ecclesiastical districts of Connecticut, New York, and Rhode Island and the fact that the faculty of these schools, largely clerical, was not subject to the draft as were the lay members of the ACTU. The number of workers new to unionism also increased tremendously with the influx of younger, black, and women workers during the war, hence there was a ready supply of students. The schools also served to maximize the proselytizing impact of that minority of ACTU members who were not in the armed forces. Another significant reason for the ACTU stress on labor education, of course, was the schools' function as important recruiting grounds for the continuing fight against the left wing in the unions.[98]

The ACTU caucus in Teamsters' local 456 in Yonkers, for example, which successfully ran Actist John Acropolis for business manager, had its origins in ACTU labor-school graduates. Similarly, an ACTU caucus and newspaper in the Brotherhood of Railway Clerks, which looked to a "major operation" on the union, originated with lodge 2125 members who were students at ACTU schools. Connecticut labor schools also produced cadre for an ACTU-supported caucus in the left-wing Mine, Mill and Smelter Workers, which intended to "get rid of all known communists in executive positions."[99]

From 1942 through 1945, the ACTU continued its preoccupation with the battle against the left wing in the unions, though the war affected the level of activity in this quarter also. The major target during 1942 was the TWU and its president, Mike Quill. Quill was attacked for a trip to the U.S.S.R., for alleged raiding, for following "communist leadership," and for his role in the expulsion of ACTU member Patrick Reilly from the TWU. Reilly had been expelled for what the union hearing board termed slanderous attacks on the TWU. CLDL attorney John Sheehan's defense of Reilly was something more than a civil-liberties fight, however. Reilly, a Fifth Avenue bus conductor, had been the campaign manager of the ACTU-supported "Rank and File of the TWU" caucus, which had unsuccessfully challenged the left wing for union office.

The ACTU campaigned to reinstate Reilly throughout 1941 and 1942 and the court case was the focus of the ACTU's struggle with the TWU leadership. The publicity around the Reilly affair and

Sheehan's success in securing a court order for his reinstatement in January of 1942 encouraged other TWU dissidents and expanded the ACTU's network of contacts in that union. By May another anti-communist caucus had been organized, in local 100 of the TWU. Sheehan defended this group against union charges that it was encouraging the UMW to raid the TWU.[100]

The ACTU continued its anti-communist activity in the UE during 1942 and began efforts also within the ACA. The ACTU had organized its own industry school for ACA members during 1941 to compete with a left-wing school in the union. This school served to recruit members for an opposition caucus in this union, which used ACTU headquarters for its meetings and leaflet production. January of that year brought electoral victory to the ACTU caucus in the large Pittsburgh UE local 601 and the defeat of the left-wing members of the executive board. In December 1942 the ACTU applauded a "right-wing victory" in the elections in UE local 1217 which elevated Actist Edward Squitieri to chief steward. ACTU Chaplain the Reverend William F. Kelly was subsequently involved in mediating a contract for the local. The UE fight developed, of necessity, more slowly than that in the TWU, since the UE was the largest and strongest left-wing CIO union, but the ACTU was gradually building contacts and caucuses in this union which would serve as a base for a major campaign in the postwar period.[101]

Through its Speakers' Bureau or assistance with meeting space and publicity, the ACTU also, during 1942, initiated or developed contacts and caucuses in the IBT, the Railway Express Clerks, the Candy Workers, and the Hotel Telephone Operators unions. This increased representation in AFL unions, in addition to its CIO network, put the ACTU in a position to approve and support an AFL "drive against communism" as well as a parallel drive to defeat the left in the New York State CIO convention of 1942. Opposition to the CIO left was drawing the ACTU generally closer to the AFL and to its position on labor unity. In January of 1942 the ACTU endorsed the AFL proposals for CIO dissolution and "regretted" the CIO executive board's continuing refusal to consider unification on AFL terms. When the 1942 CIO convention confirmed the decision, the ACTU response was that such intransigence only served the communists, since unification "means their liquidation."

Labor unity had formerly been supported by the ACTU as a measure to strengthen labor in negotiations and public policy, but was now viewed simply as the best way to defeat the communists and insure a conservative American labor movement. Increasing support for other right-wingers within the CIO followed also from the ACTU's offensive against the left wing. The ACTU therefore offered its unqualified support to the "powerful right-wing leaders" at the CIO convention, Thomas of the UAW, Rieve of the Textile Workers, and Dalrymple of the Rubber Workers, while both cultivating and pressuring centrist leaders such as President Philip Murray.[102]

The ACTU's factional battle with the left wing continued at a brisk pace during 1943, despite the effects of the war and the adherence of many union centrists and conservatives to a wartime "united front" policy. In one major effort, the ACTU organized a "save the union" caucus in the Scovill and Chase, Connecticut, locals of the left-wing MMSW. The Reverend Donnelly, director of the Waterbury Labor School, carried on an intensive campaign in that year against MMSW President Reed Robinson for his alleged communist affiliations. This campaign ultimately resulted in Robinson's defeat and Donnelly's appointment to the Connecticut State Board of Mediation and Arbitration.[103]

State authorities, such as Michigan Governor Van Wagoner, who commended the ACTU for its "stabilizing influence" on labor, were obviously attracted to the ACTU.[104] Actist priests serving as mediators could be counted on to promote class harmony and to defuse potential conflicts. The Reverend Donnelly joined ACTU priests Rice, Hensler, Boland, and Cronin on state or municipal labor-relations bodies. Their official activities were paralleled by the unofficial mediation efforts of many other ACTU priests in individual disputes. These ACTU mediators were not loath, either, to throw their offices into the fight against the left wing on occasion. The Reverend Rice, for example, upheld as arbitrator a decision by the Independent Towel Supply Company of Philadelphia to fire left-wing laundry worker Alice Burkhart for "troublemaking" on behalf of her union.[105]

The ACTU also supported caucuses during 1943 in the Oil Workers' Organizing Committee, the ILWU, the UE, the Hatters'

Union, local 32-B of the AFL Building Services Employees' Union and the Shipbuilders' Union. The ACTU Oil Workers caucus attempted in February 1943 to rescind the appointment of a leftist, Milton Kaufman, as New Jersey organizational director for the Oil Workers. They were unsuccessful. An anti-communist rank-and-file caucus was also organized in local 43 of the Marine and Shipbuilding Workers' Union in Baltimore with the assistance of Baltimore city mediator and "friend of the ACTU," the Reverend John F. Cronin.[106]

The 1943 UE convention revealed, according to the ACTU, that a "well-oiled CP machine" was "bossing the UE." The ACTU-supported opposition was defeated and the ACTU called on the rank and file to rise to the "crying need for a strong right-wing movement to clean out the sorry mob" of left-wingers. ACTU-UE members steeled themselves for a long struggle. A fight also developed in New Orleans local 207 of the ILWU. Here an ACTU priest, the Reverend Jerome A. Drolet, was active in advising members who opposed Harry Bridges' leadership of the union. Father Drolet was successful in securing a court order reinstating opposition leader Willie Dorsey, who had been expelled by the international union, and in helping the caucus organize for a prolonged fight against the union leadership. The fight lasted into February 1944 and concluded with local 207's secession from the ILWU and affiliation with the Retail Workers' Union, whose top leadership included several Actists. This was the third left-wing CIO union which had been split on the initiative of the ACTU and it would not be the last.[107]

The ACTU reached a nadir of activity in 1944 and 1945. Even the high-priority struggle against the left wing declined in the face of membership losses to the armed forces. The only major ACTU factional fighting involved UAW locals in Detroit. During 1945 Detroit Packard UAW local 190 sustained a "right-wing victory." Nine ACTU-supported conservatives were elected to union office in the spring of that year. And in June 1945 Actists were a major factor in the election of an anti-communist slate in the Ford River Rouge UAW (local 600) council elections. A number of Actists were also quietly elected to union office in these largely uneventful years. Contacts were also cultivated in the ILGWU and ILA. Otherwise the

ACTU was forced to carry on its battle with the left largely in print during the last two years of the war.[108]

A number of important themes emerged during these two years. Denunciation of the left-wing–led CIO unions, of course, continued. The preference for affiliation with the AFL, rather than with a left-wing CIO union, emerged once again in the case of an ACA campaign to organize the New York City Western Union. The ACTU recommended that the workers instead support the AFL Commercial Telegraphers' Union, in which an ACTU executive board member was active. The ACTU's campaign on behalf of the Immigration Department's attempt to deport Harry Bridges, president of the ILWU, sharpened as well. Newspaper Guild President Milton Murray's opposition to efforts to defend Bridges received an ACTU commendation and inspired a demand that the rest of the CIO "stop coddling the left-wingers." This position paralleled the ACTU's earlier denunciation of the release from prison of Earl Browder, Communist party general secretary, as "an unprecedented blow to labor."[109]

The ACTU continued its hostility to political action by labor, especially where the left was represented, in two significant actions in 1944 and 1945. The ACTU opposed a CIO executive board decision in February 1944 to organize community councils to coordinate labor's political initiatives. The Actists' opposition was caused by the fact that many of the municipal councils were dominated by the left. Left-wing political action was also the target of the ACTU when it attacked a twenty-four–hour strike of the ILWU and the NMU, to protest delays in the return of G.I.'s after VE day, as an "abuse of a legitimate labor weapon."[110]

In 1944 the Actists also began to take an interest in the political complexion of postwar Europe. In early 1944 the ACTU supported Cardinal Spellman's defense of the Franco regime in an apparent attempt to head off sentiment for an allied invasion of Falangist Spain. The Actists also endorsed the Vatican's condemnation of the Italian "Catholic Communist Party" and "Christian Left." These formations had been organized as vehicles for Catholics, many of whom had worked with the left in the resistance, to participate in a United Front coalition in Italy without running the risk of excommunication. The ACTU reminded its readers that the papal decision extended automatic excommunication to members of those two organizations as well as any would-be "Catholic Communists" in the United States.[111]

The ACTU had always opposed united action with the left and the possibility that such coalitions, based on the resistance movements, would arise in Europe sharpened the organization's attitudes on alliance with the left. The same policy held, of course, for the United States, where leftists also hoped to continue and expand united-front activities begun in support of the war effort. Such an alliance with the communists was altogether out of the question in the ACTU's view, since the Communist party was guilty of "violation of everything we hold dear." The differences were simply "irre-concilable." But the ACTU also warned Catholics against slackening their hostility to the socialists merely because the communists were worse. On the contrary, "the socialists generally form the great present danger precisely because they are patient and non-violent." Thus the ACTU, far from concluding that the postwar period might offer the possibility of work with the left, was convinced instead that the struggle between the left and the right in the union movement would intensify, and that erstwhile union centrists would be forced to follow the example of the ACTU's own uncompromising opposition to radicalism.[112]

The postwar period would demand more in the way of reconstruction policy than hostility to radicalism, however. The reconstruction debate also provided a new opportunity for the ACTU to promote the corporative organization of the American economy. By February of 1944 the ACTU had begun such a campaign. The Bishops' Statement on Reconstruction of 1919 was urged as a "solid and inspirational" basis for reconstruction discussion. As a mechanism for consideration of this and other alternatives and for implementation of reconstruction policy, the ACTU supported a tripartite committee representing labor, business, and the public.

The Actists viewed the organization of industrial councils on the pattern of Catholic corporative theory, however, as the best and most comprehensive solution for the postwar period. Voluntary action by such councils, on the basis of class harmony and reciprocity, would insure an equitable division of power and income in the postwar period. The councils would also address a long-range solution to the problems of just wages, prices, and profits, worker participation in management, self-government of the economy, radicalism, and spiritual malaise. Despite CIO President Philip Murray's support for the industrial-council scheme, however, the ACTU was not able to garner much support for it in the unions. While the corporative themes of class harmony and reciprocity were incorporated in all discussion of reconstruction policy, the postwar industrial struggle made them seem rather beside the point. The specific corporative program of industrial councils, for all the reasons previously cited, was never seriously considered. As had been the case since its founding, the ACTU proved much more successful in promoting its negative program of anti-communism than its positive program of cooperative reorganization of the American economy. The former had occupied the center stage throughout the organization's history, while the latter was treated as a "long-range solution" and relegated to an ever more distant future. In the postwar period, even more than before, it was opposition to radicalism that was to define the ACTU and to occupy its attention. [113]

The years between 1938 and 1945, then, were characterized by initially rapid, then slower expansion of the ACTU and by an increasingly sharp focus on the struggle with the left wing in the unions. The ideological and practical ambiguities of the first months of the organization's existence gave way, subsequent to the Gerson decision, to staunchly conservative aims and practices and, particularly, to a first-priority commitment to the struggle with the left, whatever the effect on the labor movement.

The consolidation of this conservative direction after the Gerson affair in 1938 laid the basis for a phenomenal expansion of ACTU organization and activity. From 1938 through 1945 the number of chapters increased from one to twenty-one. Several of these chapters organized their own publications, speakers' bureaus, and radio shows. During the same period ACTU labor education efforts increased even more significantly. The Catholic Union of the Unemployed and the Catholic Labor Defense League were initiated as well. The national conventions of the ACTU formalized the organization's structure, instituted security and discipline, adopted policy, and confirmed the anti-communist direction which had prevailed since 1938.

The ACTU's struggle against the left in the unions began in earnest during these years and accelerated until it was the major practical work of the organization. The labor schools, the CLDL, and the CUU were all, in considerable measure, initiated as alternatives to Marxist organizations and each served as an important source of ACTU union contacts and recruits for the fight with the left. The ACTU's union-support activity served a similar function.

ACTU industry conferences were organized in a large number of unions from 1938 to 1945. These conferences, which often included non-Catholics, functioned as the spearhead of more broadly-based conservative caucuses in these unions. Such caucuses were active, even during the relatively lean war years, and a considerable number of Actists were elected to local and international union offices. Apart from agitation and electoral activity against the left, these caucuses also initiated several secessions from left-wing CIO affiliates. Secessionism underlined the ACTU's commitment to defeating the radicals, no matter what the cost to the unions involved, and prefigured the ACTU's vanguard role in the purge movement of the postwar period. The ACTU's increasing virulence toward communist unionists led it also to oppose the release of Earl Browder, Communist party general secretary, from prison and to support the deportation of Harry Bridges, the left-wing ILWU leader.

The ACTU's opposition to radicalism brought it closer to the AFL in these years. AFL locals were supported over left-wing CIO unions in a number of NLRB representation contests and ACTU-led secessions in several CIO unions led to AFL affiliation. The AFL's unity campaign was likewise endorsed by the ACTU, since the radicals in the CIO might thus be more effectively isolated.

The years between 1938 and 1945 saw a period of ACTU organization, expansion, and strike-support activity, followed by a "mature" period of consolidation and preoccupation with anti-radical factional struggle within the unions. Chapter organization and union-support activity gave way by 1940 to a nearly total commitment to the anti-communist campaign. The war years imposed manpower burdens on the ACTU, particularly in 1944 and 1945, but did not affect this essential direction. By the end of the war, the ACTU was thus well established in the unions and experienced in the struggle with the left. It had graduated thousands of unionists from its many labor schools, including a large number of local leaders, and had secured additional contacts and recruits through its unemployment organizing, legal work, and union-support activity. ACTU members were officers in many AFL and CIO unions and, through a network of ACTU conferences and broader caucuses, it exerted a considerable influence on the unions, particularly those unions in which the left was strong. In 1945 the ACTU was ready to mobilize this constituency for an even more intensive struggle to expel the left-wing unions from the CIO.

NOTES

1. By 1941 both the Detroit and the Pittsburgh chapters had eclipsed the New York chapter in total membership. The Detroit chapter was probably at least as active and perhaps even more influential in the Michigan CIO than the New York chapter was in its state. "Report of the National Director," May 1941, p. 5, ACTU files; *Labor Leader* 2, no. 1.

2. *Labor Leader* 1, nos. 11, 24, and 44.

3. Ibid., 1, nos. 11, 39, and 24.

4. On Rice's activity and views see his debate with Max Schachtman, "Marxism vs. Catholicism"; Weinberg, "Priests, Workers and Communists," *Harper's*, pp. 49–56; Kampelman, *The Communist Party vs the CIO*, p. 135; Harrington, "Catholics in the Labor Movement," pp. 240–42, 253; "ACTU" (Rice's column), 1937–1966; *Labor Leader* 1, no. 35, 2, nos. 1, 17, and 20, 3, no. 17, 4, nos. 2 and 5, 5, no. 3, 12, no. 7.

5. *Labor Leader* 1, no. 22, 12, no. 9.

6. Ibid., 1, no. 22.

7. *Michigan Labor Leader* 2, no. 11.

8. *Labor Leader* 1, no. 42.

9. This chapter, too, was larger than the New York chapter by 1941. "Report of the National Director," May 1941, ACTU files, p. 5; *Labor Leader* 1, no. 42.

10. *The ACTU: A Catholic Apostolate of Labor*, p. 8; *Labor Leader* 2, nos. 1 and 8. Norman McKenna later put his speaking and organizational talents to use as the director of the United States Information Agency's Office of Labor Information. Interview with George Donahue, July 22, 1974.

11. It was O'Brien who authored the statement of the Catholic Union of the Unemployed in opposition to "private ownership [of industry], when such ownership is excessive and harmful to the common good." *Labor Leader* 1, no. 7.

12. *Labor Leader* 1, no. 7.

13. Ibid., 1, no. 13.

14. On the *Catholic Worker* and the ACTU see Day, *The Long Loneliness*, pp. 220–21. Though he appreciated *Catholic Worker* assistance in the ACTU's early months, George Donahue felt that they were "escapist" and "unrealistic." Interview, July 22, 1974.

15. There were actually three different left-wing unemployed organizations. One group was organized by followers of A. J. Muste, another by the Socialist party, and another by the Communist party. See Karsh and Garman, "The Impact of the Political Left," pp. 87–97.

16. *Labor Leader* 1, no. 14.

17. The Flint local split between a left-wing and a conservative caucus and the organizing and manuevering of the ACTU-affiliated group, led by Carl Thrasher, succeeded in dividing the leftists and securing the election of the conservative group's slate of officers, including Thrasher. *Labor Leader* 1, nos. 10 and 12.

18. *Labor Leader* 1, no. 18.

19. "The ACTU: A Catholic Apostolate of Labor," pp. 13–15,;*Labor Leader* 1, no. 40, 2, no. 17, 5, no. 15.

20. Theodore Draper, *American Communism and Soviet Russia* (New York: Viking Press, 1960), p. 181.

21. Such disputes typically pitted the CLDL and opposition forces within a local against either a left-wing or a corrupt union leadership. See *Labor Leader* 1, nos. 15, 31, and 40, 2, no. 20, 4, no. 15, 5, nos. 2, 3, 9, and 15.

22. *Labor Leader* 1, no. 24.

23. See the discussion of this shift in emphasis in chapter 5.

24. On Ryan see Johnson, *Crime on the Labor Front*, pp. 152–155.

25. Indeed, the original campaign against corruption was largely inspired by a fear that it was "threatening to foster the spread of Communism," *Labor Leader* 1, no. 34, 3, no. 15, 8, no. 17.

26. *Labor Leader* 5, nos. 2, 3, 9, and 15.

27. Ibid., 1, no. 1.

28. Ibid., 1, no. 2, 2, no. 17, 6, no. 1, 9, nos. 1 and 7, 10, no. 6. Of these schools Philip Taft remarked, "The education given is designed not merely to supply the individual with knowledge but also to equip him to meet the arguments of Communists and others who would direct the labor movement into Marxist channels." Taft, "The ACTU," p. 213. Approximately fifteen percent of the Xavier Labor School graduates were non-Catholic. This was the largest school. Johnson, *Crime on the Labor Front*, p. 216.

29. John Cort, "Catholics in Trade Unions," *Commonweal*, May 5, 1939, p. 35.

30. *Labor Leader* 1, nos. 1 and 9.

31. Ibid., 2, no. 1.

32. Ibid., 1, no. 18, 2, no. 1.

33. Ibid., 1, no. 9.

34. Ibid., 1, nos. 33 and 44.

35. Cort, "Catholics in Trade Unions," p. 35; *Labor Leader* 1, nos. 5 and 33, 2, no. 1.

36. *Labor Leader* 1, no. 38.

37. Ibid., 2, no. 7.

38. The Detroit ACTU, for example, operated thirty-six parish schools in conjunction with the diocese in 1940. *Michigan Labor Leader*, 2, no. 21;*Labor Leader* 1, no. 9, 2, nos. 17, 18, and 20; Cort, "Catholics in Trade Unions," p. 35.

39. Richard Deverall, "Commonwealth College," *Commonweal*, April 28, 1939, p. 9. The ACTU was definitely not impressed by the ideological content of the courses at Commonwealth and in September of 1938 they demanded the resignation of the school's director. *Labor Leader* 1, no. 35.

40. The possibility that such ethnic-political identification might be anti-Semitic did not

seem to occur to the editors, though on other occasions the ACTU had condemned anti-Semitism. See, for example, *Labor Leader* 2, no. 13.

41. Weinberg, "Priests, Workers and Communists," pp. 52–53; *Labor Leader* 1, no. 22, 2, no. 1.

42. Detroit Workers' School course outlines and *Information Bulletins*, Detroit ACTU Collection; *Labor Leader* 1, nos. 9 and 21.

43. The presidents of the UWU and the Newspaper Guild and regional and international offices of the UAW, the Newspaper Guild, and the RU were graduates of ACTU labor schools. Other examples of labor-school graduates quickly organizing against the left involved the TWU, the MMSW, and the largest UE local, 601 in Pittsburgh. The *Daily Worker*, March 27, 1950, p. 1; Kampelman, *The Communist Party vs. the CIO*, p. 153; *Labor Leader* 1, nos. 1, 29, and 32, 2, no. 11.

44. *Labor Leader* 1, nos. 18, 21, 23, 25, and 30.

45. Ibid., 1, nos. 30, 31, 32, and 33.

46. Ibid., 1, nos. 18, 33, 37, and 39, 2, nos. 1 and 21, 4, no. 19.

47. Ibid., 1, nos. 23, 25, 33, and 39, 2, no. 1.

48. The ACTU also attempted to recruit and establish contacts among black New Yorkers through social activities and fund-raising parties in Harlem. *Labor Leader* 1, nos. 5, 15, and 18, 2, no. 11.

49. Ironically, the TWU was left-led and the ACTU's bitter foe in other connections. "Resolution on Racial Discrimination," ACTU National Convention, Pittsburgh, 1941, Detroit ACTU Collection; *Labor Leader* 1, nos. 23, 30, and 31, 5, no. 13.

50. *Labor Leader* columnist "Syntax," in reply to one such claim by a black Office of Production Management representative, stated that "equality in job opportunity is sound trade unionism and one of the goals of the ACTU." The Actist thought the elite Protestant craft unions were worse than the Irish-dominated unions. *Labor Leader* 5, no. 3

51. *Labor Leader* 1, no. 15, 5, no. 9; *Michigan Wage Earner* 6, no. 18.

52. These tactics of containment, isolation, and opposition to the left had been Catholic practice since the 1880s. See Saposs, "Catholic Church and the Labor Movement," pp. 225–30 and 294–98; Karson, *American Labor Unions and Politics*, pp. 219–35.

53. "Bishops' Statement on Reconstruction," in Ryan, *Social Reconstruction*, pp. 225–26; Ryan, *A Living Wage*, pp. 3–4; Ryan, *Social Reconstruction*, p. 42.

54. *Labor Leader* 3, nos. 1 and 4, 4, no. 4; Ryan, *Social Reconstruction*, p. 42.

55. The Detroit chapter was unusual in the active and leading role played by women Actists. Marguerite Galagan was president of the chapter in 1947 and Helen Storen wrote a *Michigan Labor Leader* column, "Mostly for Women," which, despite its title, was largely about union organization. The figures were obtained through a survey of names of ACTU members and officers and participants in ACTU activities. *Labor Leader* 1, nos. 25, 30, and 41, 3, no. 12; *Michigan Labor Leader* 2, nos. 14 and 24, *Michigan Wage Earner* 4, no. 6; *The Leaven*, Detroit ACTU newsletter, December 21, 1949, p. 2.

56. *The Hearst Strike* (Chicago: ACTU, 1939), pp. 1–3; the Reverend John . Hayes to Paul Weber, April 24, 1939, Detroit ACTU Collection; *Michigan Labor Leader* 1, no. 7; *Labor Leader* 2, nos. 10, 14, and 17.

57. "Labor and the Church," *Newsweek*, July 31, 1939, p. 25; *Labor Leader* 2, nos. 13 and 17, 3, no. 3.

58. McKenna, *The Catholic and His Union*," pp. 7–8; *Michigan Labor Leader* 1, no. 1; *Labor Leader* 2, nos. 8, 15, 17, and 18, 3, no. 5.

59. *The Hearst Strike*, pp. 1–3; *Michigan Labor Leader* 1, nos. 1 and 7; *Labor Leader* 2, nos. 7 and 15, 3, no. 5.

60. *Labor Leader* 2, no. 13.

61. Ibid.

62. Kelly, *The ACTU and Its Critics*, p. 2; "Inter-Chapter Memorandum Number 17," September 11, 1941, p. 1; "ACTU Constitution," p. 7, ACTU files; *Michigan Labor Leader* 1, no. 3; "ACTU Transit Conference Report," August 7, 1940, p. 2; *Irish Echo*, January 24, 1942, p. 4; "Report of the National Director," 1941, p. 8; *Labor Leader* 2, nos. 16 and 18, 3, nos. 5, 6, 7, and 14.

63. *Labor Leader* 1, nos. 1, 13, 21, 35, 40, and 45, 2, no. 11, 3, nos. 5 and 6, 4, no. 10.

64. Ibid., 2, nos. 4, 7, and 18.

65. The ACTU's "Statement of Principles" itself cautioned that, while "no Catholic can remain in a union that is run along Marxist or unChristian lines," Catholics have a duty to attempt to unite with others to overthrow left-wing domination; p. 2, ACTU files.

66. Brophy to Roger Larkin, August 2, 1939, ACTU files; *Labor Leader* 2, nos. 13 and 14.

67. This ACTU-supported opposition group was led by Raymond Wescott and John Brooks of local 100. Both of them and ten other members of the opposition leadership attended the Xavier Labor School. "Transit Conference Report," ACTU files, pp. 2–4; Weinberg, "Priests, Workers and Communists," pp. 52–53; *Labor Leader* 2, nos. 16 and 20, 3, no. 5.

68. "Inter-Chapter Memorandum Number 17," September 11, 1941, p. 1; "Detroit Workers' School," brochure, pp. 1–3; *Labor Leader* 3, nos. 3, 9, 15, and 17.

69. *Labor Leader* 1, no. 7, 3, nos. 7 and 12.

70. "Inter-Chapter Memorandum Number 17," September 11, 1941, p. 1; Kelly, *The ACTU and Its Critics*, pp. 2–3; *Labor Leader* 3, nos. 7, 12, 15, and 16; *Michigan Labor Leader* 1, no. 2.

71. Carey to Roger Larkin, May 14, 1940, ACTU files.

72. Detroit ACTU "News Guild Conference," minutes, April 16, 1940, Detroit ACTU Collection; *Labor Leader* 3, nos. 9, 12, 14, and 16.

73. ACTU leaders in New York, commenting on a left-wing led ILA strike in the fall of 1945, admitted that, "when it became clear that the choice was between Joe Ryan and the Communists, our members went back to work." "The Upright Spirit," *Fortune*, November 1946, p. 188; *Labor Leader* 3, nos. 12 and 5.

74. As has been noted previously, these "Communist-Fascist-Nazi" resolutions were largely directed at the communists. Though it was strategically helpful to associate the Fascists with the left, the ACTU and the other conservatives seldom sought to act on the condemnations of Fascism expressed in these resolutions (or, in the case of the ACTU, in their own constitution and statement of principles). The ACTU did not actively oppose the Bund, the Fascist Italian-American organizations, or such native Fascists as Lawrence Dennis, nor did it place much emphasis (if some of his supporters may be considered Fascist) on opposition to Coughlin. The ACTU, in fact, was sympathetic to the Nationalists in Spain. *Labor Leader* 3, nos. 6 and 16. See also DeCaux, *Labor Radical*, p. 361.

75. Opposition to everything the left wing supported, of course, could involve the ACTU in contradictions. For example, though the ACTU initially opposed U.S. entry into World War II, it also opposed Catholic and labor participation in the communist-supported "The Yanks Aren't Coming" campaign from 1939 through 1941. Though the ACTU, like other anti-communists, would later attack the CP for its change of position on the war, its own position changed dramatically. While in September of 1939 the *Michigan Labor Leader* had argued

editorially that "there is no more democracy today in England or France than there is in Germany" (an even more extreme position than that of the CP), after Pearl Harbor the ACTU immediately pledged "our services in the nation's united effort to achieve victory over the enemies of our country"; telegram to Roosevelt, December 8, 1941, copy, ACTU files; *Michigan Labor Leader* 1, no. 1; *Labor Leader* 3, nos. 4 and 12; *Michigan Wage Earner* 4, no. 19.

76. Cort, "Catholics in Trade Unions," p. 36; *Labor Leader* 1, no. 15.

77. "On Labor Unity," "On Organizing the Unorganized," "On National Defense," "On Communism, Naxism and Fascism," 1940 Conventions Resolution, ACTU files; "Catholic Trade Unionists Meet Here," *Cleveland Press*, August 30, 1940, p. 1; *Michigan Labor Leader* 2, no. 19; *Labor Leader* 1, no. 13, 3, nos. 15, 17, and 18.

78. *Michigan Labor Leader* 2, no. 4.

79. The importance of the labor schools in the ACTU's anti-communist campaign is underlined by George Kelly in his pamphlet, *The ACTU and Its Critics*. Kelly, in the course of a passage (p. 3) defending the ACTU conferences against charges of "interference," stated that ACTU intervention within unions "begins in the labor schools." The Yonkers and Pittsburgh area schools were also to play an important role in developing leadership and support for the anti-communist struggle in the UE. "Xavier Labor School," brochure, ACTU files, pp. 1–5; *Michigan Labor Leader* 2, no. 21; *Labor Leader* 4, nos. 1, 4, and 12.

80. "The ACTU Supports Reeves' Worker," leaflet, ACTU files; *Labor Leader* 4, nos. 8, 9, and 10.

81. *Michigan Labor Leader* 2, nos. 10, 11, 20, and 24; *Labor Leader* 4, nos. 7, 9, 11 and 12, 5, no. 1.

82. On the TWU, UOPWA, and UE, see Kampelman, *The Communist Party vs. the CIO*, pp. 45, 129, 135, 153, 180; Galenson, *The CIO Challenge to the AFL*, pp. 239–65; DeCaux, *Labor Radical*, pp. 403–427, 509–513; Bernstein, *The Turbulent Years*, pp. 607–615; Taft, "The ACTU," p. 217; Weinberg, "Priests, Workers and Communists," p. 50; ACTU "Transit Conference" list, 1939, ACTU files.

83. See the discussion of the UOPWA in *Proceedings of the Tenth Constitutional Convention of the CIO*, November 22–26, 1948, pp. 336–42.

84. *Michigan Labor Leader* 3, no. 23; *Labor Leader* 4, no. 2; *Michigan Wage Earner* 4, nos. 6 and 7.

85. Victor Reisel, "Focus on Labor," *New York Post*, May 3, 1943, p. 26; "Report of the CLDL," September, 1940, ACTU files, pp. 3–5; *Labor Leader* 4, nos. 4, 5, 7, 14, 15, and 18.

86. The ACTU would prove to be the most important influence among conservatives in local 601. In Kampelman's estimation, the opposition group was "spearheaded by a branch of the ACTU, led by Reverend Rice." Harrington, "Catholics in the Labor Movement," pp. 240–42; *Labor Leader* 4, no. 5, 5, no. 3; Kampelman, *The Communist Party vs. the CIO*, p. 135.

87. On Catholic activity and influence within, and preference for, the AFL, see chapter 1. *Labor Leader* 2, nos. 4, 17, and 18, 4, nos. 1 and 4.

88. "Report of the National Director," May 30–June 2, 1941, pp. 3–13.

89. "Articles of Federation," pp. 1–3.

90. On CIO officers' tolerance for the left wing see Madison, *American Labor Leaders*, p. 327.

91. In addition to endorsing the national defense program, the 1941 ACTU convention resolved in favor of the industry-council plan (which Murray had recently endorsed), AFL-CIO unity, and a living wage. Anti-labor legislation was opposed as was racial discrimination. The

convention also directed Actists to work for prohibitions on communists in union office. The convention was held in Pittsburgh, August 30–September 1, 1941. Delegates from Detroit, New York, Milwaukee, Chicago, Cleveland, Pittsburgh, and Newark attended. "On Industry Councils," "On National Defense," "On AFL-CIO Unity," "On Living Wages," "On Anti-Labor Legislation," "On Racial Discrimination," "On Communists in Union Office," 1941 Convention Resolutions, ACTU files; *Labor Leader* 4, nos. 12 and 13.

92. "On National Defense," 1941 Convention Resolution, ACTU files; "Catholic Trade Unionists Meet Here," *Cleveland Press*, August 30, 1940, p. 1; *Michigan Labor Leader* 1, no. 1, 2, nos. 13 and 19; *Labor Leader* 1, no. 13, 3, nos. 15, 17, and 18, nos. 1, 4, and 8. The ACTU's position on national defense largely paralleled that of the CIO, especially after Murray's endorsement of the industry-council plan. See "Minutes of the CIO Executive Board, June 4, 1940," p. 4; Philip Murray, *The CIO and National Defense* (Washington, D.C.: American Council on Public Affairs, 1941); Philip Murray, *Organized Labor and Production* (New York: Harper's, 1946.)

93. The ACTU's support for wartime strikes proved to be a selective one however. For example, the 1943 anthracite strike was opposed by the ACTU, which held that it "cannot be justified on any grounds." Nearly all of the strikes which involved left-wing unions were opposed by the Actists. Morris, "Vatican Conspiracy in the Labor Movement," p. 22; *Labor Leader* 6, no. 1.

94. *Michigan Labor Leader* 3, no. 23; *Michigan Wage Earner* 5, no. 8, 6, no. 18; *Labor Leader* 5, nos. 3 and 4.

95. On the impact of the war on the ACTU see Cort, "Ten Years of ACTU," pp. 143–44; *Labor Leader* 4, no. 19, 5, nos. 1 and 3, 6, no. 5; *Michigan Labor Leader* 2, no. 13.

96. Reisel, "Focus on Labor," p. 26; *Labor Leader*, 6, nos. 1 and 5, 7, nos. 12 and 19, 8, no. 1; *Michigan Wage Earner* 4, no. 17.

97. "Newark Labor School," brochure, ACTU files, pp. 1–4; *Labor Leader* 5, no. 17, 6, no. 5, 7, nos. 4, 15, and 19.

98. This, of course, had been a major function of the ACTU's labor schools from the beginning. See Taft, "The ACTU," pp. 213–14; Johnson, *Crime on the Labor Front*, p. 216; *Labor Leader* 6, no. 11, 8, nos. 3, 11, and 17.

99. ACTU "Brotherhood of Railway Clerks Conference Report," May 1942, ACTU files, pp. 1–3; *Labor Leader* 5, no. 19, 6, nos. 1 and 5.

100. ACTU "TWU Conference Report," June 1942, ACTU files, pp. 1–5; *Labor Leader* 5, nos. 2, 5, and 9, 6, no. 5.

101. *Labor Leader* 5, nos. 3, 15, and 21, 6, no. 5.

102. ACTU "Hotel Telephone Operators Conference Report," July 1942, pp. 1–5; *Labor Leader* 5, nos. 2, 11, and 19, 6, no. 5.

103. ACTU "MMSW Conference Report," March 1943, ACTU files, pp. 2–3; *Labor Leader* 5, no. 19, 6, no. 2, 7, no. 9.

104. Several clerical mediators performed crucial functions for the federal administration. The Reverend Francis Haas, for example, was selected as a mediator by President Roosevelt during the Minneapolis Teamsters strike in 1934 and again during the unsuccessful AFL-CIO unity negotiations of 1938. See Art Preis, *Labor's Giant Step* (New York: Pathfinder, 1942), p. 30; Bernstein, *The Turbulent Years*, pp. 241–50, 700.

105. *Labor Leader* 4, nos. 2 and 9.

106. Ibid., 6, nos. 3, 15, and 21.

107. The Reverend Drolet was to play a significant role in the anti-communist struggle within the NMU also. "The Labor Priests," *Fortune*, January 1949, p. 152; *Labor Leader* 6, nos. 9, 13, and 15, 7, no. 5.

108. *Labor Leader* 7, nos. 1, 2, and 12, 8, nos. 4, 7, 11, and 20.

109. The ACTU was an important influence within the Newspaper Guild. ACTU members headed Newspaper Guild units in Chicago and Detroit. Actists Paul Weber and Robert Stern were to serve as international union secretary and Ralph Stern would become Newspaper Guild president in 1948. *The Hearst Strike*, pp. 1–3; *Labor Leader* 5, no. 11, 8, nos. 4 and 9; *Michigan Labor Leader* 1, nos. 1 and 7.

110. *Labor Leader* 7, no. 4, 8, no. 20.

111. On the Church and the French and Italian labor movements in the postwar period, see Camp, *Papal Ideology*, pp. 126–135. *Labor Leader* 7, nos. 1 and 15, 8, no. 1.

112. The ACTU's program, of course, paralleled actual developments in the postwar period. In one respect, however, they were in error. The socialists and the Schactmanite left socialists proved quite willing to follow the lead of other anti-communists in the purge that was to follow, and the ACTU eased its scruples sufficiently to allow them to join in. *Labor Leader* 7, nos. 1, 12, and 15, 8, no. 1.

113. The ACTU's corporative program was stymied by the same array of forces that opposed the prescriptions of the Bishops' Statement on Reconstruction in the post–World War I period. Anti-union employers and a communist-hunting government were loath to consider any program of "industrial cooperation," even one with the conservative implications of Catholic corporative theory. "Boulwarism" and McCarthyism, it seemed, were exclusive of "industrial cooperation." *Labor Leader* 5, no. 5, 6, no. 2, 7, nos. 4 and 11.

7 † "Throw Them to Hell Out":
The Drive to Purge the CIO Left Wing

The years 1946 through 1950 were the culmination of ACTU activity in the labor movement. From 1937 through 1945 the ACTU and its lay and clerical supporters had built a national organization and developed an important network of subsidiary organizations, schools, conferences, caucuses, and periodicals. The Actists had established themselves in significant positions within a number of unions by means of these activities, as well as their union-support work. From 1938 on the ACTU had focused on the struggle with the left wing in the CIO unions. The organization committed itself increasingly to this struggle, to the exclusion of union-support activities, during the years 1938 through 1945. By 1945 the Actists' single program plank for the unions was "dump the communists." After 1945 the ACTU was able to take advantage of the political realignment within the CIO, which favored the conservatives, to further its own organization and program. Anti-communism won increased support and powerful allies, within the union movement and without. The ACTU's position ultimately became that of the CIO itself and the left-wing unions were expelled.

The expulsion of the CIO left was not an easy event to engineer, nor was it an automatic corollary to a national policy which promoted anti-communism and confrontation with the Soviet Union. The left-wing CIO unions represented fifteen to twenty percent of the CIO membership. The left was strong also in several other important CIO unions and was a presence in most. Left-wingers, including Lee Pressman, general counsel, and Len DeCaux, editor of the *CIO News*, were national CIO officers. The left was much stronger than its

187

numbers would suggest, too, in the state and city organizations of the CIO and was an important force in the American Labor party, the Minnesota Farmer-Labor party, the Non-Partisan Leagues, and in some localities even the Democratic party. The left-wingers had been instrumental in all the CIO organizing drives and the CIO leaders were linked to them by significant organizational and often personal ties. The opponents of the leftists faced a difficult task, therefore, in seeking to dislodge them from the CIO altogether.[1]

The ACTU was the only conservative organization to concentrate on this task from the earliest days of the CIO. From its origin in February 1937 the ACTU had been committed to ideological if not active anti-communism. After the Gerson affair in March 1938, the Actists had abandoned their tentative progressive position in favor of conservative policies generally and active anti-communism in particular. The organization's constant demand was for a ban on CIO union office-holding and even membership by communists. And the ACTU consistently remained a right-wing pole within the CIO, despite the wavering of others. Some CIO figures, including Lewis, Murray, Carey, Hillman, and Reuther, might tolerate the communists because of their CIO work, a temporary factional alliance, or in the interest of CIO harmony or wartime labor unity. The Actists, however, would never work with the CP nor relax their demands for action against communists.[2]

This uncompromising position was not easily promoted in the CIO of 1937 to 1945. National CIO policy favored toleration of all political viewpoints and attacks on the "united front" were not viewed with favor. The necessity of united action in organizing drives in which the CIO faced employer and often political hostility confirmed this position even among those who detested the Communist party. To attack the communists was also to draw attention to their presence, which encouraged employer and AFL red-baiting and embarrassed political supporters of the CIO. In any case, the communists delivered organizing "results" and this counted for a great deal in the early years of the CIO. As a consequence, the left wing was treated respectfully, if not cordially, by the national CIO and shared in positions of influence and power within the organization.[3]

Those who challenged this position did so without the support of national CIO officers and usually in the face of their opposition. And they were most often unsuccessful. Homer Martin, the first president of the UAW, red-baited his opposition and ended up president of a tiny remnant of the UAW, supported largely by the Ford Motor Company. James Carey, president of the UE, promoted a resolution at the UE's 1941 convention which would have permitted UE locals to ban communists from union office. This proposal was defeated by a margin of greater than two to one and repudiated by Carey's own local. Carey himself was defeated for reelection and forced to retire to the glamorous, but letterhead position of CIO secretary. At Murray's insistence, he was quiet on the subject of communism.[4]

The ACTU faced similar opposition to its program of struggle with the communists. Some of its own members, as we have seen, challenged this direction in early 1938, but they quickly lost their reservations about the anti-communist campaign. Readers of the ACTU press and supporters of the organization, however, continued to criticize the organization's exclusive focus on combatting the left wing. The left-wingers, of course, replied in kind to the ACTU's attacks, though they were careful to try not to offend Catholic workers generally. The communist press regularly criticized the ACTU as "professional anti-communists," job hunters, religious splitters, and "clerical Fascists." The Trotskyists, before 1946, made similar criticisms. A number of unions, including the TWU, UE, UOPWA, NMU, ILWU, and ACA, rejected the ACTU's anti-communism and several complained that their attacks only helped employers and the AFL. Quill went so far as to characterize the ACTU as a "scab outfit" and a "company union." Even Carey was moved to protest the ACTU's anti-communist "boring-from-within." Murray, too, reprimanded the organization for its unbending anti-communism, which had led the Actists to circumvent union procedures and to oppose legitimate strikes led by left-wing unions.[5]

Despite such opposition, the ACTU maintained its fire on the communists. From 1938 through 1945 the Actists devoted an ever-increasing proportion of their resources and efforts to anti-communism. The organization's contacts and supporters were gained and trained through this issue. Since other potential anti-communists within the CIO adhered to official tolerance, or even depended on CP support, the ACTU during this period was the only national focus for conservatives in the CIO. The anti-communist issue was virtually ACTU property through 1945. This situation encouraged non-Catholic anti-communists, as well as Catholics who might not otherwise have chosen to work with a religious-based union faction, to join with the ACTU. The ACTU, therefore, was able to utilize the vacuum of conservative leadership to extend its own organization and support base. The result, as one Actist modestly put it, was that "Catholics in 1945 were in fair measure prepared to participate fruitfully in the anti-Communist campaign."[6]

The situation within the CIO in the postwar period made the prospects for such a campaign increasingly favorable. The wartime alliance with the Soviet Union was rapidly changing to confrontation and Cold War. Foreign-policy issues were increasingly interjected into CIO discussions and served to open a wedge in the "united front." At the same time, at least in the North, the CIO had concluded its most important organizing drives and the need for left-wing participation and militance became much less pressing. Walter Reuther in the UAW and other centrists and conservatives had freed themselves of dependence on internal left-wing support and were prepared also to "participate fruitfully" in the anti-communist campaign. Political divisions, especially the left's support for the Wallace campaign, also exacerbated the hostility of the CIO center and right. Finally, the passage of the Taft-Hartley Act placed severe restraints on labor and made it abundantly clear that the campaign against communism was now national policy.

The unions, then, were facing serious limitations on their freedom of action. The CIO leadership was subjected to considerable government pressure to toe the line on foreign-policy issues and anti-communism. The press and employers were crusading against communism and red-baiting the CIO and "public opinion" was responding accordingly. At the same time, considerable pressure was mounting internally, on the part of the ACTU and others, to purge the left-wing unions. The CIO leadership ultimately capitulated to this pressure. They hoped to minimize the impact of Taft-Hartley and anti-labor sentiment generally by disassociating the CIO from the left and joining the orgy of anti-communism and "Americanism." In doing so, they retreated from further CIO organizing, especially in the South, abandoned the CIO's traditional policies in support of militance and independent political action, and severely curtailed both union autonomy and membership democracy. The broad social and political involvement of the early CIO was also much reduced. Soon after the expulsions the CIO would rejoin the AFL under George Meany's leadership, which had the effect of cementing the conservative victory.[7]

During the postwar period, then, the ACTU was able to promote anti-communism in a climate favorable to its objectives and with the support of important figures within the CIO, ultimately President Murray himself. While the Actists had hardly pulled their punches previously, they were now able to count on CIO support for more extreme measures, including secession from the left-wing unions and even national CIO intervention against the left in individual unions. The ACTU also enjoyed the support of employers, the press, Congressional committees, and the Taft-Hartley machinery in their struggle with left-wing unions. Many other CIO members were now won to the anti-communist program and they tended to join the existing anti-communist caucuses, many of which had been initiated by the ACTU. The situation was entirely favorable to an anti-communist campaign and the Actists, the CIO's original anti-communists, threw their energies, resources, and experience into that struggle. The ACTU's role in the movement to expel the left-wing unions proved to be a crucial one.

PRELIMINARIES, 1946–1947

In 1946 and 1947 the ACTU carried out its own postwar organizational "reconstruction" and participated in the national reconstruction debate. ACTU armed forces veterans were reintegrated into the organization, suspended chapters were revived, and labor schools were begun or expanded. The ACTU also fought for the maintenance of price and rent controls and equal-employment safeguards. The most important arena of intensified activity, however, was the struggle with the left.

Some important developments occurred in this quarter in 1946 and 1947. ACTU conferences and caucuses were expanded and in several different unions the Actists expanded their contacts and organization among non-Catholic anti-communists. ACTU anti-communist campaigns for the first time began to be assisted by the national CIO and by some Trotskyists. The ACTU also muted its advocacy of union democracy and membership self-determination where left-wing unions were concerned. The Actists developed a model of "communist machine" control which served to justify national CIO intervention, secession, and raiding against these unions when the membership proved unwilling to depose their left-wing leaders. During 1946 and 1947 the Actists endorsed increased restrictions on the civil liberties of left-wing CIO members and demanded government intervention within the CIO should the CIO unions prove unwilling to "clean house." In every respect the ACTU's anti-communism became more virulent until the organization ceased to view the communist issue as an in-house CIO problem, but rather a matter of treason, sedition, and evil. The organization was approaching a position of "any means necessary" to defeat the left.

During 1946 the ACTU reorganized chapters and expanded its activities on several fronts. The New York chapter alone provided speakers on thirty occasions during the year to unions and Catholic organizations. The CLDL provided legal assistance to workers in local 895 of the ILA, local 138 of the IBT, and locals of the TWU, UE, the Brotherhood of Railway Clerks, and the Plumbers, and ACTU lawyers also defended employees of Consolidated Edison, Hudnut, White Cross, Wanamaker's, and the New York City Police Department. ACTU conferences were established or reorganized in the ILA, the ACA, the Steel Workers, the Retail Workers, the Drug and Warehouse Workers, the News Guild, the UAW, the UE, and the IBT. Actists also worked in a number of other, more broadly based caucuses in these and other unions. Most of these groupings, as we shall see, concentrated on the anti-communist issue.[8]

The roster of ACTU members holding important union offices increased. Tom Doherty, for example, was elected a member of the Michigan CIO Council and Paul Weber won the position of secretary of the Newspaper Guild. The ACTU increased the number of its labor schools in the New York area to thirty, including six in Manhattan, six in the Bronx, and schools in White Plains, Staten Island, Yonkers, New Rochelle, Peekskill, and Haverstraw. Two special schools were established for members of the ACA and the UE in order "to cure a problem of Communist infiltration." In addition, ten Brooklyn labor schools were maintained as a joint ACTU-diocese project under ACTU chaplains William Kelly and Joseph Hammond. Schools established earlier in Buffalo, Detroit, San Francisco, Connecticut, and Rhode Island continued to function and the Pittsburgh chapter considerably expanded its network of labor schools. A regular labor forum was also begun in Jersey City by ACTU chaplain John Monaghan.[9]

The ACTU took strong positions during 1946 on behalf of the maintenance of price controls and the continuation of federal equal-opportunity regulations. The postwar inflation, particularly in industries with frozen wage contracts, was severely undercutting workers' purchasing power. Since profits were increasing, these high prices seemed unjustifiable. The Actists, therefore, called for continuation of the Office of Price Administration and its price regulations. In its continuing battle against discrimination in employment, the ACTU also took up the issue of retention of a federal anti-discrimination authority. The House of Representatives' vote to cut such funding in May 1946 was criticized and, noting that discrimination was still rampant in the building trades and elsewhere, the ACTU supported the call of the New York Committee for a Permanent Fair Employment Practices Commission (FEPC) for a Madison Square Garden rally in June.[10]

The ACTU's renewed organizational activity and expansion paralleled the postwar strike wave and the ACTU found itself once again manning picket lines. Actists contributed money, marched on the picket lines, mobilized support, and addressed meetings during strikes by Anaconda workers at Hastings-on-Hudson, UAW members at GM's Tarrytown plant, UE members at the Mergenthaler Corporation in Brooklyn, and bus drivers in Spring Valley. ACTU members also supported News Guild strikes in Camden and Philadelphia, while George Donahue, ACTU member and international organizer for the Retail Union, led strikes by local 25 at the Safeway stores and Sunshine Biscuit Company in Philadelphia. The ACTU also actively supported maintenance of contract fights against anti-union drives at Grace Lines, Remington Rand, Heide Candy Company, and several chains of drugstores and warehouses in New

York, Philadelphia, and Pittsburgh. An organizing drive of the United Financial Employees, an independent union, among Wall Street employees in the fall of 1946 also received ACTU assistance. These efforts represented a substantial increase in ACTU union-support activities after the relative inactivity of the war years. In comparison to the enormous increase in strikes, however, the ACTU's efforts were relatively modest and none of these campaigns involved the heavy commitments and sustained activity of several of the support actions of 1937–39. [11]

Though the ACTU supported these specific strikes, the organization's long-standing ambivalence about the strike weapon and its preference for mediation, arbitration, and class harmony led them to oppose George Meany's call for postwar reaffirmation of the unlimited right to strike. While the ACTU opposed some of the more severe measures proposed to curtail that right at the crest of the postwar strike wave, the Actists were considerably to the right even of AFL officials such as Meany in supporting both legal and voluntary limitations on strikes, boycotts, and the closed shop. This position led the ACTU to condemn what it regarded as extreme contract demands in several strikes involving the left wing, and contributed to their continuing focus on faction fighting in the unions rather than strike-support work. The ACTU's level of activity in such internal union struggles, in fact, increased several-fold in 1946 over that of 1944 and 1945. [12]

Untypically, corruption and "bossism" were the issues in the ACTU's ongoing struggle in the ILA. The long-smoldering antagonism between a group of ACTU-led insurgents and President Ryan erupted anew in January of 1946 with Ryan's expulsion of five opposition members of local 895. The ACTU ILA conference condemned the action and called a protest meeting, while CLDL attorney Edward Scully initiated a suit against Ryan. This pressure resulted in reinstatement for the five unionists. Scully and other Actists subsequently assisted an opposition slate in local 895 which secured the election of Actist Marty Lynch as secretary-treasurer of the local. [13]

Apart from the ILA fight, however, the ACTU's intra-union activities were directed against left-wing unionists, rather than corruption or authoritarianism. These had become relatively minor issues compared to the preeminent issue of "communist domination." One such fight against communist leadership involved the MMSW. During 1944 graduates of the ACTU's Waterbury, Connecticut, labor school and their supporters, under the direction of the Reverend Donnelly, had "jolted the Communist control almost completely out of the Connecticut district" of the MMSW. Secure in this district, the Actist-led conservative faction began a sustained campaign in 1946 to oust left-wing MMSW president Reid Robinson.

The factional battle did not always go so smoothly however. In the case of the Retail Workers' Union, in which Actists Martin Kyne and George Donahue were officers, the right wing was divided and concerted efforts against the left-wing locals proved impossible. This division also undercut organizing efforts by the Retail Workers' Union, which served to justify the efforts of the left-wing ILWU to represent workers at Montgomery Ward, to the chagrin of the ACTU.[14]

The ACTU's struggle within the Shipbuilders' Union illustrates the increasing militance of the Actists' attacks on the left wing and their propensity during these years to call in external assistance when they were faced with stalemate or defeat. The campaign in the Shipbuilders' Union was directed against the communists and their allies, but was complicated by Left Socialist party (Schactmanite) as well as ACTU support for the opposition. The Communist party was strong in several locals of the Shipbuilders' Union in the New York City area and, beginning in January 1946, the ACTU moved to challenge their leadership. In that month communist-supported incumbents were defeated in one local by a combination of the ACTU, other conservatives, and the left socialists, with the support of international president John Gwen. In June the opposition also upset the communist-supported leadership in local 39 and soon, the ACTU noted approvingly, the local union paper was promoting the "American way."

Several other shipbuilder locals reelected their communist-supported officers, but the Actists did not permit this to decide the issue. In one such local, number 13 in Brooklyn, the reelected left-wing president, Irving Velson, was removed by international president Gwen, with the support of the ACTU and others in the opposition. Following this series of local campaigns, the Shipbuilders' Union opposition improved its position by electing fifteen of the twenty local delegates to the national convention.[15]

The struggle within the Shipbuilders' Union was noteworthy for two reasons. One was the unprecedented alliance between the ACTU and the Schactmanite left socialists, a small left-wing grouping which had split from the Trotskyist Socialist Workers' party. The ACTU remained genuinely opposed to all forms of Marxism. The left socialists, however, though no less reprehensible doctrinally than the communists in the ACTU's view, were weaker and instrumentally useful in the fight against the CP. The ACTU's commitment to fighting the communists had been underlined during the Gerson affair of 1938 by the organization's willingness to welcome anti-union employers into the "anti-communist front." Eight years later the same single-minded opposition to the communists encouraged the ACTU to embrace the Schactmanites, on the other end of the political spectrum, as members of the "anti-communist front." This coalition, stretching from Schactmanites through the ACTU to anti-union employers, the press, and the government did not bode well for the communists. The Schactmanites were to duplicate their role in the Shipbuilders' Union in several other unions in the next four years. The UE was one such union.[16]

The other important aspect of the struggle in the Shipbuilders' Union was the intervention of a national CIO officer on behalf of the anti-communist opposition. Previously, the ACTU had urged such action in vain. The national CIO and most of the international unions had been loath to join the factional fighting at the local level, though local unions had occasionally been placed in receivership in cases of corruption or racketeering. On this occasion, however, the ACTU successfully secured the removal of an admittedly honest, duly elected local officer by the international union president. In the case of those international unions led by the left wing, where the ACTU had focused its activities for some time, such a procedure was obviously unlikely to aid the opposition. But the jump from political intervention in a local by the international officers to political intervention by the national CIO in the affairs of an international union was not a very long one. The action of the president of the Shipbuilders' Union brought the ACTU a number of steps down the road to CIO intervention against the leftist international unions, a goal it had been seeking since 1938. If democratic opposition were to prove ineffective against left-wing local or international union leadership, or if the membership were to wish to retain its left-wing leadership, such intervention could hand the opposition a victory from without.[17]

This is exactly what occurred in the case of the left-wing UE. In 1946, however, the ACTU and other conservatives still hoped to overthrow the UE administration from within. Actists had been involved in the internal struggle in the UE since 1939. ACTU members were active in the opposition in five New York City locals, the largest UE local, number 601 in Pittsburgh, and several others, and had organized an electrical-industrial ACTU conference. The chief steward of local 1217 in New York City was Actist Edward Squitieri. In local 601 the Reverend Rice had been instrumental in the organization of an opposition caucus. Under Rice's leadership the conservatives had won executive-board seats in the local in 1941 and 1942. The Pittsburgh ACTU has also established two labor schools in the vicinity of the Westinghouse plant.[18]

In 1946, the ACTU began to increase substantially its activity in the UE, building on the base of this existing ACTU electrical-industry conference. In February of that year John Page, a non-Catholic leader in an independent caucus in Yonkers UE local 453, sought the ACTU's help against the UE left-wing leadership. The Reverend Thomas J. Darby of the New Rochelle Labor School worked with Page to organize an ACTU labor school in the union hall. The following month Page and two other local 453 members, Helen Reynolds and David Fellmeth, met with George Donahue of the ACTU. Donahue proposed a program for the UE opposition of building its membership, making contacts with other locals, contesting as many local and national UE elections as possible, and contacting other unions with a "problem of Communist activity."[19]

This network of contacts was extended further to include Bart Enright and Edward Ruggirico of local 404 in New York and members of local 456 in Jersey City. By March 1946, UE members from seven New York–New Jersey locals (453, 404, 456, 419, 1237, 1202, and 475) were ready to begin a renewed fight with the left wing in the union. The following month the ACTU began publication of the *Searchlight*, the bulletin of this caucus, now called the "UE Committee for Rank and File Democracy." The committee's anti-administration campaign in the pages of the *Searchlight* and the *Labor Leader*, combined with factional activity in the locals, secured the defeat of the left-wing president of local 456. By June several more locals, including local 428 of White Plains, site of an ACTU labor school, had affiliated with the committee and a national caucus was proposed.[20]

This proposal met with approval from UE opposition elements outside district 4 (New York–New Jersey) and resulted in a meeting to found the UE Committee for Democratic Action or Members for Democratic Action(MDA) on August 10 and 11, 1946. Participants included the Actists, other conservatives and centrists (among them James Carey, former UE president and now CIO secretary, and Harry Block, a UE international vice-president) as well as Socialists and the Schactmanite left socialists. Block was elected chairman of the MDA and James W. Click of local 1102 in St. Louis became secretary. The group adopted a "statement of principles," which reflected the MDA's exclusive concern with the issue of communist control in the UE. The statement indicated that UE members had a choice between "returning the UE to the ranks of respectable CIO unions with sound union objectives or allowing the UE to hurry along to its own destruction as a front for the American Communist party." The MDA and the ACTU spent the next month girding for the September UE convention and contesting local elections for convention delegates. The ACTU forces, for example, were instrumental in the right-wing victory in delegate elections in local 453 of Yonkers, which represented 1,800 Otis Elevator workers. Yonkers was the site of an ACTU labor school and its graduates were active in this campaign.[21]

The convention itself was something of a disappointment for the opposition. The left-wing UE administration maintained a margin of between four and six to one in the voting for officers and policy positions. The ACTU, however, took heart in the fact that the opposition "has increased in strength during the last year" by over 100 percent. Members of the original ACTU-initiated Committee for Rank and File Democracy, the founding group of the MDA, were prominent among the opposition leaders at the convention. Bart

Enright of Local 456 was a floor leader and the MDA's slate of candidates for UE office included William Boulter, secretary-treasurer of Actist-led local 1237. Local 1237 also initiated the unsuccessful convention resolution to prohibit communists from holding office in the UE. [22]

Though the UE administration retained the support of between seventy-five and eighty-five percent of the membership, the ACTU and MDA had good reason for regarding the convention results as something of a victory. The oppositions's vote had doubled and, more importantly, it was now unified, nationally organized, and competently led. The largest part of the credit for this organizing work certainly went to the ACTU. The Actists had begun their work in the UE in 1938 and had continuously cultivated contacts through several strike-support efforts on behalf of UE locals and through their labor schools. These schools were closely related to the factional struggle: in the case of local 453 the school met in the union hall and a similar school was organized by Rice in the vicinity of the Westinghouse plant in Pittsburgh.

The contacts made through their strike-support and educational activities were consolidated in 1940 in the ACTU electrical industry conference. Elections were then contested and won in local 601 in 1941 and local 1217 in 1942. With this preexisting base, and with extensive experience in the fight against the left wing in other unions, the ACTU naturally served as the focus of the efforts of other New York and New Jersey locals to oppose the UE administration. Donahue and the Reverend Darby were thus the crucial links in the organization of the Committee for Rank and File Democracy. [23]

This group was the largest and most coherent element in the UE opposition and sparked the formation of the MDA. Together with Rice's group in local 601, they also formed the largest single bloc in the MDA. While the socialists and left socialists provided MDA cadre, they were weak within the UE itself. Block had no local base and was isolated among UE officers. Carey, as a past officer (he had failed reelection in 1941), was well known in the UE and could count on the prestige of his national CIO office. Nonetheless, as CIO secretary from 1941 to 1946, he had been far removed from UE affairs and had no effective base to deliver. The ACTU bloc was the one coalition component which had long experience in the struggle in the UE and a significant base in the locals of district 4 (New York–New Jersey), the largest UE district, and in the largest single UE local, number 601 in Pittsburgh. Organizationally, the Actists were the ones who provided the MDA with the cohesion and direction that had been lacking in the earlier phases of the UE fight. The Actists were not merely boasting when they assigned themselves the major part of the credit for the "tide turning in the UE."[24]

Though the tide might have turned, the UE struggle was hardly over. The MDA was handicapped in particular by its exclusive concentration on red-baiting attacks on the UE administration. This was the primary focus of the ACTU and had been their past practice in the other left-wing unions. Anti-communism had, furthermore, been the sole issue which had brought the components of the MDA together, since the participants varied from ideological conservatives to opportunistic office seekers to left-wing Schactmanites. But in the case of the UE it was apparent that fighting communism was not going to be a sufficient program to win the membership. Consequently, as a kind of afterthought, the MDA began to develop other policy positions. On November 10 and 11, 1946, four months after the founding of the caucus, forty MDA delegates gathered at Dayton to draw up a broader program. The program they adopted included organizing the unorganized, more aggressive union action, support of Murray for CIO president, a shorter work week, and a guaranteed annual wage. But in practice the MDA did little to implement, or even to publicize, this program and continued its almost exclusive concern with the Communist issue.[25]

The conflict in the UE continued on the local level through the end of 1946. In early December the huge General Electric UE local in Schenectady elected MDA candidate William Hodges to the post of local vice-president by a vote of 3,845 to 3,685. Six other locals in New York, Pennsylvania, and Connecticut also had contests during the month which resulted in MDA victories. Yonkers local 453, one of the original locals of the Committee for Rank and File Democracy, ousted all of its remaining left-wing officers and elected David Fellmeth local president by a two-to-one margin. Fellmeth had been meeting with Donahue and other Actists since March and the ACTU played an active role in the election campaign, providing speakers and assistance in the publication of *Searchlight Junior*, a caucus paper. A second session of the ACTU labor school at the local 453 union hall was begun after the election.

The 6,000 GE workers of local 203 in Bridgeport also defeated left-wing incumbents by a vote of approximately 2,600 to 1,500 and returned MDA member Michael Berescik as head of the local. The 500-member local 452 of Long Island City elected the entire MDA slate, including Sam Horn, one of the MDA floor leaders at the convention. In local 425, also of Long Island City, Actist John Dillon was elected head of the local along with the rest of the MDA slate by a three-to-two vote. In local 601 Rice's Actist-based group was successful in defeating six of eight left-wing officers and electing Philip Conahan as president by a vote of 3,495 to 2,811. Ed Timnes, business agent of local 1237 in Manhattan, one of the original ACTU electrical-industry conference locals, retired at the end of the month and was replaced by a former communist, Actist Jim Conroy.[26]

While the struggle within the UE was the ACTU's major front in the campaign against the left wing during 1946, the organization continued to play a role in other phases of that campaign. The factional fighting within the CIO as a whole had sharpened, just as it had in the UE. Several of the state CIO councils which had large left-wing components were scenes of factional fighting during 1946. ACTU members played a role in the contention within both the Massachusetts and the New Jersey CIO councils. The former barred communists from office and the latter pledged to fight communist interference. The Wisconsin State CIO Council, with the support of the Milwaukee ACTU, also removed its communist officers. The ACTU had sought such action since 1938 and now commented that "this is more like it." The prewar and wartime center-left CIO coalition was beginning to come apart and the left seemed definitely to be on the run.[27]

Several other CIO developments during 1946 seemed to bear out the left's declining fortunes. The Utility Workers' Union, one of the first in which an ACTU conference had been organized, followed the Actists' advice and barred communists from office. Then the CIO convention in November adopted a resolution "resenting and rejecting the efforts of the Communist party or other political parties and their adherents to interfere in the CIO." The ACTU, however, thought this resolution, with its implication that Democratic party interference was as culpable as that of the communists, much too weak. A ban on office-holding in the CIO unions by communists or even pro-communists was what was needed, in the ACTU's opinion. The ACTU had urged that the convention take a first step in this direction by firing leftists Len DeCaux, CIO publicity director, and Lee Pressman, CIO general counsel. The CIO's failure to do so was regarded by the Actists as "nothing less than treasonable."[28]

The ACTU's anti-communist campaign was thus proving quite successful in building a conservative opposition, isolating the left wing, and embarrassing the centrists. The left wing, however, still retained most of its positions of strength in the unions it dominated at the close of 1946. Nor had the CIO leadership undertaken a full-scale purge campaign as the Actists wished. The anti-communists still had their work cut out for them. An alteration in anti-communist ideology helped to ease that task somewhat. Originally, the ACTU had dealt with the communist issue largely as an internal union matter. Communism had been viewed as an erroneous response to social injustice which would decline with the rise of intra-union efforts to educate workers in Catholic social doctrine and "common sense unionism." The communists had to be opposed, said the Actists, but their civil liberties ought to be respected and the government should stay out of the internal struggle in the unions.[29]

By 1946 this position had changed considerably. During the war, the Navy's dismissal of a thousand left-wing seamen in the militarized Merchant Marine had been applauded. Harry Bridges' deportation, originally opposed by the ACTU, was endorsed by them in February 1945. Similarly, Earl Browder's release from prison was opposed by the Actists. In March 1946 the ACTU also endorsed the House Un-American Activities Committee (HUAC) investigations of the Communist party, which it had earlier held to be anti-union in motive, as having "served a useful purpose." The Actists thereafter regularly denounced the movement to abolish the committee and in an April *Labor Leader* editorial went even further. According to the editors, the existing legislation and common law were inadequate to the task of fighting the communists. What was necessary was a "redefinition of subversion" to remove the legal "loophole" which required the commission of overt revolutionary acts. For the ACTU the communists' intentions were a priori subversive and the law should be changed to cover them regardless of the consequences to First Amendment rights. [30]

Thus, the ACTU's anti-communist perspective in 1946 was considerably more uncompromising than that of 1939. The communists were now more than wrong or misguided. They were subversive and treasonous. Therefore, the Actists now argued, their civil liberties ought to be curtailed and the unions ought to take measures to bar them from office, or even from membership. The communist issue was no longer seen merely as an internal union problem, but as a problem that demanded government intervention. This position reflected the growing strength of the conservatives in the CIO and the increasing anti-communist campaign in the country at large.

Paradoxically, it also reflected the continuing relative weakness of the conservative opposition in the left-led unions. In none of these unions had the opposition been able to defeat the left-wing leadership democratically. To continue to regard the communist issue as an internal union matter and the communists themselves as legally protected by the Constitution could well condemn the opposition to continued defeat in the unions. The new strategy, which defined the communists as subversive and illegitimate, served to justify extraordinary measures which were not consistent with membership self-determination, but promised success for the opposition. If communism in the unions were seen as an international conspiracy, rather than an expression of the members' honest beliefs, then expulsions, splits, dual unionism, and government interference in the CIO on behalf of the conservative opposition could all be more easily defended.

The tenth-anniversary celebration of the ACTU in March of 1947 was the occasion for a renewed effort to reorganize chapters which had lapsed during the war and to reconsolidate the national organization. Representatives of chapters in New York, Cleveland, Detroit, Gary, Pittsburgh, San Francisco, and New Orleans attended the celebration. The delegates heard James Carey, CIO secretary and ACTU ally in the UE-MDA, and made plans for a national conference to prepare for the third national convention. This national planning conference was held in New York on March 28. Delegates attended from the above ACTU chapters and from two fraternal groups, the Catholic Labor Alliance (CLA) of Chicago and the Catholic Labor Guild (CLG) of Boston. Plans for a summer convention were made and the Actists passed resolutions favoring price cuts and supporting the right of civil service employees to strike in New York state.[31]

The projected convention convened over the July fourth weekend in Pittsburgh. Sixty delegates participated including representatives of Actists in Cleveland, New York, Pittsburgh, Detroit, New Orleans, Washington state, and Kansas City, as well as the CLG and CLA. The convention delegates elected Roger Larkin as national chairman. They also adopted a number of resolutions, including one which expressed "vigorous opposition" to the Taft-Hartley Act, though they called on the unions "to reject the advice of those who propose general strikes and similar techniques of violence and class war as a means of opposing this Act."[32]

The ACTU's struggle with the left wing continued to occupy the organization's main attention during 1947. A victory on this front occurred in January in the New York local of the Hotel and Restaurant Workers' Union when the ACTU-supported conservatives prevailed on the international to remove the left-wing editors of the New York *Hotel and Club Voice*. A more significant battle continued throughout the year in the MMSW. The ACTU had previously established contact with members of the MMSW in the Connecticut region through its labor schools and had organized opposition caucuses in the Scovill and Chase locals. These caucuses had been successful in defeating left-wing incumbents, but despite the growing strength of the opposition, the MMSW reelected left-winger Reid Robinson as president in January 1947. The ACTU called on the opposition to "press the fight," but several locals were disheartened enough at this defeat to secede from the MMSW in the following month. The ACTU originally opposed this secession, as it usually did in cases where conservative victory seemed possible within the union, as "a tactical mistake." But the secession movement soon grew to encompass forty-six locals representing one-third of the MMSW's 90,000 members. At that point the secessionists secured the approval of both the Connecticut CIO Council and the ACTU. Robinson resigned in an effort to stem the tide and was replaced by another leftist, Maurice Travis. Three members of the MMSW executive board also resigned to join the secessionist Provisional Metal Workers' Council. [33]

In the course of this secession movement CIO president Murray threatened the removal of MMSW president Travis, though he did not remove him, and he suggested for the first time that unions which had a problem with the Communist party should "throw it to hell out." Though it was not the ACTU's preferred tactic, secession did serve their purposes: the disruption "rescued" 30,000 workers from the MMSW and weakened the left-wing union considerably. And the ACTU could certainly claim a significant share of the credit for these events. The campaign to oppose Robinson had been their initiative, through the Reverend Donnelly of the Waterbury Labor School. The original opposition caucus had been organized by graduates of the school who represented several of the seceding locals. The 30,000-member secessionist unit could certainly stand on its own and, with the support of the national CIO, the remainder of the MMSW membership could probably in time be either won to the secessionists or at any rate lost to the MMSW. Murray's intervention was also an extremely important result of the MMSW dispute. The ACTU was now armed with the precedent of a CIO presidential threat to remove a left-wing international union president. [34]

Raiding was another weapon in the ACTU's battle with the left wing during 1947. The left-wing TWU and ACA were raided during 1947 by UMW district 50 and the AFL Commercial Telegraphers' Union, respectively, and the ACTU threw its support to the raiders. In the case of the TWU, the ACTU had attempted to promote anti-communist opposition for years, while supporting tthe union's organizing efforts. The opposition had never been much of a threat to President Mike Quill, however, and the ACTU now decided that a policy of raiding would be more successful than one of continued "boring from within." The ACTU's support for the UMW's raiding drive sparked a vehement speech by Quill in which he attacked the ACTU as a "strike-breaking outfit." The ACTU replied that they had simply concluded that he was a communist and that the TWU was communist-dominated. They could, therefore, no longer support the union, even if this meant divided employee representation in the New York City transit lines.

The ACA situation was similar. The ACTU had members in the union and had supported past organizing drives and strikes by the Western Union local. They had concluded that the union was radical–dominated, however, and that it indulged in "irresponsible" strikes. This analysis led the ACTU to support the AFL Commercial Telegraphers' Union raid, despite the protests of the ACA that ACTU opposition was tantamount to "a threat of the displeasure of the Church" toward Catholic members of the ACA. In furtherance of this position, Bill Shinnick, an ACTU executive-board member active in the ACA opposition for several years, took a position as Western Union organizer for the AFL unit. [35]

Actists also fought a major factional battle in the Newspaper Guild in 1947. The ACTU had long been active in this union in New York, New Jersey, California, Ohio, Massachusetts, Louisiana, Illinois, and Michigan. An ACTU News Guild conference had existed since 1939 and several ACTU members were officers of the union. Paul Weber, president of the Detroit ACTU, was also president of the large Detroit News Guild local, ACTU member Lyan Hogan was a New Orleans Guild officer and Gene Kelly, a Cleveland Actist, was president of the Cleveland News Guild. Actist Ralph Novak was secretary-treasurer of the International Union. Inconclusive fighting against the left wing in the Guild had occupied the Actists for years, especially in the large, radical–dominated New York unit. [36]

Successful battles with the left in other unions in 1946 and 1947 sparked a renewed enthusiasm by Actists and other conservatives in the Guild. Several opposition members were elected to the New York News Guild executive board in April 1947 with the support of the ACTU. This victory was followed by the election of eight of the New York local's fifteen convention delegates on a slate pledged to "opposition to Communist maneuvers to control or sway the Guild." Among those elected were Lawrence Delaney of *Time*, an ACTU executive-board member who had been an active opponent of the left in the Guild, and Robert Stern, an Actist who worked for the *Herald Tribune*. The ACTU congratulated its own partisans and their allies and ironically, considering their developing role in the CIO purge, embraced their statement that "we will not fall into the trap of employing fascist or Soviet purge methods. We will expose communists and vote against them. We rely on the methods of democracy." [37]

These victories in New York set the stage for the national Guild elections in September. The *Labor Leader* informed its readers that "ACTU members are supporting the 'pro-guild slate' down the line" since it was "free of any communist taint." This slate won all the executive-board posts, except for that held by left-winger John Manus of New York, whose defeat the Actists had regarded as "particularly important." The ACTU had no reason to complain, however. Two Actists, Robert Stern of New York and Ralph Novak of Detroit, were elected secretary-treasurer and vice-president, respectively, of the Newspaper Guild. The year's activity in the Guild was rounded off in December when the ACTU-supported Committee for Guild Unity won all the local offices in the New York City News Guild. [38]

The ACTU's role in the Newspaper Guild effectively undercuts the argument made by some writers that this organization was of minor importance, that it was merely a club for Catholics, or that it was merely "a faction" among many in the unions. As was the case with several other unions, the ACTU was a pivotal anti-communist force in the Newspaper Guild. The Actists in the Guild had functioned for five years as a relatively disciplined caucus. They included officers of several of the largest Guild locals and their strength was significant enough in the national union to have secured the election of members to the secretary-treasurership and vice-presidency. The ACTU's position in the union was one of considerable strength and they were crucial in the defeat of the left in the New York City local, its strongest base. [39]

The battle within the UE also continued to rage during 1947. The ACTU extended its own organization in order to participate most effectively in the UE fight. For example, the Pittsburgh chapter, led by William J. Hart, the Pittsburgh district director of the USW, and John Duffy, the UE-MDA leader in the Pittsburgh area, organized ten parish sub-units of the ACTU, in order to influence Pittsburgh unionists. The chapter also organized a meeting, attended by 200 unionists, which heard speeches on the communist question by the Reverend Rice and Gene Kelly, chairman of the Cleveland ACTU. Kelly called for the expulsion of the CIO unions which were "playing the Communist game," and their replacement with new unions with "proven allegiance to American principles." This was the first time that purges and dual unionism had been suggested as a program against the left-wing unions and it is significant that it was raised by the ACTU. [40]

In January four UE locals shifted to the opposition column with the election of MDA-supported local officers. These included locals 901 (General Electric) and 910 (Magnavox) in Fort Wayne, local 801 (General Electric) in Dayton, and local 419 (General Electric, Rex and Dubarry) in Mount Vernon, New York. As opposition strength grew, so too did impatience with the strategy of working within the UE. Thus in the same month, despite MDA pleas to remain within the UE and see the fight through, the Rahway, New Jersey, local (411) withdrew from the union. In February, contrary to both the UE constitution and the advice of the MDA, the Bridgeport, Connecticut, local (203) jumped the gun in a different manner by expelling twenty-seven members of the Communist party. A prompt UE suspension of the local led the opposition to reconsider and readmit the left-wingers. These difficulties in maintaining discipline among secession-prone opposition locals contributed to the MDA's defeat at the September 1947 UE Convention. The major problem, however, was simply that the majority of UE locals continued to support the left wing. The MDA slate of officers, including Harry Block for president, James Click for secretary-treasurer, and Bart Enright of the original ACTU Committee for Rank and File Democracy for vice-president, was thus defeated by a substantial margin. [41]

The ACTU's struggle with the left wing continued on other fronts as well during 1947. The Actists' regular sniping at Joe Curran, president of the NMU, was transformed into "warm applause" when Curran denounced the Communist party and resigned from the co-chairmanship of the Committee for Maritime Unity, which the ACTU regarded as a communist front. [42] The ACTU threw its weight also into the competition between the Progressive Citizens of American (PCA), supported by the communists, and the Americans for Democratic Action (ADA), which disallowed communist membership. The Labor Leader predictably denounced the PCA as another communist front and endorsed the ADA, indicating that it was "glad to see an impressive galaxy of American progressives and labor leaders" join together "on a clearly liberal and anti-Communist basis."

On the international front, the ACTU endorsed the organization of Christian trade unions in France as an antidote to communist influence. The Actists also attacked a speech by Louis Saillant, secretary-general of the World Federation of Trade Unions (WFTU), in which he had criticized Turkish and Greek trade unions as neither "democratic nor free." The ACTU dismissed the speech as an attempt to influence American foreign policy toward these countries to the advantage of the Soviet Union. Foreign policy and the international struggle in the trade-union movement were beginning to play a larger role in the ACTU's views and comments on the left wing in the American unions. [43]

The year 1947 was marked by the continuation of the ACTU's campaign against the left and by the beginnings of an organizational response to the initiatives which were to become the Taft-Hartley Act. A comparison of these two campaigns may shed some light on the priorities of the ACTU. The communist question was the primary issue facing the unions, according to the Actists. All the ACTU-supported union caucuses, but one, were concerned almost exclusively with the struggle against the communists. The ACTU's important work in the News Guild and the UE was organized entirely on such a basis, and the organization's schools and publications reflected the priority assigned to anti-communist work. During 1947 the ACTU had given its support to raiding against the left-wing unions and to secession from one of them, the MMSW. The organization had called for national CIO intervention against the left-wing unions and ultimately had demanded that they be expelled and replaced by new unions.

Anti-communism was the issue, then, that engaged the attention and activity of the ACTU. It demanded, in their view, the disciplined commitment of unionists and the most extraordinary measures by the unions themselves. Secession, suspension, and expulsion had never before been undertaken by the CIO, and such extraordinary measures promised to bring disorganization and loss of members to the labor unions at a time when employers were seeking their utmost to weaken them. The ACTU was thus willing to make enormous demands on itself and its supporters on behalf of the anti-communist campaign. The Actists encouraged the most drastic measures of union discipline and were willing to court a great deal of trouble for union members in the form of weakened unions, lost contracts, and lack of unity, in order to carry through the struggle against the communists.

Let us compare this response to the communists with the ACTU's reaction to the Taft-Hartley Act, a set of restrictive amendments to the Wagner Act passed in 1947. This act embodied features which had been urged by conservative employers since the Wagner Act was passed and represented a significant retreat from the trade union gains of the 1930s. Taft-Hartley prohibited both the closed shop and strikes by government workers. It exempted domestic, agricultural, and health employers from NLRB requirements. The act required separate union representation for craft, professional, and other workers, barred political contributions by the unions, and in some cases provided for a lengthy "cooling off" period before strikes. Union meetings on company time were prohibited and extremely detailed financial and other information was required of the unions. Taft-Hartley made illegal several categories of "unfair labor practices" by the unions, including jurisdictional strikes, mass picketing, "wildcat" strikes, and secondary boycotts. One important provision required the filing of non-communist oaths by the officers of any union seeking to use the NLRB machinery. The act was the capstone of the postwar employers' offensive and was understood by both the CIO and the AFL to represent the most serious threat to the unions since the open-shop drive of the 1920s. [44]

The ACTU shared in the opposition to the Taft-Hartley Act expressed by both the AFL and the CIO. The organization indicated its disapproval of the Taft-Hartley measures as early as January 1947 and, when Congressional approval appeared imminent, urged union members to write to President Truman demanding a veto of the legislation. The ACTU also took part in the mass rally sponsored by the AFL and CIO in New York city in June 1947, which urged Truman to veto the bill. At their own July 1947 convention, too, the Actists resolved "vigorous opposition" to Taft-Hartley. [45]

Despite its stated opposition to the Taft-Hartley Act, however, the ACTU supported several of the act's provisions which most other unionists found objectionable. These included limitation of both the closed shop and the right to strike, mandatory arbitration of some disputes, and the ban on jurisdictional and "wildcat" strikes and on secondary boycotts. In part, this position reflected a strategy of supporting the lesser of two evils. Since some regulatory legislation seemed inevitable, the ACTU probably hoped to forestall the

Taft-Hartley provisions by accepting Truman's milder labor program.

The modification of the closed shop, however, was sought because of ACTU experience with the ILA and a number of other unions in which expulsion of rank-and-file opponents under closed-shop provisions brought automatic dismissal from employment. The ACTU's support for compulsory arbitration, limitation of the right to strike, and the ban on jurisdictional and "wildcat" strikes, as well as secondary boycotts, had other sources. The ACTU's long-standing policy of discouraging strikes and militance, especially "wildcat" strikes, its penchant for arbitration and mediation, and the ideological commitment to class harmony underpinned these positions.[46]

The ACTU thus held an ambiguous position on the provisions of the Taft-Hartley Act, despite its public opposition to the act. Nor did the Actists undertake any extraordinary measures to combat it. The convention resolution expressing ACTU opposition to the act also cautioned unionists to "reject the advice of those who propose general strikes and similar techniques of violence and class war as a means of opposing this Act." The ACTU contemplated no special action against Congressmen who voted for Taft-Hartley, and once the bill had been passed over Truman's veto, they were prepared to accept defeat. The organization did not favor the policy of non-compliance which the majority of the CIO as well as the AFL unions initially pursued. While the Actists continued to criticize Taft-Hartley after its passage, the burden of their criticism was that the required non-communist affidavits were unsuccessful in removing communists from positions of influence.[47]

The Actists' energetic and uncompromising struggle against the communists thus stood in marked contrast to their modest and ambiguous reaction to the Taft-Hartley Act. Opposition to the communists, was by far the more significant issue to the ACTU. That fight superseded all other internal union issues and the most extraordinary means were considered legitimate in its prosecution, including raiding, secession, and expulsion, even though these measures would inevitably weaken the protection the unions could offer their members.

In contrast to the all-encompassing struggle with the communists, the ACTU's campaign against the Taft-Hartley Act hardly amounted to a campaign at all. Despite the universal belief within the trade-union movement that the act was the most serious attack on labor in decades, the ACTU actually endorsed several important provisions and mounted no large-scale organizational campaign against it. Once the act was passed, the ACTU opposed the joint AFL and CIO policy of noncompliance, denounced proposals for a general strike or demonstrations against the act, and confined its criticisms to the functional limitations of the anti-communist provisions. Thus, while in the context of the anti-communist campaign the ACTU was willing repeatedly to mobilize its supporters around an extreme position, to expose the labor movement to serious risks and to demand extraordinary measures from the unions, it was unwilling to do these things to bring about the defeat or unenforceability of the Taft-Hartley Act.

FROM SECESSION TO EXPULSION, 1948–1949

The ACTU continued its organizational expansion during 1948 and 1949, added two international branches and held its fourth convention. These events, however, were merely a sideshow compared to the expansion and culmination of the anti-communist campaign. The CIO left wing was increasingly isolated from its former allies in these years. The operation of the Taft-Hartley anti-communist oaths and the effects of government, AFL, employer, and finally CIO opposition cost the left-wing unions members, leaders, and contracts and, in some cases, threatened their very existence. The left's support for the Progressive party campaign of Henry Wallace and their opposition to the Marshall Plan and the Truman Doctrine also undercut their position within the national CIO and upset the structure of many local alliances.

While the left lost support in every quarter in these years, the ACTU gained supporters and allies everywhere. The Actists virtually took control of the Newspaper Guild. They were unable to dent the popularity of the left wing within the UE, but were able successfully to implement a policy of raiding, secession, and eventually expulsion and dual unionism whose effect was to reduce the UE's membership by ninety percent. The ACTU was even more successful in its campaigns against the UOWPA and the left-wing locals of the RU, and in its role in the "conversion" of the TWU and the NMU to the right wing. The Actists also spearheaded the attack on the New York City CIO Council, the left's last remaining base of support in the city outside of the garment trades, and helped thereby to destroy the left-wing American Labor party, a longtime ACTU goal. The organization saw its program of anti-communism and expulsion adopted by the national CIO and enjoyed the added fillip of CIO endorsement of the industry-council plan. These two years represented the apogee of ACTU influence and support. Once the ACTU's anti-radical demands had been adopted by the CIO, however, it was without *raison d'être*. It is ironic, and indicative of the ACTU's preoccupation with anti-communism, that, once there were no more CIO communists, its influence and organization should simply collapse.

The year 1948, however, began mundanely enough with several episodes of union-support work. In February the Pittsburgh ACTU joined in the picketing of the Rodgers Dairy Company by striking members of the AFL Hotel and Restaurant Employees Union. The New York chapter continued its work with the AFL United Financial Employees' Union, which conducted an unsuccessful strike on Wall Street during April. The closing of three New York piers in January inspired a major ACTU campaign in support of idled members of ILA local 895, who demanded that the piers be reopened under public auspices so that no jobs would be lost. The ACTU, working with several parish priests, organized a mass meeting of protest at St. Veronica's Church on January 27 which was successful in bringing about the reopening of the piers in early February.

The most significant ACTU strike-support action involved a strike at the Sunshine Biscuit Company on Long Island, which lasted through October and November of 1948. The strikers, 2,000 strong, were members of local 25 of the CIO Retail Union, whose business manager was *Labor Leader* editor George Donahue. Despite attempts by the management to divide the workers, who were, among other backgrounds, Polish, Italian, Irish, Puerto Rican, and black, the strike remained solid for five weeks until the employer agreed to hourly raises of between 8½ and 17½ cents and a system of plantwide seniority. While this strike involved a CIO union, the other three union-support efforts were on behalf of AFL affiliates. The previous year, too, the ACTU had assisted members of AFL unions, the Office Employees' Union and the Independent Association of Telephone Equipment Workers. This declining emphasis on

CIO organizing and strike-support activities, within a generally declining emphasis on all such efforts, reflected the ACTU's concentration on the struggle with the left within the CIO, as well as a wait-and-see attitude toward the New York CIO affiliates, all of which had strong left-wing components. [48]

The ACTU convention in July 1948 was marked by internal consolidation, the internationalization of the ACTU, and the ACTU's condemnation of the Wallace campaign and endorsement of the Marshall Plan, two issues which were to figure importantly in the campaign against the left in the CIO. The delegates also voted to support President Truman's civil-rights declaration. The convention urged the repeal of the Taft-Hartley Act and endorsed both family allowances and AFL-CIO cooperation. The internationalization of the ACTU reflected the convention participation of an English ACTU, which had been organized in April. The continuing emphasis on internal consolidation and cohesion, in preparation for the denouement of the fight with the left, led the delegates to endorse a regular internal ACTU bulletin. This publication, titled *Between Ourselves*, appeared in September. [49]

During 1947 the ACTU increased its influence within the Newspaper Guild at the national level and tightened its organization in that union's New York locals. Nonetheless, the left made something of a comeback. The communist-supported slate won a majority of the seats on the New York Guild executive committee in January 1948, despite the December election of anti-communist local officers on the ticket of the ACTU-supported Committee for Guild Unity. As part of a campaign to end this standoff, the ACTU New York Guild conference began publication of a caucus newspaper, *The Masthead*. The ACTU's position in the national Newspaper Guild was consolidated with the election of Actist Ralph Novak to the presidency of the union, while ACTU member Robert Stern remained secretary-treasurer. Actist Paul Weber also served in the powerful position of chairman of the resolutions committee during the 1948 News Guild convention. The ACTU's influential role in the Newspaper Guild was further evidenced by the union's endorsement of the industrial-council plan, the current version of the ACTU's corporative program. It was the first CIO union to do so. [50]

The struggle against the left in the UE was undercut during 1948 by the growing secessionist trend among opposition locals, a tendency which had characterized the MDA from the beginning. The secession movement gained impetus from the Taft-Hartley provision requiring non-communist affidavits to be signed by the officers of unions seeking NLRB certification as bargaining agents. Initially the left-wing unions chose to ignore the affidavits. Since the majority of AFL and CIO unions responded similarly, because of the general Taft-Hartley non-compliance policy, no disadvantage had resulted to the left. By February of 1948, however, 79 of 105 AFL unions, 23 of 41 CIO unions, and 41 independent unions had filed non-communist affidavits. This meant that UE plant representation rights might be challenged with impunity by any of these unions. As a noncomplying union, the UE would have no recourse to an NLRB representative election or even to the maintenance of current contracts against such a raid. This open season on UE bargaining units frightened many UE members, who were fearful of losing contract protection, and encouraged those opposition leaders who were seeking a justification for secession. The result was an increase in secessions by UE locals and a rush by other unions, especially the UAW and the IBEW, to raid the UE.[51]

In February, New York local 1237 withdrew from the UE in the face of threatened court action by Remington-Rand to void the contract on the grounds of UE noncompliance with the non-communist affidavit requirement. The business agent of local 1237 was Actist John Conroy and the local had been an original member of the ACTU-sponsored Committee for Rank and File Democracy. The ACTU regarded these secessions as a "serious blow to the anti-communist movement represented by the UE-MDA." Each secession weakened the MDA bloc in the UE while the left-wing locals all maintained their standing in the union.

The ACTU blamed the Taft-Hartley anti-communist oaths for this result. The burden of the ACTU's criticism of the affidavit provision was that it was "ineffective" in purging the left-wing from the unions. The Actists did not oppose this purpose, nor did they oppose the oaths in principle, as some did, as an intrusion into the right of workers to choose their own representatives. Rather, they believed the communists to be hopelessly unregenerate: they might quit the party and thus formally meet the requirements of the non-communist oath while continuing to promote the communist program. In the case of those left-wing unions which refused to file the affidavits, the ACTU believed that the victims would be the anti-communist opposition, as was the case in the UE. The Actists thus opposed the oaths as an ineffective measure against the communists and one which actively damaged opposition prospects in left-wing unions.[52]

While the ACTU's struggle against the communists was stalled in the UE, it proceeded in other quarters of the labor movement with increasing strength during 1948. In January, the New York State CIO withdrew from the American Labor party (ALP). The ALP had been supported by most CIO and many AFL unions in New York as a labor alternative to the Democratic and Republican parties. The ALP normally endorsed the Democratic national ticket, while successfully fielding its own candidates, including socialists and communists, for New York office. The ACTU had always opposed the Labor party as an example of the class politics condemned by the papal encyclicals, and more specifically as a source of legitimacy and power for the communists. The Actists had continually called for cessation of labor-movement support for the ALP. George Donahue, Actist vice-president of the Retail Union, had been a leader of the floor fight against ALP affiliation within the New York State CIO Council for several years. The disaffiliation of the New York State CIO represented a signal victory for the Actists' drive to isolate the CP and to end this provocative precedent of class politics.[53]

The major justification for the New York State CIO's break with the ALP was the latter's support for the campaign of Henry Wallace for president. This issue was also central in the split in the New York City CIO Council. This CIO council had long been dominated by the left, and the ACTU had opposed most of its projects on that account, even those mandated by the national CIO. The minority position of the conservatives in the New York City CIO Council changed dramatically, however, with Michael Quill's repudiation of the communists.

As president of the TWU and of the CIO council, Quill had been a leading left-wing figure and a continual target of ACTU criticism. His position in the TWU had remained impregnable despite the best efforts of the ACTU to mount an internal opposition movement. The organization finally despaired of this approach and instead threw its support to the transit-raiding of the UMW's district 50. By 1948, however, the pressure on Quill had begun to have its effect. "Red Mike," despite his reputation, had always "played politics as they were" and politics now dictated a turn to the right. His position within the union might momentarily be secure, but he was certainly vulnerable to the opposition of the national CIO and to raiding by other CIO affiliates. Raiding became especially effective when the closed shop was banned on the transit lines. As a pariah left-wing union, the TWU now could expect to face a coalition of the open-shop Transit Authority, raiding CIO and AFL unions, the national CIO leadership, the Taft-Hartley NLRB, and the courts, all determined to terminate its representation of the city's transit workers. In an attempt to preserve the TWU and his own position within it, Quill choose to repudiate the left and Henry Wallace and to announce his support for the national CIO leadership and the Marshall Plan.[54]

Quill's resignation from the New York City CIO Council in April sparked a series of complicated secessions and counter-secessions. By June, CIO affiliates representing 85,000 workers had withdrawn from the council. Despite these secessions, the conservatives within the council were actually strengthened by the defection of former left-wingers who were beginning to feel the pressure from the national CIO. The right wing was therefore able to carry a council vote for a referendum of the members of affiliated unions on Wallace's campaign and the Marshall Plan. Following this vote, a countersecession movement began with the withdrawal of the radical-led New York local of the News Guild. The struggle culminated in November when the national CIO executive board withdrew the council's charter, to the "applause" of the ACTU. The left thus lost control of a major union institution in its strongest local base, largely through the defection of its own most prominent local leader. Quill himself took over leadership of his erstwhile opposition in the TWU, including the ACTU, and in December successfully shifted his base of support by defeating an "unreconstructed" left-winger, Austin Hogan, for TWU president. The ouster of the left-wingers from staff and elective positions in the TWU, "something that the ACTU has worked and fought and prayed for since its founding," followed the elections.[55]

The issue of the Wallace campaign was crucial in both these

defeats for the CIO left wing. Together with the Marshall Plan, it had become the litmus test of loyalty or disloyalty to national CIO policy. The ACTU had left no doubt as to where it stood in this division. Wallace's candidacy made him a "tool of the Communist party" and a "poisonous influence." The ACTU's attack on Wallace ironically illustrates the degree to which left-wing support was the kiss of death for people and ideas otherwise unobjectionable to the Catholic activists. Previous to his 1948 candidacy, the ACTU had strongly supported Wallace. He had been viewed as an exemplary fighter for social justice whose program "largely paralleled our own." While Wallace had not altered his program in any significant respect, his willingness to campaign as the presidential candidate of a third party supported in part by the communists rendered him "no longer worthy of support" in the view of the Actists.[56]

The Actists had a very good year in 1948. They had tightened their own organization at the national and the industrial-conference levels and had gone "international." They had also consolidated their position within the New York and the national Newspaper Guilds. The struggle with the left in the UE, it is true, had been stalled by the secession movement, but since internal opposition had not got the opposition very far since 1946, the secessions may not have been so unwelcome to the ACTU and the rest of the MDA as they appeared to be. In any case the secessions did serve to justify the alternative policy of expelling the UE from the CIO and also provided a base for the organization of that alternative union "with proven allegiance to American principles," which some Actists had been promoting since September 1947. The setback in the UE, then, was more apparent than real.

A more clear-cut victory had been won during 1948 in the TWU, where long-term ACTU opposition activity provided a base of support for a reformed Michael Quill. The TWU's defection from the left-wing column precipitated the split and dissolution of the left-wing power base in the New York City CIO council and in the state council. The Actists played a significant role in both of these struggles. The ACTU's maritime conference had also scored a victory in the NMU. Actists had been involved in the opposition in that union since 1940, particularly in New Orleans, and their support was instrumental in Curran's break with the left wing.[57]

In addition the ACTU could count several victories in the national CIO. Leftwinger Lee Pressman, whose removal had been demanded by the ACTU for years, resigned under pressure in February. The CIO's Portland convention in November, 1948, moved considerably closer to the ACTU's position on the anti-communist issue. The delegates condemned the U.S.S.R., endorsed the Marshall Plan by name, and issued ultimatums to the left-wing CIO unions which left little doubt that expulsion was in the offing. The ACTU took pride too in the convention's endorsement of the industrial-council plan, a version of the Catholic corporative program, which had long been favored by Murray. While the national CIO's adoption of the ACTU's anti-communist demands in effect tended to deprive the Actists of a program and to undercut their *raison d'être*, victory certainly had its consolations. Since the ACTU's major purpose had long been the defeat of the CIO left wing, the dissolution of the organization in the context of that defeat was not unexpected, either. The ACTU's work was not actually done by 1948, however. The Actists still had a role to play in the coming year.[58]

In fact, no decline was apparent in early 1949. The ACTU continued an active program and organization during the year. A new chapter was organized in St. Johns, Newfoundland, in May and the ACTU's communion breakfast in New York City that month drew the usual one thousand participants. Students assembled for classes at ACTU labor schools from San Francisco to Detroit and New York to Baltimore. Twenty-nine schools opened for the new term in the New York City area, thirteen in Connecticut, and thirty-six in Detroit, while there were several each in Chicago, Buffalo, San Francisco, Rhode Island, Milwaukee, and Pittsburgh. Other chapters maintained at least one school and all of them continued to feed recruits into the internal union struggle with the left.

The San Francisco ACTU chapter registered a membership of over 400 for the year and internal chapter bulletins were begun in New York and Detroit. As internal fighting against the left moved toward a climax in several unions, ACTU industrial conferences were also expanded and increased in number. The Detroit chapter, for example, sponsored three separate conferences in the UAW and two in the teacher's union. Others were established in the News

Guild, the chemical and municipal worker's unions, and among college students and lawyers. The strength of the Detroit ACTU was illustrated in the career of its first president, Paul Weber, who by 1949 had become vice-president of the Michigan CIO.[59]

The organizational resources represented by this summary did not, for the most part, go into union-support activities. Pure and simple union-support efforts by the ACTU had diminished in number and significance since 1940, as the ACTU increasingly emphasized the intra-union struggle with the left. The number of instances of such activity reached a new low in 1949. The ACTU did take up, once again, the case of ILA members on New York City piers 42, 45, and 46. These piers had been closed in January 1948 for lack of business and the ACTU had played a major role in the campaign to reopen them under city control. This had been done, but the rental demanded was so high that no takers had come forward. Consequently the ACTU began a campaign to lower the fees. A rally was held in January 1949 at which ACTU National Director Roger Larkin and *Labor Leader* editor George Donahue spoke. The resulting pressure convinced the city to lower the pier rents. The ACTU found itself opposing the ILA leadership in March, however, and supporting the demands of black workers who charged the ILA with discrimination in job assignments at the hiring halls.[60]

Other instances of ACTU support for organizing drives during 1949 were actually part of the ongoing drive against the CIO left wing, which continued to be the nearly exclusive concern of the ACTU. In April, for example, the Actists supported the efforts of the AFL National Federation of Life Insurance Agents to secure bargaining rights at Prudential Insurance Company offices in New York City. These workers had already been organized, however, by the left-wing United Office and Professional Workers' Union, CIO. In fact the ACTU had contributed significantly to the initial organizing of this union and Actists were among the membership. Nonetheless, as in the UE, secessionism was the result after attempts to promote internal opposition to the left-wing leadership had proved fruitless. Two other locals of the UOPWA had previously been split and in this case also the Actists decided on a strategy of raiding the "Communist-dominated outfit." The raid proved successful and the UOPWA lost the ensuing NLRB election to the AFL affiliate.[61]

In an even more significant case of secessionism, the ACTU abandoned a union it had helped to build, the Retail Workers' Union (RU), in order to further its struggle against the left. The ACTU had been heavily involved in organizing drives of the Retail Union since 1939. The Actists had played a significant role in the organization of several retail chains, including the Weisbecker and Wanamaker Department Stores, the Barricini and Loft candy stores and the Whelan Drug chain. RU organizing was also supported by the ACTU at Sears in San Francisco, Montgomery Ward in Chicago, and several stores in Camden. Several Actists had worked as organizers for the RU. George Donahue had served as international organizer, business agent of local 25, and international vice-president, and had run for president of the union. Martin Kyne, another Actist, was also an RU vice-president. As late as 1943 and 1944 the ACTU had been the prime mover in a major RU drive in New York and New Jersey.[62]

Despite this heavy stake in the union, the relative success of ongoing efforts in New York, and the need to increase the organization of retail workers nationally, the ACTU once again chose to support a policy of raiding by certifiably anti-communist AFL unions. George Donahue resigned his positions in the CIO Retail Union in February and became international representative of the AFL Retail Clerks. This union then began to challenge the representation rights of the left-wing New York locals of the RU. Raiding can be a highly competitive business, however. The CIO Amalgamated Clothing Workers' Union also moved in on the RU jurisdiction. The Actists supported the Amalgamated's bid for representation of the workers of the Namm Department Stores in April. Though the Amalgamated's membership was wholly in the garment trades and the union had no intention of organizing retail workers, other than those it could pick up from the weakened, left-wing RU locals, the Actists, correctly believed it could be counted on to purge the communists.[63]

The ACTU's support for the raids and secessions in the CIO Retail Union was unusual in one important respect. Though the ACTU had supported raiding and secession before, the victimized unions—MMSW, UOPWA, NMU, UE, TWU, and ILWU—were all led by the left wing on the national level. The Retail Workers' Union, in contrast, did not have a left-wing leadership. In fact, the ACTU was more prominent on the national level than the communists. The union had a poor record of organizing retail workers and this was often cited by the ACTU as justification for raiding, secession, and the hostile attitude of the national CIO. But other CIO unions, such as the Textile Workers' Union, had poor organizing records yet were not made subject to wholesale dismemberment.

The difference between the right-wing Textile Workers' Union and the Retail Union was that a strong left-wing contingent dominated most of the larger New York City RU locals. Though they were not represented in the national leadership of the union, the left was secure in New York, having beaten back several attempts to defeat it. The ACTU and others of the conservative opposition were unable to win a democratic victory against the left in these locals. The conservatives were both unsure of the national RU leadership's ability to carry out a purge and unwilling to mobilize for a national struggle to win leadership themselves, despite the fact that this would have been considerably easier than it had proved to be in the UE or the other unions actually led by the left.

This was not simple laziness on the part of the ACTU. The RU, rather, was a victim of the Actists' abandonment of democratic opposition within left-wing unions. The earlier commitment of the ACTU to defeating the left within the CIO unions through democratic means had by this time been superseded by the desire to oust them by any means necessary. In 1946 the ACTU had been willing to organize within the unions most decisively controlled by the left. Actists had advised others to remain in these unions and criticized locals which seceded and unions which indulged in raids. By 1949, however, the ACTU was unwilling to mobilize internal opposition, even in a union which merely had a strong left-wing minority, and chose instead to promote and organize the raids and secessions it had earlier condemned. The ACTU's commitment to union democracy proved to be contingent on the opposition's ability to win democratically. Where it could not, the ACTU supported the dismemberment of the CIO union involved and the division of its membership among AFL unions on a first come, first served basis, even though the effect would be a decline in overall union membership.

Significantly, AFL unions were the beneficiaries of the ACTU's raiding policies in both the RU and the UOPWA.[64] In its first two years the ACTU had been strongly identified with the CIO, to the degree that the Actists felt it necessary to point out to fearful AFL leaders that they supported all "bonafide trade unions."[65] ACTU organizing and strike-support activities in those years had almost invariably involved CIO unions, whose commitment to industrial unionism and militance the Actists found preferable to AFL craft divisions and passivity. By the late 1940s, however, the ACTU was moving toward a position considerably more favorable to the AFL. The belief that the organization generally supported secession of CIO affiliates to AFL unions was so widespread by 1947 that the *Labor Leader* editors were forced to issue a denial that the ACTU was abandoning the CIO.[66] Explanation of this change of direction requires a little backtracking.

While Catholic labor activists of the early twentieth century had operated exclusively in the AFL unions, the ACTU had been formed as a CIO-oriented Catholic labor organization. The CIO was a new and potentially radical union federation, but its membership was probably more heavily Catholic even than that of the AFL. It was thus imperative that a Catholic CIO presence be established to promote a "sound trade union" alternative to the ominously strong CIO left wing. Though the early ACTU was unlike the Militia of Christ for Social Service or the German Central Verein in that it favored industrial unionism and criticized the AFL's "conservatism," it followed the same Catholic labor strategy which these organizations had utilized in the AFL. This program had underpinned the Church's accommodation with the Knights of Labor and subsequently with both the AFL and CIO. The strategy was to unite with conservative unionists within "nonsectarian" unions in order to defeat the socialists.[67]

European Catholics had to contend with a labor movement dominated by socialists and communists from the outset and were thus forced to organize their own conservative unions. In the United States, on the other hand, Catholics faced a multidenominational working-class and conservative trade unions which nonetheless included substantial radical minorities. The unusual papal dispensation which American Catholics received to join the Knights of Labor, and by extension the AFL and the CIO, was designed to assure the continued conservative domination of these union federations and the defeat of the radical wings.[68]

The ACTU's commitment to the CIO, rather than the AFL, had been essential to combat the left and reinforce the conservatives in the CIO. Unlike the socialist-led AFL unions, however, which gradually succumbed to business unionism, the CIO left stubbornly refused to be defeated or corrupted. The ACTU recognized the endurance and discipline of the CIO left wing and had always argued for the CIO's rejoining the AFL to increase the conservative balance of power. But most of the CIO unions, even the most conservative, resisted this amalgamation because of fear of the dismemberment of the new industrial unions among the AFL craft unions. The problem, then, was to defeat a well-organized left wing which was heavily entrenched in unions representing a substantial minority of the CIO membership. When internal opposition failed to deliver any victories to the conservative opposition, except in the Newspaper Guild, the ACTU gave up the democratic approach and called for national CIO action to circumvent the memberships and "clean up" these unions. [69]

The AFL unions, of course, were eager to win members from CIO affiliates, and from the point of view of the ACTU, these unions were admirably suited for the purposes. With the assistance of the Church, they had long since defeated and expelled their own radicals and settled comfortably into conservative unionism. By aiding the AFL unions in their raids on the CIO unions, the ACTU also put more pressure on the national CIO leadership to undertake the purge which the ACTU had long demanded. The ACTU's growing support for the AFL unions, when they competed with left-wing CIO unions, thus did not represent a fundamental change in policy so much as an altered tactical application of a quite consistent policy of anti-communism. The ACTU's commitment to the industrial unionism of the CIO had simply never been so strong as its commitment to the struggle against the left.

The denouement of this struggle occurred in the UE in 1949. The UE was the largest left-wing CIO union and hence the crucial battleground in the purge campaign. The struggle there would determine the course of events in all the smaller left-wing unions, whose combined membership was less than half that of the UE. The ACTU had long understood the pivotal role of the UE. The Actists had made contacts within the union in their first months of existence and had developed conferences, periodicals, and finally a full-scale movement in opposition to the UE left wing. The ACTU-supported Committee for Rank and File Democracy proved to be the crucial pivot in the unification of the various anti-communist factions in the UE into the MDA. The MDA then extended its organization throughout the country, with the active participation of several ACTU chapters, from 1946 through 1948. The opposition had elected local officers and convention delegates and contested the left wing's control of the UE at several conventions during these years.

Despite the favorable conditions which the opposition enjoyed (national CIO support, the employer offensive against the UE, AFL and CIO raiding, anti-communist hysteria in the press and pulpit, and NLRB and court attacks on the UE), however, they were not able to win. The left wing was capable and tenacious and the UE had an excellent organizing and bargaining record. The membership was reluctant to abandon its union leadership and support the MDA, especially since the latter focused almost exclusively on anti-communism. Anti-communism, the members perhaps realized, would not fight the Taft-Hartley Act, GE, or Westinghouse, and the MDA's later development of an economic program was clearly something of an afterthought. The UE leadership, on the other hand, did have an economic program and it was resisting the Taft-Hartley Act and confronting the electrical employers. Much of the support, too, which the MDA did secure represented members' fears that the UE would be unable to defend them because of attacks against it, rather than positive support for the MDA's recent economic program or its anti-communism.

The majority of the UE membership, in any case, remained unimpressed with the MDA and gave their votes to the left wing. This fact encouraged the ACTU and the other conservatives, first reluctantly and then wholeheartedly, to support secession from the UE and ultimately the organization of a dual electrical union, the International Union of Electrical Workers (IUE). The exclusive commitment of the ACTU and MDA to anti-communism thus caused them, when rejected by the UE membership, to abandon membership democracy, autonomy, and self-determination. Their strategy, instead, depended on national CIO support, and that of raiding CIO and AFL unions, employers, and the Taft-Hartley machinery, and resulted in the disruption of the UE through succession and contract nullification. Since it did not depend on the support of the union's members, still largely loyal to their left-wing leadership, this strategy was successful in weakening, isolating, and expelling the UE, and in turn the other left-wing unions, from the CIO.

The anti-communist struggle in the UE continued to be waged internally by the MDA during 1949, however, though secession and the threatened expulsion of the UE were always in the background.[70] The MDA gains were relatively substantial. In January the ACTU could take heart in a "swing to the anti-communists" in a significant number of locals. MDA or affiliated slates were successful in election contests in eleven locals in that month.[71] The ACTU was an important factor in several of these struggles, including that in the largest UE local, number 601 in Pittsburgh. Under the leadership of the Reverend Rice the Actists had been active in local 601 since 1940. The struggle in this 17,000-member local was especially bitter and involved two brothers, the FitzPatricks, as leaders of the opposing sides. The ACTU-supported MDA slate elected its three candidates, Philip Conahan, Charles Copeland, and Mike FitzPatrick, as officers of the local in January, but the left made a comeback the following month when they elected Mike's brother, Tom FitzPatrick, chief steward and won a majority of the executive board seats. A similar stalemate occurred when the left won the executive board of the large Schenectady local 301, whose other officers were MDA members.[72]

The continued strength of the left in these two large locals, and in others where the opposition had won elections, engendered instability in the MDA forces. This instability was reinforced by continued secessions. Pittsburgh UE locals 613 and 628, for example, gave up the internal struggle and affiliated with the UAW in April, despite the opposition of the ACTU and of Actist John Duffy, the vice-president of local 613 and the leader of the Pittsburgh MDA. The MDA representatives met at a national conference in Dayton on May 8 and 9 under the pale of this chronic organizational and programmatic weakness. The 250 MDA delegates represented thirteen states, thirty-nine cities, and ten of the thirteen UE regional districts. The meeting was intended to prepare opposition forces for the upcoming September 1949 UE convention. The situation had certainly never been more propitious for the opposition. The UE was under attack by the national CIO leadership, the major electrical industry employers, and the government. It was losing contracts through noncompliance with the Taft-Hartley non-communist affidavits and the raiding of both CIO and AFL affiliates, and losing locals through secessions. The UE administration had never been more vulnerable to opposition challenge. [73]

The result of the convention, however, was another victory for the administration. Albert Fitzgerald was reelected president over Fred Kelly of the MDA by a vote of 2,335 to 1,500. By similar tallies, Mike FitzPatrick of local 601 and the MDA lost to Julius Emspak for the position of secretary-treasurer, and Actist John Dillon was defeated for organization director by James Matles. Though the MDA candidates had doubled their vote of the previous year, they had fallen considerably short of victory. The convention also endorsed a stiff resolution to the national CIO demanding an end to raiding on the UE by CIO affiliates. In a move which took some of the wind out of the MDA's sails, the delegates also voted for UE compliance with the Taft-Hartley non-communist oaths. [74]

The 1949 convention made rather plain what the ACTU had feared for some time. It was not going to win a majority vote for MDA candidates for national office in the UE. As a result, the MDA began to function more like an alternate union than the UE opposition caucus. Just after the convention the *Labor Leader* reported that,

> the minority re-elected ten delegates on a geographical basis to meet with the officers of the CIO and attend the CIO Convention. The delegates are also to determine the best way to provide a CIO international union in the electrical industry free from the domination of the Communist party.

The secession-expulsion strategy which the ACTU had originally sought to defeat had now been adopted as the only one likely to give the conservative opposition a victory. Two months later, in November 1949, the CIO convention expelled the UE from the CIO and proceeded to organize a dual electrical union, the International Union of Electrical Workers (IUE) from seceding MDA-dominated UE locals. The expulsion of the remaining left-wing CIO unions, as well as that of many individual left-wingers in other unions, followed within the year. [75]

NOTES

1. Bernstein, *The Turbulent Years*, p. 783; Kampelman, *The Communist Party vs. the CIO*, p. 45; Galenson, *The CIO Challenge to the AFL*, pp. 239, 265. See DeCaux, *Labor Radical*, for an account of the left and its role within the CIO; also, Preis, *Labor's Giant Step*; Matles, *Them and Us*; Richard Boyer and Herbert Morais, *Labor's Untold Story* (New York: UE Press, 1955).

2. On CIO leadership toleration of the left wing see Madison, *American Labor Leaders*, p. 327; "Labor Leaders Rebuff the ACTU," *Daily Worker*, July 28, 1947; Bernstein, *The Turbulent Years*, p. 607. Both Lewis and Hillman had fought the communists in the 1920s and early 1930s, but were willing, in a limited way, to let bygones be bygones where CIO organizing was concerned. Bernstein, *The Lean Years*, pp. 106–138; Madison, *American Labor Leaders*, pp. 349–50.

3. Madison, *American Labor Leaders*, p. 327. Both Mathew Woll and Joseph Ryan of the AFL made virtual careers of testimony before Congressional panels on communist influence in the CIO.

4. Bernstein, *The Turbulent Years*, p. 527; *Proceedings of the Seventh International Convention* (UE), p. 172.

5. Harry Read to Thomas Doherty, October 19, 1940, ACTU files; "When Red Baiting Failed," editorial, *Daily Worker*, September 7, 1947; "List Fifteen Renegades From Waterfront CP," *Daily Worker*, April 5, 1948; "ACTU Ignores Pay Proposal," *Daily Worker*, March 3, 1949; George Morris, *Where is the CIO Going* (New York: New Century, 1949), pp. 26–27; Morris, "Vatican Conspiracy in the Trade Union Movement," p. 22–24; Morris, "The ACTU," pp. 252–63; Preis, *Labor's Giant Step*, pp. 327, 331; DeCaux, *Labor Radical*, 326, 327, 513, 487, 488; *Labor Leader* 1, nos. 26 and 41, 3, no. 9; "Open Letter to Mr. Murray," leaflet, 1948, ACTU files.

6. Abel, *American Catholicism and Social Action*, p. 275.

7. On the realignment of the CIO, postwar conditions, and the expulsions, see Madison, *American Labor Leaders*, p. 327; DeCaux, *Labor Radical*, 336, 378, 487–490, 509, 513; Boyer, *Labor's Untold Story*, 329–350; *Proceedings of the Eighth, Ninth, Tenth and Eleventh Constitutional Conventions of the CIO*.

8. "Report of the CLDL," September 1946; Reports of ACTU conferences in the TWU, UAW, News Guild, and UE, 1946; *Labor Leader* 9, no. 8, 10, no. 4.

9. Ever since the establishment of the Tarrytown Labor School in February 1938, many of the ACTU's schools had direct relationships with union locals. Special schools for members of specific unions had also been established previously for the Office and Professional Workers' Union, the Transit Workers, the Railway Clerks, and several other unions. Donahue viewed the schools as an "open sesame" for organizational contacts with unionists. Interview with George Donahue, July 22, 1974; "ACTU Labor Schools in the New York Area," brochure, 1946, pp. 1–5, ACTU files; "The Detroit Workers School," brochure, 1946, pp. 1–3, ACTU files; *Labor Leader* 1, no. 9, 2, no. 1, 6, no. 5, 9, nos. 1, 17, 19, and 20, 10, no. 40.

10. Committees for a Permanent FEPC were formed in many cities and were endorsed by the 1946 CIO convention. *Proceedings of the Eighth Constitutional Convention of the CIO*, p. 84; *Labor Leader* 9, nos. 8, 9, 11, and 21.

11. "Stern Unfair to Labor," "ACTU Supports Electrical Workers," other leaflets, 1946, ACTU files; *Labor Leader* 9, no. 14, 10, no. 4.

12. The communists were accused by the ACTU, for example, of destroying the "good will" of the employer at one Allis-Chalmers UAW local. *Labor Leader* 9, nos. 17 and 21, 10, no. 1; Reports of ACTU Conferences in the TWU, UAW, Newspaper Guild, and UE, 1946.

13. *Labor Leader* 9, nos. 1, 5, 17, 19, and 21.

14. The RU was also subject to the particular organizing problems facing white-collar unions, including the UOPWA. The Actists, however, once they were among the leadership of the RU, were more charitable in their analysis of that union than they were with regard to the left-wing UOPWA, which was attacked by the ACTU and the CIO national leadership for "not fulfilling [its] responsibilities" to white-collar workers. *Proceedings of the Tenth Constitutional Convention of the CIO*, pp. 336–341; *Labor Leader* 7, no. 9, 9, nos. 2 and 3.

15. "Support the American Way," "Defeat Velson-Stalin's Agent," leaflets, ACTU files; *Labor Leader* 9, nos. 1, 11, and 15.

16. The ACTU's alliance with the Schactmanites was interesting also because the Church had rejected any such alliance with socialists in order to defeat Fascism. Communism apparently was a different matter. Indeed, since this period the Church-supported parties have joined with the socialists in several countries, notably Italy and Portugal, to oppose the Communist party, and even, informally, with the communists to oppose the ultra-left. Camp, *Papal Ideology*, pp. 60–80; Harrington, "Catholics in the Labor Movement," p. 247.

17. The ACTU's anti-communist ideology provided a ready explanation for such disregard of internal union democracy. The communists *could not* have membership support—that was axiomatic—therefore they must be running the union undemocratically. In that case external intervention could be justified to rescue the membership. This was the logic that was to inform the ACTU's activities in the UE. See, for example, "Communists Boss UE," leaflet, 1947, ACTU files.

18. Rice was the acknowledged leader of union anti-communists in Pittsburgh and took up the struggle against the left with a zest which he has only recently reconsidered. Charles Owen Rice, "Ecumenism in Labor," *Pittsburgh Catholic*, June 9, 1966. See also Harrington, "Catholics in the Labor Movement," p. 240; Taft, "The ACTU," p. 217; DeCaux, *Labor Radical* p. 427; *Labor Leader* 1, nos. 23, 25, 37, and 39, 4, nos. 5, 15, and 16, 5, no. 3.

19. "Electrical Industry Conference Report," May 1946, ACTU files. Interview with George Donahue, July 22, 1974; *Labor Leader* 10, no. 40.

20. Harrington, "Catholics in the Labor Movement," pp. 245–246; *Labor Leader* 10, no. 4.

21. The UE administration's response to the MDA was the pamphlet *The Members Run This Union*, which argued that the MDA sought to promote secession, raiding, and "CIO interference in the UE." Matles, *The Members Run This Union*, 1947, pp. 1–4; Harrington, "Catholics in the Labor Movement," p. 246; *Labor Leader* 9, nos. 14 and 17. DeCaux and Bernstein confirm that the UE was in fact one of the most democratic CIO unions and that Matles and James Emspak were extremely able union leaders. DeCaux, *Labor Radical*, pp. 509–513; Bernstein, *The Turbulent Years*, p. 607.

22. Kampelman confirms that "in a number of communities, the opposition UEMDA group was spearheaded by [branches] of the ACTU." The ACTU played a leading role in the MDA in New York–New Jersey (district 4), the largest UE district, and was also active in Pittsburgh, Bridgeport, and Saint Louis. Kampelman, *The Communist Party vs. the CIO*, p. 135; DeCaux, *Labor Radical*, p. 496; *Labor Leader* 9, no. 18.

23. *Labor Leader* 2, no. 17, 4, no. 5, 5, nos. 3 and 21, 10, no. 4.

24. Harrington, "Catholics in the Labor Movement," p. 248; *Labor Leader* 10, no. 4.

25. "Minutes of the MDA Meeting," November 10–11, 1946, ACTU files, pp. 1–9; *Labor Leader* 9, no. 20.

26. Conroy was but the first of many Catholic leftists who would recant and join the ACTU. Virtually the entire ACTU leadership in the NMU deserted from the left wing. "Renegades From Waterfront CP," *Daily Worker*, April 5, 1948; *Labor Leader* 9, nos. 21 and 22, 10, no. 1.

27. The ACTU had been active within the state CIO council in New York as early as 1938 and helped in the defeat of the left wing at the 1940 meeting. DeCaux, *Labor Radical*, p. 361; *Labor Leader* 9, nos. 21 and 22.

28. From its first UWU steward in 1938 the ACTU had expanded its influence until one of its labor school graduates became UWU president in 1945. Weinberg, "Priests, Workers and Communists," p. 53; *Proceedings of the Eighth Constitutional Convention of the CIO*, p. 113; *Labor Leader* 9, nos. 7, 14, and 20.

29. *Labor Leader* 1, no. 5.

30. The Reverend William J. Smith, Director of the ACTU's Crown Heights Labor School, prefigured the ACTU's position on the first amendment in his 1938 pamphlet, *American or Communist? You Can't Be Both*. Smith argued that "a federal statute [must] be drawn up" to cover communism, which "itself is worthy of criminal title." The Sedition Act "loophole" which required that "danger of violence and insurrection should be immediate and proximately threatening" should be "plugged." Smith, *American or Communist? You Can't Be Both*, pp. 1–2; *Labor Leader* 1, nos. 5 and 7, 5, nos. 7 and 11, 8, no. 4, 9, nos. 6 and 7.

31. The Boston Catholic Labor Guild and the Chicago Catholic Labor Alliance had both originally been ACTU chapters. They had separated amicably largely because of localist sentiment, though the Chicago group had also had reservations about the stress the ACTU placed on anti-communism. By 1946, however, these groups fully shared the ACTU's perspective on the left wing and they cooperated in the campaigns under way. Harry Read to Thomas Doherty, October 9, 1939; Doherty to Read, October 14, 1939; Read to Doherty, October 19, 1940; *Labor Leader* 10, nos. 6 and 7.

32. "Minutes of the National Convention," 1947, ACTU files, pp. 1–11; *Labor Leader* 10, no. 13.

33. *Labor Leader* 10, nos. 1, 3, 4, 5, and 8.

34. Ibid., 10, no. 10.

35. James Freeman, *No Friend of Labor* (New York: Fulfillment Press, 1949), p. 1; "Reports" of the ACA and TWU Conferences, 1947, ACTU files; *Labor Leader* 10, nos. 1, 2, and 3.

36. *The Hearst Strike*, pp. 1–3; "Reports" of the News Guild Conference 1945, 1946, 1947, ACTU files; *Labor Leader* 10, nos. 13 and 16; *Michigan Labor Leader* 1, no. 1.

37. "Clean-Up The News Guild," ACTU leaflet, 1947, ACTU files; *Labor Leader* 10, nos. 7, 8, 11, 13, and 16.

38. *Labor Leader* 10, nos. 13, 16, and 22.

39. Harrington, for example, minimizes the role of the ACTU, particularly in the faction fighting in the UE. He argues that people merely "used its name," that the Reverend Rice was a "one-man ACTU" in Pittsburgh, and that "at no time did the ACTU create a stable, national organization." The evidence suggests that he has underestimated the ACTU's role. Harrington, "Catholics in The Labor Movement," pp. 237, 239, 242.

40. *Labor Leader* 10, nos. 13 and 16.

41. Block was Jewish. He was one of several non-Catholics whom the ACTU supported in the anti-communist campaign. As the ACTU extended its activities to wider caucuses within the

unions it was necessary for them to build ties with non-Catholic workers. Indeed, beginning in 1946 this had become a priority item for the Actists. The criticism of the left wing, that the ACTU was sectarian, cleric-controlled, and a source of religious splitting, reinforced this direction. "The Labor Priests," *Fortune*, p. 151; Morris, "Spotlight on the ACTU," pp. 252–63; Freeman, *No Friend of Labor*, pp. 2, 5; *Labor Leader* 10, nos. 1, 4, 10, and 16.

42. On Curran's defection from the left wing, see Barbash, *Unions and Union Leadership*, pp. 216–18; DeCaux, *Labor Radical*, p. 422; *Labor Leader* 10, no. 1.

43. The WFTU united the trade unions of the socialist and Western powers and, almost as soon as it was organized, became an issue among conservatives in the British and American labor movements. The CIO executive board disaffiliated the CIO from the WFTU in late 1948. *Proceedings of the Eleventh Constitutional Convention of the CIO*, p. 10; *Labor Leader* 10, nos. 1, 2, and 4.

44. The 1947 CIO convention unanimously approved a resolution protesting the Taft-Hartley Act, which Murray characterized as an "inestimable threat to the existence of labor organizations" and "a triumph of repression." *Proceedings of the Ninth Constitutional Convention of the CIO*, pp. 87–88, 187–88; *Labor Leader* 10, no. 11.

45. The *Labor Leader* characterized the act as "hastily drawn, ill-considered legislation" that "endangered the economic future of millions of Americans." *Labor Leader* 10, nos. 1, 10, 11, and 13.

46. *Labor Leader* 9, no. 21, 10, no. 1.

47. The ACTU complained, in February 1948, that the non-communist oaths were a "serious blow to the anti-Communist movement represented by the UE-MDA," since their effect was to promote secession, which strengthened the left-wing administration. *Labor Leader* 10, nos. 13 and 15, 11, no. 3, 12, no. 7.

48. "Support the Wall Street Strike," "Open the Piers," leaflets, 1947, ACTU files; Interview with George Donahue, July 22, 1974; *Labor Leader* 10, no. 8, 11, nos. 3, 7, 18, 19, and 20, 12, no. 9.

49. "Minutes of the 1948 Convention," pp. 1–11, ACTU files; *Labor Leader* 11, no. 13, 12, no. 11.

50. ACTU "Conference Reports" for the Newspaper Guild, April and November 1947, ACTU files; *The Masthead* 1, nos. 1 and 3; *Labor Leader* 10, no. 22, 11, nos. 2, 7, and 13, 12, no. 11.

51. The UE, despite the secession of many locals, did not do badly during this period. The union actually won 84.1 percent of its bargaining elections in 1946, one of the highest proportions in the CIO. The union lost many more members through secession than through contract nullification, even in 1948 and 1949. *Proceedings of the Eighth Constitutional Convention of the CIO*, p. 209; *Labor Leader* 10, no. 15, 11, nos. 3 and 13.

52. *Labor Leader* 11, no. 3, 12, nos. 1, 7, and 11.

53. Two communist councilmen and a left-wing Congressman, Vito Marcantonio, were elected on the ALP ticket. "When Red-Baiting Failed," editorial, *Daily Worker*, September 12, 1947; *Labor Leader* 5, no. 13, 10, no. 15, 11, no. 1. DeCaux, *Labor Radical*, p. 361.

54. On ACTU activity in the TWU see, Weinberg, "Priests, Workers and Communists," pp. 49–56. On Quill's defection from the left see Preis, *Labor's Giant Step*, pp. 343, 359; DeCaux, *Labor Radical*, p. 427; *Labor Leader* 11, no. 7.

55. In July of 1949 Joe Curran, the former left-wing leader of the NMU, was able to execute a similar series of maneuvers and win reelection as president of the seamen's union on an anti-communist slate supported by the ACTU and other conservatives. *Labor Leader* 12, no.

11; "TWU Conference Report," May, 1948, ACTU files; *Labor Leader* 11, nos. 12, 18, 23, and 24.

56. The left wing was equally strong in support of Wallace, who was viewed as the most progressive of the New Deal figures, a strong anti-monopolist, and supporter of labor and an opponent of Truman's Cold War initiatives, including the Marshall Plan. Matles, *Them and Us*, pp. 171–73, 187–89, 197; *Labor Leader* 11, nos. 1 and 5.

57. *Proceedings of the Sixth Convention of the NMU*, p. 108; "The Labor Priests," p. 152; Barbash, *Unions and Union Leadership*, pp. 216, 218; DeCaux, *Labor Radical*, 422; Preis, *Labor's Giant Step*, p. 359; *Labor Leader* 10, no. 16.

58. *Proceedings of the Tenth Constitutional Convention of the CIO*, pp. 228, 232, 263–264; *Labor Leader* 11, nos. 3, 7, and 20.

59. Gary ACTU labor school brochure, ACTU files; Cort, "Ten Years of ACTU," p. 143; *Labor Leader* 12, nos. 3, 7, 8, 9, 10, and 16.

60. The ACTU was involved in a similar campaign during 1948 on behalf of a black worker at the Transit Authority who had been repeatedly passed over for promotion. James C. Jefferson to Roger Larkin, November 30, 1948; Larkin to Jefferson, December 15, 1948; ILA Conference Report, April, 1949; *Labor Leader* 12, nos. 2, 6, and 11.

61. John Cort, a vice-president of the ACTU and editor of the *Labor Leader*, and Margaret McGarry, ACTU treasurer, were both UOPWA members. In the course of the UOPWA struggle the *Labor Leader* reported, rather pointedly and perhaps to good tactical effect, that Catholics who "knowingly and freely" give aid to the communists or their doctrines "incur automatic excommunication." *Labor Leader* 1, no. 39, 2, nos. 11 and 18, 12, nos. 7 and 13.

62. *Labor Leader* 1, nos. 1 and 9, 4, nos. 8, 9, 10, and 18, 5, nos. 1 and 3, 6, no. 1, 7, no. 19, 8, no. 1, 12, no. 4.

63. *Labor Leader* 12, nos. 4 and 8; Interview with George Donahue, July 22, 1974.

64. This was not always the case, however. In the fall of 1949 the ACTU supported raiding on the left-wing United Public Workers by another CIO affiliate, the American Civil Employees Union, in "hopes that this is really the beginning of a concerted drive by the right-wing to oust the left-wing UPW." (The ACTU's preferred description of itself and its allies in the anti-communist campaign was "right-wing.") *Labor Leader* 12, no. 14.

65. *Michigan Labor Leader* 1, nos. 20 and 25.

66. *Labor Leader* 10, no. 1.

67. See the introduction for a fuller explication of Catholic strategy in the labor movement.

68. Cross, *Liberal Catholicism in America*, p. 117; Karson, *American Labor Unions and Politics*, p. 269.

69. Gene Kelly, president of the Cleveland ACTU, called for expulsion of those CIO unions which were "playing the Communist game," as early as September 1947. The *Labor Leader* editors referred approvingly to the "liquidation" of the left-wing unions even earlier, in 1942. *Labor Leader* 5, no. 19, 10, no. 16.

70. Internal opposition also remained the policy of the San Francisco chapter and other Actists within the left-wing ILWU. *Labor Leader* 12, nos. 11 and 14.

71. These included numbers 601, 502, and 628 in Pennsylvania, 607, 608, and 627 in West Virginia, 301 in New York, 1117 in Minnesota, 1140 in Maine, 755 and 801 in Ohio, and 201 in Massachusetts. *Labor Leader* 12, no. 1; Harrington, "Catholics in the Labor Movement," pp. 253–58.

72. *Labor Leader* 12, nos. 1 and 3.

73. *Labor Leader* 12, nos. 7, 9, and 10; "Minutes of the MDA Meeting," May 8–9, 1949, ACTU files. On the UE's difficulties with the courts, raiding unions, employers, and redbaiting, see DeCaux, *Labor Radical,* pp. 509–513; Matles, *Them and Us,* pp. 153–227.

74. *Labor Leader* 12, no. 16.

75. These unions included the UE, the UOPWA, the UPW, the Fur and Leather Workers, the ACA, the Food and Tobacco Workers, ILWU, MMSW, Marine Cooks, Fishermen, and Farm Equipment Workers. Kampelman, *The Communist Party vs the CIO,* p. 160; *Proceedings of the Eleventh Constitutional Convention of the CIO,* pp. 302–305, 334–35, 347; *Labor Leader* 12, no. 16.

Conclusion

This book began with the proposition that the conservative orientation of the United States labor movement has never been adequately
explained. The assumption that labor conservatism was natural and
necessary in America, it was argued, has inhibited serious investigation of the sources of that conservatism. The active and, at times,
successful struggle of the left to win union leadership and the efforts
of conservatives to defeat them, it was pointed out, have both been
slighted because of the presumed inevitability of American labor's
business unionist and "nonideological" perspective. This book has
investigated one source of conservative ideology, organization, and
action in the American labor movement—the Catholic Church and
its lay apostolate to labor—and has argued that the partisans of the
Church were a crucial factor in the conservative direction taken by
the CIO unions during the period 1937–1950.

The important role of the Catholic Church in the labor movement
of the late nineteenth and early twentieth century has received
scholarly attention. Marc Karson's study of the Church's part in the
struggle for conservative dominance in the AFL shows the Church to
have been "a vital force accounting for the moderate political
position of American labor."[1] The Church in this period approved or
banned Catholic participation in particular unions. The clergy
agitated for a specific brand of unionism and for particular positions
on such disparate issues as socialism, women's suffrage, and free
public-school texts, as well as against a labor party. Churchmen
wrote articles for labor periodicals and addressed union conventions. Schools, seminars, and religious functions for unionists
encouraged a trade unionism consistent with Catholic social doctrine. Lay Catholics organized the Militia of Christ for Social Service

and, among German Catholics, the Central Verein. These and other Catholic organizations worked among Catholic unionists and union leaders to defeat socialist influence and support the conservative direction of the AFL leadership.

The Church's important role in the struggle between left and right in the pre–World War I AFL has thus been established as a crucial one. This book examined the influence of the Catholic Church in the CIO unions in the 1930s and 1940s. The investigation indicates that the Church and its lay partisans were able to duplicate the earlier structure of influence in the AFL unions in the CIO as well. The ACTU, in particular, became an effective vehicle for the education of unionists within the Catholic labor tradition and a spearhead in the internal struggle against the left wing. Catholic influence proved to be a significant factor in the conservative direction of American industrial unionism.

The Association of Catholic Trade Unionists was the largest, the "officially" sanctioned, and the most active Catholic organization in the labor movement in the 1930s and 1940s and was especially strong in the CIO unions. The group has received many footnotes in the history of the CIO and was generally assumed by contemporaries to have played a relatively significant role, especially in the struggle with the left wing.[2] But published historical studies of the ACTU are few and meager and do not provide a general assessment of the organization.[3] Nor have any of the former Actists published their own histories or memoirs.[4] The present study, then, depended heavily on primary sources, periodical literature, and union records. The major sources were the ACTU's organizational records, the *Michigan Labor Leader*, and the national ACTU *Labor Leader*.

The first question, naturally, was whether the ACTU, in the context of the CIO of the 1930s and 1940s, was a "conservative" organization. During 1937, the first year of the organization's existence, the ACTU tended toward a "progressive" or a "center-left" position. The charged atmosphere of the initial CIO organizing drives, the relative fluidity of the young ACTU, and the group's extensive union-support work, particularly the ACTU-CIO organizing in Jersey City, helped to encourage this position among a portion, at any rate, of the membership. The progressive position was characterized by hostility to business, clerical, and AFL conservatives and by a priority commitment to the fight for "social justice." The progressives rejected political anti-communism and indicated willingness to work with all supporters of industrial unionism. The ACTU in its progressive period expressed a strong partisan commitment to working-class interests and militance in pursuit of them, and endorsed a mild socialism.

By February 1937, however, the Gerson affair had provided the occasion for a conservative reaction among ACTU members. In the course of the ACTU debates over the protest of Gerson's appointment the progressives abandoned their position and ultimately joined with the conservatives in denouncing Gerson's appointment. The conservative position, which was quickly consolidated following the Gerson protest, attached first priority to the fight against communism over "social justice." The mild socialism of the first year was abandoned and erstwhile opponents in the AFL, the business community, and the right wing of the clergy were welcomed into a new "anti-communist" front. The early ACTU's militantly pro-worker attitude gave way to a pronounced stress on nonviolence, mediation, and class harmony.

In practice this conservative direction was manifested in the beginnings of ACTU anti-communist factional fighting in the unions, coalition work with other anti-communists, renewed red-baiting, and in a friendlier relationship with the AFL and conservative clergy. The new conservative orientation was consolidated through organizational expansion around this program and the adoption of a formal structure and constitution.

Investigation of the Gerson debate, the most significant internal division in the ACTU, and of the background of both progressives and conservatives indicated that the commitment of both groups to the Church and its labor doctrine virtually assured the dominance of the conservative position. While there were elements in the background of the progressives (college, unskilled work, participation in strike-support and organizing work, and the experience of having been red-baited) which disposed them to a center-left position, they were unwilling to entertain any break with the Church. Since the position of the Church and the whole weight of past Catholic labor action favored the conservatives and placed anti-communism before all other questions, the progressives were in an untenable position.

Despite experience which tended to confirm a center-left position, then, the ACTU readily returned to the conservative orientation which had characterized its earliest position papers as well as the work of previous Catholic labor groups. This was accomplished without a split in the organization or even a change of leadership, since the progressives, despite their earlier radical statements and actions, fundamentally agreed with the conservative premises of the Church's labor ideology.

The ACTU derived a number of organizational strengths from Catholic affiliation and Church support. Among these were a sense of history, a preexisting body of doctrine which spared them the pains of theoretical dispute, the coherent world view which sprang from a parallel social and religious commitment, a defined constituency which was prepared for the ACTU's religiously framed union program, and the institutional and personnel resources of the Church.

The official Catholic status of the organization, however, contributed some difficulties as well. Catholicism promoted a tendency to see union issues in moral and theological, rather than political or strategic terms and the Church encouraged the ACTU's stress on class harmony, cooperation and mediation, rather than working class self-determination. The theological definition of communism and socialism as evil also foreclosed the possibility of common work with these tendencies.

The confessional limitation on membership presented no serious internal problems for the ACTU, but it made more difficult the organization's attempts to work with wider sections of the labor movement. Suspicion of religious sectarianism and dual unionism was widespread in the unions, and the ACTU was often viewed as the agent of Church interference. In response to this problem the ACTU initially focused on issues which tended to unite Catholic with non-Catholic workers: corruption and authoritarianism among union leaders, and organizing the unorganized. Ultimately, however, the ACTU's solution to religious limitations on its constituency was to focus on anti-communism, which was at once the cardinal tenet of Catholic labor strategy and a nonreligious issue with which the ACTU could build ties with conservative, but non-Catholic workers.

The clergy had a significant impact on the ACTU. Clerical control over and participation in the ACTU was extensive and most ACTU activities and positions bore the stamp of their influence. Especially important among these were the ACTU's labor schools, whose faculties were predominantly clerical, and the organization's union-support activities. Clerical influence in both cases was demonstrably conservative. The schools were a major locus of the conservative faction during the Gerson debate and were centers for recruitment to factional fighting against the left wing in the unions. Clerics were often the leaders of such factional fighting. In the case of union-support efforts, clerical influence was strongly on the side of mediation and against militance. Nearly all the ACTU's strike-support efforts were terminated by mediation, and in every such case the mediator was a Churchman. In a more general way, the extensive participation of the clergy and the ACTU's emphatic support for their authority tended to reinforce conservatism among Catholic workers. Since most clergy were relatively conservative, the ACTU's support for clerical authority in all matters tended to reinforce the hold of conservative Catholicism among parishioners. The role of the clergy in the ACTU's activities also contributed to Catholic workers lack of self-confidence, passivity, and inexperience with union struggle and democratic forms (which the ACTU itself had cause to lament), since the clerics tended to dominate the strikes they supported and to subordinate them to their ideas of class harmony. The clerical members of the ACTU were also responsible for the especial vehemence of the organization's anti-communism, for its favorable position toward the Franco forces in Spain, and, in general, for the ACTU's staunch adherence to the spirit and letter of Catholic social doctrine.

Portions of the social encyclicals, the Bishops' Program for Reconstruction of 1919, and the works of Monsignor John A. Ryan, as well as the ACTU's own formulations of Catholic social doctrine, seemed to imply sweeping social changes. These included support for cooperative enterprise in industry and a wider distribution of property, opposition to monopoly, and the concepts of fair prices and profits and a living wage. In the development of these ideas, however, their critical edge was almost entirely lost. A staunch commitment to private property, classical economics, authority and hierarchy, and hostility to socialism and communism subordinated the radical elements of Catholic theory to the conservative ones.

The Catholic social ideology which emerged was thus a fundamentally conservative ideology. Price and profit regulation as well as action against monopolies were abandoned. The living-wage concept offered a Catholic critique of prevailing wage rates, but this was undercut by the concept's ambiguity, its subsistence orientation, and its lack of connection to workers' increasing productivity. At its best the living-wage doctrine served to justify minimal increases for the most ill-paid workers. At worst, it served as a rationale for prevailing wage rates or even lower wages. The doctrine was further complicated, and made more conservative in impact, because of the corollary ideas that a differential "family wage" should be paid to male wage earners and that a living wage varied with one's "station in life." The more radical forms of cooperation, such as cooperative ownership or management, were ultimately dismissed as impractical. As Church authorities admitted, the requirement of voluntary assent by employers made any serious reform in management impossible. Similarly, the commitment to private property and opposition even to compensated nationalization, meant that, while formally supporting a wider distribution of property, the Church remained hostile to any possible scheme of accomplishing it.

The fullest expression of Catholic social ideology was the concept of the corporative society and this model brought the often latent conservatism of Catholic social thought into sharp focus. The corporative society was to be one of self-managing economic councils representing both workers and employers and functioning in an atmosphere of class harmony with minimal interference by the state. Since the prerogatives of ownership and management of property were to remain unchanged, however, the corporative society appeared far more attuned to the interests of the propertied than those of workers. Indeed, since unions were to be replaced by employer-employee guilds, while the regulatory role of the state was to be lessened, the position and power of workers promised to diminish significantly. Corporative ideology was conservative, even reactionary, in its stress on hierarchy, authority, national unity, class harmony, and discipline. Corporative theory subordinated political representation in favor of an economic representation which gave employers a relative advantage, and it promoted the virtue of satisfaction with one's social station over social mobility. The explicit connection of corporative doctrine to Italian Fascism and Spanish Falangism emphasized the conservative content of the theory.

The ACTU's own version of Catholic social ideology fully paralleled the conservatism of this body of doctrine. The ACTU supported and promoted the corporative or industrial-council plan as its long-range program. In the short range it promoted class harmony through its stress on mediation and its hostility to a labor party, class conflict, militance, and the organized left wing. The ACTU was equally committed to private property, to hierarchy, authority, order, and acceptance of one's social position. While the organization supported the industrial unionism of the CIO, in every other respect the ACTU's positions dovetailed with earlier Catholic doctrine developed during the struggle with the left wing in the AFL before World War I. Indeed, the Actists supported the renewed subordination of the CIO to the AFL. In particular, the ACTU maintained the commitment of earlier Catholic labor activists to the "fundamental issue" of Catholic union work: opposition to the left wing. The ACTU's ideology, before all else, was an anti-socialist and anti-communist one.

Catholic doctrine placed first priority on the struggle against the left wing within the unions, rather than the fight with employers and their conservative supporters. Much of Catholic social doctrine was, in fact, a reaction to the theories of the Marxists and the anti-radicalism of Catholic social thinking was its most characteristic element.

Apart from the ideological impact of the Catholic doctrine, the Church and the ACTU promoted a conservative program and a conservative style for the labor movement. Class consciousness and class politics were illegitimate and militance and violence were unjustifiable. Labor's role in politics was to be strictly limited and should not include support for an independent labor party. Strikes were to be avoided and the preferable solution to industrial disputes was mediation. In general, labor should accept its place and its condition and work with employers in class harmony, accepting whatever employers were willing to grant in the way of co-management of industry.

The ACTU proved to be a relatively coherent, effective, and disciplined national force in the late 1930s and 1940s. They organized over twenty chapters in the important industrial centers, published several periodicals, worked within all the major CIO unions, elected members to local and international union office, and maintained a continuous organizational presence and a consistent program throughout the period, even during the wartime years. While this program initially stressed organizing the unorganized and hence strike support and union organizing activity, after the first ten months the ACTU threw its main energies into the struggle with the left wing in the unions. The lack of any other organized cadre of union conservatives heightened the influence of the Actists in the internal struggle within the CIO unions. This vacuum permitted the ACTU to function as a catalyst and organizer for the broader conservative coalition which ultimately expelled the left-wing unions and secured conservative dominance in the CIO.

The ACTU's early strike- and organizing-support work served to establish its union credentials and to recruit workers to the organization. Three other major organizational activities were important in recruiting and promoting the ACTU's ideology: the labor-school network, the Catholic Labor Defense League, and the Catholic Union of the Unemployed. Each of these institutions was in part a response to initiatives by the left wing, whose influence the ACTU sought to counter. The Catholic Union of the Unemployed was unsuccessful largely because the left-wing unemployed councils had preempted the field. The CLDL, however, was quite active and was often the source of contacts for ACTU caucuses in local unions. Despite the CLDL's commitment to legal defense for unionists, it mainly functioned as a legal arm for the anti-communist forces in the unions.

The labor schools were the ACTU's most successful initiative. The schools taught a curriculum which included union basics, parliamentary procedure, labor history, the social encyclicals, and Catholic social doctrine. They were run either directly by the ACTU or by ACTU clerics operating under diocesan authorities. Scores of these schools functioned all over the country, as well as in Canada. They served to promote Catholic social doctrine among thousands of active trade unionists and local union officers, many of whom were non-Catholic, who subsequently formed the core ACTU caucuses in many unions.

All these branches of the ACTU served the organization's major focus: the internal struggle with the CIO left wing. To this struggle the ACTU brought a committed cadre, a far-flung network of contacts gleaned from its strike-support, legal, and educational activities, and the support of the Church. The Actists advanced an anti-communist position far to the right of any other organized force in the unions and the history of the organization from 1939 to 1950 was largely a history of promotion and increasing support for this position.

The ACTU organized its own caucuses in nearly all the important CIO unions and many AFL unions. It assisted other conservatives and spearheaded the unification of the right-wing forces in several CIO unions. The Actists ran their own candidates against the left wing and supported other conservatives. When success did not come at the local level, the organization sought assistance from international union and national CIO officers. During these eleven years the ACTU increasingly centered its attention on the fight with the left and favored increasingly extreme policies of intervention, raiding, secession, and purges to defeat the radicals. Positions which the ACTU had previously endorsed favoring union democracy, membership autonomy, and CIO versus AFL affiliation, and opposing raiding and secession, were abandoned in practice when they came into conflict with the struggle against the left.

From 1938 through 1945 the ACTU extended its base throughout the trade-union movement. From 1945 through 1950, favored by the national and international situation, it was able to play a crucial and leading role in the drive to purge the left wing from the unions. Actists were prominent in the national leadership of the News Guild and the Retail Union and they were a major conservative force in many other unions including the UAW, UWU, UOPWA, NMU, USW, MMSW, ILA, ILWU, UE, TWU, and IBT. Actists were the major factor in anti-communist victories in the News Guild, the Retail Union, and the MMSW. They were the best established force in the MDA, the anti-communist coalition in the UE, which they had initiated. The ACTU was also an important contributing force in conservative gains in the NMU, UOPWA, TWU, and UAW. Actists initiated and supported splits, secessions, raids, purges, and international union discipline in many of these unions and, in the CIO as a whole, were the major force promoting an extreme solution to the communist issue. Since the expulsion of the left-wing unions and the left-wing members of other unions was the most significant factor in the conservative direction of the CIO after 1950 and its subsequent amalgamation into the AFL, the ACTU's central role in the anti-communist drive serves to justify the conclusion that the ACTU was an important source of the conservative direction of American industrial unionism. In addition to its opposition to radicalism, however, the ACTU's conservative influence was felt in its stress on mediation, nonviolence, and class harmony, in its opposition to militance, class politics, and independent political action, and in its promotion of the fundamentally conservative tenets of Catholic social doctrine.

The ACTU's history as a significant force in the American labor movement ended with the expulsions. The organization had been founded in 1937 to propagate Catholic social doctrine and promote trade unionism and had contributed to a great many strikes and organizing drives, but its real genius had been the struggle against the trade-union left. Prior to the Gerson affair the ACTU had held its fire against the left and directing it largely toward the practitioners of social injustice. Thereafter the group had given way to the weight of the Catholic labor tradition and had embraced the implications of the slogan "opposition to socialism is the fundamental issue in the unions."[5]

From 1938 through 1949 the Actists had focused their major efforts on the fight with the communists. By 1946 anti-communism was virtually the sole issue which occupied the organization. The greater part of *Labor Leader* coverage in these years was polemic against the left. The ACTU's strike-support and organizing work languished while every organizational resource was thrown into the battle against the communists. During these years too the ACTU gradually abandoned its positions favoring union democracy and autonomy, and civil liberties for communists, as well as its opposition to dual unionism, interference in union affairs by the government or the national CIO, secession, and raiding. In the struggle against the communists, all means were justified and no holds were barred. In the course of this struggle against the radicals the ACTU had virtually ceased activity in any other arena. The organization thus became little more than an anti-communist vanguard within the labor movement.

Once their object—the expulsion of the radicals—had been

achieved, the ACTU's *raison d'être* was at an end. Thus it is not very surprising that the ACTU entered into a precipitate decline after 1949. Many Actists became or continued as union officers, especially in the new IUE. Others became mediators, lawyers, judges, labor-relations consultants, or writers for the State Department and the Voice of America. The ACTU itself continued to exist, though only in New York City on a very small scale, until 1973. The group organized labor schools for the Spanish-speaking in New York City during the 1950s and was involved in the poverty program in the city in the 1960s. But after 1949 the organization had outlived its purpose and was moribund.[6]

The story of the Calvary Cemetery strike may serve as an epilogue to the history of the ACTU. This strike broke out in January 1949 among gravediggers at Calvary Cemetery in the Borough of Queens, New York City. The gravediggers, members of local 293, United Cemetery Workers, were affiliated with the CIO Food, Tobacco and Agricultural Workers' Union. They demanded a wage increase and hours reduction in the form of "48 hours pay for 40 hours work." Their average weekly wage was $59.40. Approximately 250 workers were involved.[7]

The manager of the cemetery, Monsignor George C. Ehardt, refused, with the support of Cardinal Spellman, to recognize the union or negotiate. Instead, he fired the members of the negotiating committee. Ehardt sent several letters to the strikers charging that their union was communist-controlled and threatening them with dismissal if they did not return to work. The workers, all Catholics and nonradicals, refused.

Instead, they sought the support of the ACTU in their strike. CLDL attorneys John Harold and John Sheehan attempted to intervene with the cemetery's clerical management and secure an agreement to negotiate. They were rebuffed and accused of being communists themselves, though both were practicing Catholics, ten-year ACTU veterans, and graduates of Catholic colleges and law schools.[8]

The strike remained at an impasse until March 3, 1949. On that date Cardinal Spellman led 100 seminary students through ACTU-supported picket lines at Calvary and personally supervised the burying of several hundred bodies. This continued for three days, to the accompaniment of considerable publicity for the Cardinal's remarks that the strike was communist-inspired, "anti-American," "evil," "anti-Christian," and "a strike against the Church."[9]

This action and the resulting publicity effectively broke the strike. The workers voted to disaffiliate from their international union and "took an oath that they were opposed to Communism." These actions did not satisfy the cardinal, however, who stated that "their tactics seem to be Communist in nature." The demoralized workers attempted to meet with the cardinal several times as did Sheehan and Harold. On one occasion they succeeded, only to have the cardinal refuse again to recognize their reconstituted union or rehire the members of the negotiating committee. The strike was utterly lost.[10]

The ACTU suffered considerably from the after-effects of this strike. Its relations with the cardinal, of course, and the hierarchy in general were strained severely and its reputation with the Catholic rank and file plummeted. Ironically, the inveterately anti-communist Actists had been red-baited in the full glare of publicity and linked with what a cardinal of the Church termed a communist, anti-Christian, and un-American strike. They lost recruits, credibility with the faithful, and thousands of dollars in contributions. The Calvary strike inaugurated a period of financial and organizational instability from which they never recovered and they received red-baiting mail for years thereafter.[11] The anti-communist hysteria which the Actists themselves had promoted so enthusiastically had rebounded with a vengeance to hasten the already advanced decline of the ACTU.

NOTES

1. Karson, *American Labor Unions and Politics*, p. xi. See also Commons, *History of Labour*, pp. 201, 453, 456; Foner, *History of the Labor Movement*, 3:111–35; Saposs, "The Catholic Church and the Labor Movement," pp. 225–30; Morris, *Where Is the CIO Going?*, p. 26.

2. See Matles, *Them and Us*, pp. 200, 202, 258–59; DeCaux, *Labor Radical*, pp. 326–27; 362, 487–88; Preis, *Labor's Giant Step*, pp. 327, 331, 336; Kampelman, *The Communist Party and the CIO*, p. 135; Taft, "The ACTU," pp. 210–18.

3. The published scholarly studies are limited to Phillip Taft's "The Association of Catholic

Trade Unionists" (*Industrial and Labor Relations Review*, January 1949, pp. 210–18) and Michael Harrington's "Catholics in the Labor Movement: A Case History" (*Labor History*, Fall 1960, pp. 231–67). Taft's article is a general introduction to the ACTU, its philosophy, and its activities. Taft tends to overestimate its influence, though this author would agree with his general conclusion that the ACTU was "an important factor in a number of unions," that it gave "direction and support to dissidents" who opposed left-wing leaders, and that it was largely effective in its campaign to defeat these left-wing leaders. Taft argues further that the ACTU did not promote religious divisions in the unions or create factionalism. Harrington's monograph is a limited treatment of the ACTU's role in factional fighting in the UE and in the formation of the International Union of Electrical Workers (IUE) and is largely confined to the post–World War II period. While Harrington believes that the ACTU "played a central role in the factional struggle which shook the UE in the [nineteen] forties," he states that the Actists never created a "stable national organization." Their influence, he argues, was exaggerated by other principals in the UE struggle. In fact, he suggests, the ACTU name was merely a matter of convenience for many groups, while the organization itself seldom operated in a unified, consistent, or coordinated fashion. The Actists, in Harrington's view, contributed in an eclectic way to the opposition in the UE, but the group did not "build a religious faction in the UE," nor was it a significant center of "organizational power" in the electrical union. This author believes that Harrington has underestimated the unity of purpose, direction, and activity of the ACTU members and their impact on CIO union factionalism. There are two noteworthy unpublished studies of the ACTU. Richard Ward's doctoral dissertation "The Role of the Association of Catholic Trade Unionists in the American Labor Movement" (University of Michigan, 1958) is largely concerned with whether the ACTU promoted religious sectarianism, whether it was directed by the Church, and whether the organization was "inimical" to the American labor movement. His conclusions are in the negative on these counts. His argument has considerable merit as far as religious sectarianism is concerned. The question of whether the ACTU was "inimical" to the American labor movement is a more curious one and, though Ward writes about it at length, it does not seem to this author to be an answerable question. This author differs with Ward in his conclusion that the Church did not direct the activities of the ACTU. Frank Emspak's master's thesis "The ACTU and the United Automobile Workers" (University of Wisconsin, 1968) is concerned with the ACTU's role in factional struggle in the UAW. His conclusions are that the ACTU had some strength in the large Ford River Rouge local (number 600) and that Actists worked closely with Reuther to defeat the center and the left in the UAW. They were not, however, a "crucial" or a "decisive" factor in the UAW as a whole. Emspak considered the wider role of the ACTU in his doctoral dissertation "The Breakup of the CIO: 1945–1951" (University of Wisconsin, 1972). His conclusions are that the ACTU had some strength in a number of CIO unions, that they energetically joined or organized opposition to the left in unions in which the left dominated, and that, particularly in the UE, the Actists "played a considerable role" in the defeat of the left and the expulsions of the left-wing CIO unions. This author is in agreement with these general conclusions and with Emspak's assessment of the ACTU role in the UAW, though the ACTU influence in the largest UAW local, a stronghold of the left, suggests that the organization had a fair amount of leverage, if not a "decisive" role, in the factional struggle in the UAW as a whole. Emspak is the son of Julius Emspak, secretary-treasurer of the UE from 1936 to the present.

4. John Cort, however, is said to be writing such a memoir. Interview with George Donahue, July 22, 1974.

5. McQuade, "American Catholic Attitudes on Child Labor", p. 50.

6. Interviews with George Donahue and John Donahue, July 22, 1974.

7. "Minutes of the Calvary Strike Support Committee," March 1949, ACTU files; *Labor Leader* 12, no. 5.

8. George C. Ehardt to Calvary employees, February 3, 1949, ACTU files; *Labor Leader* 12, no. 5.

9. "Calvary Strike," *New York Telegram*, March 4, 1949.

10. "Calvary Strike," *New York Telegram*, March 4, 1949, *Labor Leader* 12, no. 5.

11. Interview with George Donahue, July 22, 1974.

Selected Bibliography

PAMPHLETS

ACTU. *The ACTU: A Catholic Apostolate for Labor*. New York: ACTU, 1940.

———. *The Story of ACTU*. New York: ACTU, 1958, ACTU files.

———. *What is the ACTU?* New York: ACTU, undated.

———. *Questions and Answers About the ACTU*. Detroit: ACTU, 1945.

———. *The Hearst Strike*. Chicago: ACTU, 1939.

———. *The ACTU Creed*. New York: ACTU, undated.

Bishops' Program for Reconstruction of 1919, reprinted in Ryan, John A., *Social Reconstruction*. New York: MacMillan Co., 1920, pp. 217–238.

Clancy, Raymond S. *The Actist Catechism*. Detroit: ACTU, 1939.

Freeman, James Morton. *No Friend of Labor*. New York: Fulfillment Press, 1949.

Kelly, George. *The ACTU and Its Critics*. Detroit: ACTU, 1945.

Lucy, George E. *The Catholic and His Trade Union*. New York: The American Press, 1958.

Matles, James J. *The Members Run This Union*. UE Publication No. 94, March 1947.

McKenna, Norman C. *The Catholic and His Union*. New York: Paulist Press, 1948.

Morris, George. *Where is the CIO Going?* New York: New Century, 1949.

Murray, Philip. *The CIO and National Defense*. Washington, D.C.: American Council on Public Affairs, 1941.

Oberle, Joseph. *The ACTU*. New York: Paulist Press, 1941.

Rice, Msgr. Charles Owen. *How to De-Control Your Union of Communists*. Pittsburgh: ACTU, undated, ACTU files.

Shiel, Bernard. *A Society of Free Men*. Washington, D.C.: Catholic University, 1944.

Smith, William, S. J. *The Catholic Labor School*. New York: Paulist Press, 1941.

―――. *American or Communist? You Can't be Both*. Brooklyn: Catholic Truth Society, 1938.

ARTICLES AND PERIODICALS

Abel, Aaron. "The Reception of Leo XIII's Labor Encyclical in America, 1891–1919." *The Review of Politics*, October 1945, pp. 164–195.

―――. "Ryan." *The Review of Politics*, January 1946, pp. 128–34.

Alter, Karl. "The Industry Council System and the Church's Program of Social Order." *Review of Social Economy*, September 1952, pp. 97–107.

ACTU. *The Labor Leader*, official newspaper of the ACTU, 1938–1950.

―――. *Michigan Labor Leader* (after 1946 *Wage Earner*), 1939–1950, Detroit ACTU publication.

―――. *The Gist Mill*, erratic, San Francisco ACTU publication.

―――. *The Catholic Trade Unionist*, erratic, Cleveland ACTU publication.

―――. *Actist Bulletin, the Leaven*, erratic, Detroit ACTU publications.

Bauer, D. C. "The ACTU." *New Catholic Encyclopedia*, pp. 968–69.

Browne, Henry J. "Peter E. Dietz, Pioneer Planner of Catholic Social Action." *The Catholic Historical Review*, January 1948, pp. 448–56.

"How Catholics Work in the Labor Movement." *Business Week*, July 18, 1953, pp. 122–24.

Catholic Action. National Catholic Welfare Conference, Washington, D.C., 1941–1950.

"Catholic Infiltration Disturbs Union." *Christian Century*, May 9, 1945, pp. 572–73.

Cort, John. "Catholics in Trade Unions." *Commonweal*, May 5, 1939, pp. 34–36.

―――. "Labor and Violence." *Commonweal*, November 10, 1939, pp. 68–70.

―――. "The Fight for Ford 600." *Commonweal*, March 22, 1946, pp. 576–77.

―――. "Nine Years of ACTU." *America*, April 6, 1946, pp. 4–5.

―――. "What Kind of Labor." *Catholic Digest*, April, 1946, pp. 24–26.

―――. "Ten Years of ACTU." *Commonweal*, May 23, 1947, pp. 143–44.

"Labor Leaders Rebuff ACTU." *Daily Worker*, July 28, 1947, p. 4.

"When Red-Baiting Failed." *Daily Worker* editorial, September 12, 1947, p. 7.

"List Fifteen Renegades from Waterfront CP." *Daily Worker*, April 5, 1948, p. 7.

"ACTU Ignores Pay Proposal at Westinghouse UE Meeting." *Daily Worker*, March 2, 1949, p. 7.

Deverall, Richard L. G. "Commonwealth College." *Commonweal*, April 28, 1939, pp. 9–10.

Donnelly, James L. "Condition of Labor: Reconstructing the Social Order." *Vital Speeches*, August 1, 1944, pp. 16–20.

"Upright Spirit." *Fortune*, November, 1946, p. 188.

"Labor Priests." *Fortune*, January, 1949, pp. 150–52.

Frommelt, Horace A. "The Future of Our Catholic Workers." *The Sign*, December, 1938, pp. 263–64.

———. "Catholic Workers in the Unions." *The Sign*, January, 1939, pp. 339–40.

Harrington, Michael. "Catholics in the Labor Movement: A Case History." *Labor History*, Fall 1960, pp. 231–67.

Karson, Marc. "The Catholic Church and Unionism, 1900–1918." *Industrial and Labor Relations Review*, July 1951, pp. 527–42.

———. Reviews and letters to the editor, *New Republic*, April 12, May 4, June 21, August 2, 1954.

———. "The Catholic Church and the Political Development of American Trade Unionism (1900–1918)." *Industrial and Labor Relations Review*, January 1949, pp. 527–42.

Kelly, Reverend George A. "The ACTU and Its Critics." *Commonweal*, December 31, 1948, pp. 298–302.

LoPinto, Victor. "Catholic Trade Unionists." *Sign*, March 1939, p. 498.

McKenna, Norman. "The Story of the ACTU." *The Catholic World*, March 1949, pp. 453–59.

Morris, George. "Spotlight on the Association of Catholic Trade Unionists." *Political Affairs*, March 1947, pp. 252–63.

———. "Vatican Conspiracy in the American Trade Union Movement." *Political Affairs*, June 1950, pp. 16–24.

Montgomery, David. "The Shuttle and the Cross." *Journal of Social History*, Spring 1972, pp. 441–47.

"Labor and the Church." *Newsweek*, July 31, 1939, p. 25.

Rice, Charles Owen. "Ecumenism in Labor." *Pittsburgh Catholic*, June 6, 1966, p. 6.

Rovere, Richard H. "Labor Catholic Bloc." *The Nation*, January 4, 1941, p. 13.

Saposs, David J. "The Catholic Church and the Labor Movement." *Modern Monthly*, May, June 1933, pp. 225–30; pp. 294–98.

Schachtman, Max. "Marxism vs. Catholicism." *The New International*, January 1949, pp. 3–14.

Smith, William. "The Catholic Labor School." *Catholic Mind*, July 1949, pp. 392–97.

Sturzo, Luigi. "Corporatism—Christian, Social and Fascist." *The Catholic World*, July 1937, pp. 394–99.

Taft, Philip. "The Association of Catholic Trade Unionists." *Industrial and Labor Relations Review*, January 1949, pp. 210–18.

Weinberg, Jules. "Priests, Workers and Communists." *Harper's Magazine*, November 1948, pp. 49–56.

BOOKS

Abell, Aaron. *American Catholicism and Social Action*. Garden City, New York: Hanover, 1960.

Alinsky, Saul D. *Reveille for Radicals*. Chicago: University of Chicago, 1946.

Barbash, Jack. *The Practice of Unionism*. New York: Harper's, 1956.

———. *Unions and Union Leadership*. New York: Harper's, 1959.

———. *Labor's Grass Roots*. New York: Harper's, 1961.

———. *Universities and Unions in Workers' Education*. New York: Harper's, 1955.

Beard, Mary R. *A Short History of the American Labor Movement*. New York: Macmillan Co., 1924.

Bernstein, Irving. *The Lean Years*. Boston: Houghton-Mifflin, 1960.

———. *The Turbulent Years*. Boston: Houghton-Mifflin, 1970.

Bok, Derek, and Dunlap, John. *Labor and the American Community*. New York: Simon and Schuster, 1970.

Boyer, Richard O. *The Dark Ship*. Boston: Little, Brown and Co., 1947.

———, and Morais, Herbert M. *Labor's Untold Story*. New York: UE Press, 1955.

Broderick, Francis. *Right Reverend New Dealer*. New York: Macmillan Co., 1963.

Browne, Henry Joseph. *The Catholic Church and the Knights of Labor*. Washington, D.C.: Catholic University, 1949.

Bruehl, Charles. *The Pope's Plan*. New York: Devin-Adair, 1939.

Camp, Robert. *The Papal Ideology of Social Reform*, Leiden, Holland: J. Brill, 1969.

Cochran, Bert. *American Labor in Midpassage*. New York: Monthly Review Press, 1959.

Colman, Barry. *The Catholic Church and German Americans*. Milwaukee, Wisc.: Bruce, 1953.

Commission on the Church and Social Service of the Federal Council of Churches, et al. *What Is the Christian View of Work and Wealth*. New York: Association Press, 1920.

Commons, John. *History of Labour in the United States*. New York: Macmillan, 1935.

Conkin, Paul. *The New Deal*. New York: Crowell, 1967.

Cronin, John. *Catholic Social Principles: The Social Teaching of the Church Applied to American Economic Life*. Milwaukee, Wisc.: Bruce, 1950.

———. *Catholic Social Action*. Milwaukee: Bruce, 1948.

Cross, Robert. *The Emergence of Liberal Catholicism in America*. Cambridge, Mass.: Harvard, 1958.

Darby, Thomas J. *Thirteen Years in a Labor School*. St. Paul, Minn.: Radio Replies Press, 1953.

Day, Dorothy. *The Long Loneliness*. New York: Harper's, 1952.

DeCaux, Len. *Labor Radical*. Boston: Beacon, 1970.

Derber, Milton, and Young, Edwin. *Labor and the New Deal*. Madison, Wisc.: University of Wisconsin, 1961.

Flagler, John J. *The Labor Movement in the United States*. Minneapolis, Minn.: Lerner, 1970.

Foner, Philip. *History of the Labor Movement in the United States*, vols. I and III. New York: International, 1964.

Foster, William Z. *American Trade Unionism*. New York: International, 1947.

Fountain, Clayton, *Union Guy*. Viking, 1949.

Fox, Mary Harrita. *Peter E. Dietz, Labor Priest*. South Bend, Ind.: Notre Dame, 1953.

Galenson, Walter. *The CIO Challenge to the AFL*. Cambridge, Mass.: Harvard, 1960.

———. *1937: The Turning Point for American Labor*. Reprint No. 120. Berkeley, Calif.: Institute of Industrial Relations, University of California, 1959.

Gearty, Patrick W. *The Economic Thought of Monsignor John A. Ryan*. Washington, D.C.: Catholic University, 1953.

Gleason, Philip. *The Conservative Reformers: German-American Catholics and the Social Order*. South Bend, Ind.: Notre Dame, 1968.

Gregory, Charles O. *Labor and the Law*. New York: Norton, 1958.

Grob, Gerald. *Workers and Utopia*. Evanston, Ill.: Northwestern University, 1961.

Harris, Herbert. *Labor's Civil War*. New York: Knopf, 1940.

Husslein, Joseph. *The Catholic's Work in the World*. New York: Benziger, 1917.

————. *The World Problem: Capital, Labor and the Church*. New York: Kenedy, 1918.

Johnson, Malcolm. *Crime on the Labor Front*. New York: McGraw-Hill, 1950.

Kampelman, Max. *The Communist Party vs. the CIO*. New York: Praeger, 1957.

Karson, Marc. *American Labor Unions and Politics*. Carbondale, Ill.: Southern Illinois University, 1958.

Laslett, John, and Lipset, Seymour. *Failure of a Dream?* Garden City, New York: Doubleday, 1974.

Lens, Sidney, *Left, Right and Center*. Hinsdale, Ill.: Regnery, 1949.

Litwack, Leon. *The American Labor Movement*. Englewood Cliffs, N.J.: Prentice-Hall, 1962.

Madison, Charles. *American Labor Leaders*. New York: Harper's, 1950.

Marshall, Ray. *The Negro and Organized Labor*. New York: Wiley, 1965.

Matles, James. *Them and Us*. Englewood Cliffs, N. J.: Prentice-Hall, 1974.

Miller, Raymond J. *Forty Years After: Pius XI and the Social Order*. St. Paul, Minn.: Radio Replies Press, 1947.

Moody, Joseph N. *Church and Society: Catholic Social and Political Thought and Movements, 1789–1950*. New York: Arts, 1953.

Munier, Joseph D. *Some American Approximations to Pius XI's Industries and Professions*. Washington, D.C.: Catholic University, 1943.

Murray, Philip. *Organized Labor and Production*. New York: Harper's, 1946.

O'Connor, Reverend Daniel A. *Catholic Social Doctrine*. Westminster, Md.: Newman Press, 1956.

Paul, Reverend John. *Production for Use and Not for Profit*. Washington, D.C.: Catholic University, 1931.

Perlman, Selig. *A History of Trade Unions in the United States*. New York: Augustus M. Kelley, 1922.

Preis, Art. *Labor's Giant Step*. New York: Pathfinder, 1942.

Radosh, Ronald. *American Labor Unions and United States Foreign Policy*. New York: Vintage, 1969.

Raymond, Allen. *Waterfront Priest*. New York: Holt, 1955.

Reuther, Walter. "How to Beat the Communists," in Christman, Henry M., *Walter P. Reuther: Selected Papers*. New York: Macmillan Co., 1961.

Ryan, John A. *Social Reconstruction*. New York: Macmillan Co., 1930.

———. *A Better Economic Order*. New York: Harper's, 1935.

———. *A Living Wage: Its Ethical and Economic Aspects*. New York: Macmillan Co., 1906.

———, and Husslein, Joseph. *The Church and Labor*. New York: Macmillan Co., 1924.

Saposs, David J. *Left-Wing Unionism*. International, 1926.

Seidman, Joel. *American Labor From Defense to Reconstruction*. Chicago: University of Chicago, 1953.

Seven Great Encyclicals. New York: Paulist Press, 1963.

Siefer, Gregor. *The Church and Industrial Society*. London: Darton, Longman, Todd, 1964.

Stieber, Jack. *Governing the UAW*. New York: John Wiley and Sons, 1967.

Thomas, Hugh. *The Spanish Civil War*. New York: Harper's, 1961.

Ware, Norman J. *Labor in Modern Industrial Society*. New York: Heath, 1935.

Whittemore, L. H. *The Man Who Ran the Subways: The Story of Mike Quill*. New York: Holt, Rinehart and Winston, 1968.

UNPUBLISHED MATERIAL

Crosby, Donald. "Angry Catholics." Ph.D. diss., Brandeis University, 1973.

Emspak, Frank. "The ACTU and the UAW." Master's thesis, University of Wisconsin, 1968.

———. "The Breakup of the CIO: 1945–1951." Ph.D. diss., University of Wisconsin, 1972.

Irons, Peter. "America's Cold War Crusade." Ph.D. diss., Boston University, 1972.

Leonard, Jeande Lourdes. "Catholic Attitude Toward American Labor." Master's thesis, Columbia University, 1946.

McQuade, Vincent. "American Catholic Attitudes on Child Labor Since 1891." Ph.D. diss., Catholic University, 1938.

Ward, Richard. "The Role of the ACTU in the American Labor Movement." Ph.D. diss., University of Michigan, 1958.

UNION RECORDS

Minutes of Executive Board Meetings and Proceedings of Conventions of: the AFL; the CIO; the UE; the NMU; the Newspaper Guild.

COLLECTIONS

ACTU Collection. ACTU, New York, New York.

Detroit ACTU Collection. Wayne State University, Detroit, Michigan.

New York Public Library ACTU Holdings, New York.

The Tamiment Collection. New York University Library.

Wisconsin Historical Society CIO Holdings, Madison, Wisconsin.

Holdings of Columbia University, Saint Peters College, University of Minnesota, Rutgers University, Detroit Public Library, Milwaukee Public Library, Princeton University, the University of Wisconsin, and Fordham University.

Index